IMAGES
of America

Portland's Chinatowns

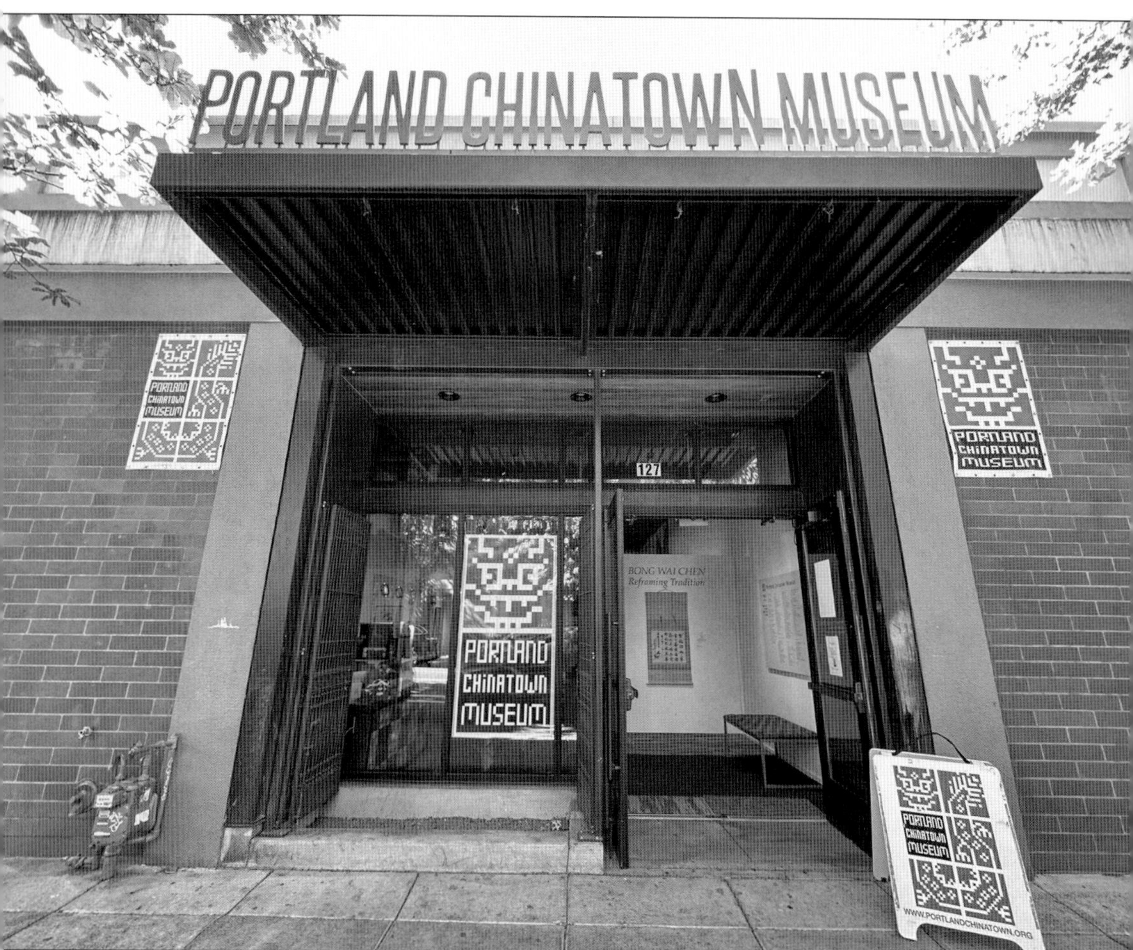

The Portland Chinatown Museum at 127 Northwest Third Avenue is in the New Chinatown/Japantown Historic District. Dedicated to preserving the rich history of Portland's Chinatowns, the museum has rotating exhibits exploring the contributions of the Chinese community past and present, as well as collections, archives, and a research library. Its permanent exhibit, "Beyond the Gate: A Tale of Portland's Historic Chinatowns," offers an in-depth look into this vibrant cultural history. Please visit www.portlandchinatownmuseum.org. (Kristin Wong.)

On the Cover: The Portland Rose Festival's "electric parade" debuted in 1907 before evolving into the Merrykhana Parade, a name it held until 1973. In 1976, it was rebranded as the Starlight Parade. The Shang Gee Shan youth group took part in the inaugural Merrykhana Parade in 1937, proudly celebrating their cultural heritage. Today, the Starlight Parade remains a beloved tradition, bringing the Portland community together. (Oregon Historical Society, No. 0029P429.)

IMAGES
of America

Portland's Chinatowns

Kristin Wong, PharmD, and
the Portland Chinatown Museum
Foreword by Chuimei Ho, PhD

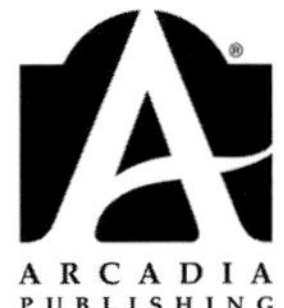

ISBN 978-1-4671-6288-3

Published by Arcadia Publishing
Charleston, South Carolina

Printed in the United States of America

Library of Congress Control Number: Applied for

For all general information, please contact Arcadia Publishing:
Telephone 843-853-2070
Fax 843-853-0044
E-mail sales@arcadiapublishing.com

Visit us on the Internet at www.arcadiapublishing.com

This book was inspired by my father's family history in Portland's Chinatown. The stories of individuals, families, and their contributions to this historic area ensure their legacies live on—preserved, shared, and celebrated for generations to come.

Contents

Foreword

In 2003, Fred M. Wong, an old-timer of Portland's New Chinatown, met me at a restaurant on Northwest Fourth Avenue. Fred told me about his decades of working at salmon canneries in Alaska while holding down a regular teaching post in Portland: "It was a good job. It paid for my college degree and my children's. All my kids have done summer jobs at canneries, too." In 2025, one of those kids, Kristin, the author of this book, asked me to write a foreword. I was delighted for several reasons.

While there are many long-term residents of US Chinatowns who do their best to memorialize the communities they grew up in, it is unusual for their Americanized children to follow suit. Kristin, a pharmacist, is a refreshing exception among the younger generations.

Kristin told me, "My goal is to share the rich history of the Chinese community in Portland's Chinatowns." She has done just that, passionately, and with the viewpoint of an insider. Kristin deviates from earlier writings on the subject by providing a broader time frame, ranging from the 19th century to the present day, and by focusing more sharply on individual Chinatown residents, viewed through over 200 photographs.

Those earlier writings include *Sweet Cakes, Long Journey: the Chinatowns of Portland, Oregon*, Marie Rose Wong's frequently cited history published in 2004. Then, in 2007, the Chinese Consolidated Benevolent Association in Portland produced a bilingual volume, *Dreams of the West, A History of the Chinese in Oregon 1850–1950*. I myself, with Bennet Bronson, in 2014, summarized Portland's early Chinese history in *Coming Home in Gold Brocade, Chinese in Early Northwest America*. More recently, the 2021 winter issue of *Oregon Historical Quarterly* included Portland in two articles. Clearly, there are still a lot of Portland-focused stories to be told, especially those after World War II.

Kristin's stories are more than her own family. Her vision extends to relationships between individuals and organizations in Chinatown. Her great-grandparents resided in Portland's first Chinatown before the family relocated to the second Chinatown, where Fred later lived. After having moved away to East Portland, Fred continues to play a leading role in various Chinatown organizations, often attending Chinatown events together with his family. Kristin's knowledge comes from deep personal awareness of generations of family history.

—Chuimei Ho, PhD

Acknowledgments

My deepest appreciation goes to the Portland Chinatown Museum and also Norm Gholston, a member of the board of directors, for invaluable guidance and for generously providing many of the images. I would also like to thank executive director Anna Truxes and vice president Sarah Chung for their support.

I would like to acknowledge the following for their contributions: Chinese Consolidated Benevolent Association (Neil Lee and JoAnn Ngan Lee), Chinese Consolidated Benevolent Association Museum, Chinese American Citizens Alliance (Helen Ying), Lan Su Chinese Garden (Christine Nickerson, Elizabeth Nye, Venus Sun, and Lilly Joynes), Portland Archives and Records Center (Ayshea Khan), Oregon Historical Society (Robert Warren), APANO (Alisa Kajikawa), Lee Family Association (Janet Lee), Lee Family Association Dragon and Lion Dance (Terry Lee and Eric Lee), Japanese American Museum of Oregon (Lucy Capehart), Metro (Karen Vitkay), Soo Yoon Association (Richard Louie), International Lion Dance (Michael Choi), the Society Hotel (Jessie Burke, Jonathan Cohen, and Micah Cruver), the *Oregonian* (Sean Meagher), Oregon State University (OSU) Special Collections (Anna Dvorak), and Museum of History and Industry, Seattle (Adam Lyon and Aurora San Miguel).

Thank you, Victor Leo, for the translation, and to authors Chuimei Ho, PhD, and Marie Rose Wong, PhD, for their generosity.

It was an honor to meet the families and people of Chinatown, who graciously shared memories: Carol Lee (Lee Lung); Robert Hugh Leong (George W. and Mary N. Leong); Carey Wong (Gordon Wong); Allison Wong Toso; Robert Luck and Jean Heilig-Luck; Marcus Lee (Joe Lae); Keith Lee (Pak On Lee); Franklin Quan; Norman Locke; Joe Leong (Wing K. Leong); Steven Louie, Judy Louie, and Estee Louie; Roberta May Wong (Francis Gang Wong); G.G. Rowe (Billie Chin and Fred Chin); Fred B. Wong (Sun and Rosie Wong); Ellen Wong Lee (Harry and Eva Wong Woo); Ron Wong; Tommy Ly; Alice Cheong, Mary Louie, and Kristena Louie (Henry and Diane Choi); and Gloria Wong and Shelley Wong-Kamikawa, PhD (Wong On).

My heartfelt gratitude goes to my family for their support: parents Fred M. and Jane S. Wong, sisters Lisa Woo, PharmD, and Staci Wong, Ray and Nancy Pfortner, Dale Wing, Verna Lee, Victoria Wong, Michele Bernstein, and Sharon Hsu. Thank you, David Wing, Elvis Duong, and Wendell Woo, for countless airport rides.

Thank you, Arcadia Publishing, for supporting this project.

Introduction

In the mid-1850s, Portland became the prime location along the Columbia and Willamette Rivers, establishing itself as a major hub for commerce and trade and attracting settlers and immigrants, including Chinese merchants and laborers. Chinatown emerged as a sanctuary, offering protection from discriminatory laws and practices. It provided essential services, helping residents navigate legal obstacles and city ordinances while supporting them with jobs, housing, and a sense of community.

Chinese American history is intertwined with China's struggles and the establishment of Chinatowns in the United States, like the one in Portland. During the Qing Dynasty, Guangzhou (Canton) in Guangdong Province served as China's sole international trade port, exporting tea, silk, and porcelain. However, civil unrest, economic hardship, natural disasters, British imperialism, and the Opium Wars (1839–1842 and 1856–1860) drove many Chinese to seek opportunities abroad.

Chinese immigration increased significantly during the California Gold Rush in the 1850s. By 1857, Chinese laborers comprised 90 percent of the Central Pacific Railroad workforce. They often performed more hazardous tasks and earned lower wages than their white counterparts. Others worked in mines, agriculture, salmon canneries, and laundries. Early immigrants, who were primarily men, sent earnings home to their families in China. Facing racism and segregation, Chinatowns emerged as protective community enclaves.

Economic turmoil in the 1870s fueled anti-Chinese sentiment, culminating in the Chinese Exclusion Act of 1882. This law barred the immigration of laborers, prohibited naturalization, and restricted family reunification, with exceptions for those such as merchants and diplomats. Later laws, like the Scott Act (1888) and the Geary Act (1892), further tightened restrictions. Early enforcement of these laws was inconsistent due to insufficient funding, while confusion at immigration stations and courts allowed limited but continued immigration despite the restrictions.

Then, in 1943, the Chinese Exclusion Act was repealed through the Magnuson Act, permitting naturalization but limiting immigration to a total of 105 annually. Full repeal came with the Immigration and Nationality Act of 1965, which prioritized skilled workers and family reunification and introduced broader immigration reforms. These changes transformed the landscape for Chinese American communities and allowed them to further increase their contributions to US society in various ways.

Chinese immigration to Portland began in 1850 with just two individuals, marking them as some of the city's earliest non-native settlers, predating Oregon's statehood in 1859. The city's first Chinatown emerged in 1851, with the heart of the enclave spanning from Taylor to Oak Streets and from Second to Fourth Streets. By 1900, it had grown into the second-largest Chinatown in the United States, housing nearly 8,000 residents, second only to San Francisco's 14,000. Chinese businesses fostered community growth, offering housing, groceries, medicine, and entertainment, while labor contractors facilitated employment opportunities. These immigrants contributed significantly to the economic and infrastructural growth of Portland.

In Portland's Chinatown, the merchant class emerged as the ruling elite, maintaining a cordial relationship with city officials. This helped mitigate the violence and riots experienced in other areas like Mount Tabor, Albina, Oregon City, and other West Coast cities such as San Francisco, Tacoma, and Seattle. Over time, Chinatown's population grew as individuals migrated to Portland seeking opportunities and a relatively more tolerant environment.

However, discriminatory laws persisted. In 1859, laws were enacted restricting property ownership for Chinese residents while also denying them the right to vote, hold public office, or attend public schools. In 1862, an annual $5 state tax was imposed on Chinese residents, and in 1863, a $25 quarterly fee was mandated for Chinese laundries in the city. These laws were meant to marginalize the community both economically and socially.

Organizations like the Chinese Consolidated Benevolent Association (CCBA) and the Chinese American Citizens Alliance (CACA) established local branches in Portland's Chinatown to provide support, help navigate immigration challenges, and foster kinship within the community. Family and regional associations further strengthened ties among immigrants from the same village or area in China.

Several factors contributed to the relocation of Portland's Chinatown in the late 19th and early 20th centuries to an area north of Burnside Street, known as Nihonmachi or Japantown. Japantown was a vital hub for Japanese immigrants who, like their Chinese counterparts, faced exclusion, racism, and discriminatory laws while seeking economic opportunities. This relocation marked the establishment of Portland's second Chinatown, now recognized as the New Chinatown/Japantown Historic District.

The original Chinatown, situated near the Willamette River, frequently suffered flooding and experienced a devastating fire in 1873 that destroyed 22 blocks of downtown. Restrictive city laws barred Chinese residents from owning property, forcing them into rental agreements. Rising rents, fueled by urban development, worsened these challenges, and after the catastrophic flood of 1894, residents and businesses started to migrate north over the next several decades. A bronze plaque at Second Avenue between Pine and Ash Streets commemorates this historic site.

Throughout the 19th and 20th centuries, Chinese, Japanese, and African Americans each faced unique and explicit barriers to immigration and citizenship. In Portland's second Chinatown, these groups worked and lived in close proximity, partly as a result of Union Station being nearby, where African Americans were employed by the railways. During segregation, Chinese restaurants provided a unique space, offering an inclusive environment. This created a distinctive cultural and social connection between Black and Chinese communities.

Despite hardships, Portland's Chinese community thrived, with Chinatown hosting cultural events for Chinese New Year, Mid-Autumn Moon Festival, and the Lantern Festival. By 1939, restrictive property laws were lifted, allowing areas like Ladd's Addition in Southeast Portland to become informally accessible to Chinese residents. Also, descendants of immigrants gained opportunities to pursue higher education and professional careers in fields such as healthcare, politics, technology, and business. Many started to move outside of Chinatown as they achieved the American Dream.

Following World War II, Chinese immigration reflected a broader diaspora, including ethnic minorities from China and those from regions like Hong Kong, Taiwan, Vietnam, and Malaysia. These groups brought blended cultures and traditions, enriching American society. In recent decades, Chinese immigration has increasingly included professionals, students, and families seeking opportunities amid a shifting economic and social landscape.

Today, immigrants do not necessarily use Portland's Chinatown as a gateway to achieving the American Dream. Over the years, Chinese families and businesses have dispersed across the greater Portland metropolitan area, with a prominent enclave forming at Eighty-Second Avenue and Division Street, now known as the Jade District. Services and support systems are more widespread across the region than they were in the 1850s, when systemic discrimination centralized these resources to Chinatown.

With the demographics of recent Chinese immigrants encompassing a more diverse diaspora and often with limited traditional ties to Chinatown, this creates an opportunity to reimagine this historic neighborhood. The loss of legacy businesses and cultural spaces threatens to sever vital connections to the past. Both local and national Chinese organizations can develop strategies to engage these newer immigrants and inspire their active participation in preserving Chinatown's rich history. Possible approaches include hosting events that combine traditional Chinese culture with modern influences, such as food festivals showcasing both classic dishes and innovative fusion cuisine or music performances blending traditional instruments with contemporary sounds.

Creating modern community spaces like coworking areas and art galleries infused with traditional Chinese motifs could provide welcoming environments for younger generations. Using digital platforms, social media, and influencers can be leveraged to share stories, promote events, and spotlight local businesses by connecting with younger audiences and newer immigrants. Partnerships with schools, universities, and organizations can engage students and young professionals in activities such as urban development, preservation of historical landmarks, and revitalization of cultural areas. Businesses and restaurants can enhance downtown engagement by offering unique shopping and dining experiences, such as exclusive in-store events, product tastings, and interactive workshops. These initiatives not only attract residents but also strengthen the local economy and help preserve cultural heritage.

Organizations continue to engage the community through events like the CCBA-cosponsored Lunar New Year festival at the Oregon Convention Center and the Portland Chinatown Museum's long-standing Chinese New Year parade in Chinatown. The Portland Chinatown Museum serves as a cultural cornerstone, preserving the community's history through exhibitions, research, and archives. Meanwhile, the Lan Su Chinese Garden hosts educational workshops, seasonal celebrations, and performances. Portland's lion dance teams also play a crucial role by preserving and passing down this art form to younger generations, ensuring the tradition thrives and connects the community.

Chinese family associations are organized by shared surnames, ancestral villages, family lineages, and tongs, which were established to provide mutual support and protection for Chinese immigrants. These still exist in Chinatown but now focus on cultural preservation and fostering community engagement.

As one of Portland's foundational districts, Chinatown deserves preservation efforts to sustain its role as a vital crossroads of history, culture, and identity. Achieving this vision will require collaboration from city officials, community leaders, multi-generational individuals, younger generations, and newer immigrants to reimagine this historic area, ensuring future generations can appreciate and connect with this part of Portland's rich history, which began over 175 years ago.

—Kristin Wong, PharmD

One

First Chinatown and Early Pioneers 1850–1905

Chinese immigrants have been present in Portland since before the city's incorporation in 1851, initially seeking better opportunities during the Gold Rush of 1848 and then later during the construction of the transcontinental railroad in the 1860s. Portland's strategic location at the confluence of the Columbia and Willamette Rivers made it a vital trade and transportation hub, supporting the movement of goods like lumber, hops, and wheat. Steamer ships brought immigrants and travelers from San Francisco and abroad, further cementing Portland's role as a center for commerce and cultural exchange. Early Chinese settlers primarily worked in professions that required minimal skills or English proficiency, with the intention to earn money and send it back to their families in China before returning themselves. In Portland, they operated businesses like Hop Wo Washing and Ironing on Front Street, worked in domestic service for wealthy white residents, and grew produce to sell locally. Despite their contributions to major infrastructure projects like the railroads on the West Coast, anti-Chinese sentiment grew in California and Washington, culminating in violent riots like the Tacoma incident of 1885. This led to 200 displaced Chinese residents seeking safety in Portland, aided by Moy Back Hin, a prominent Chinatown merchant and labor contractor. Portland's Chinatown business elites established ties with city officials, mitigating some violence that was seen elsewhere. The Chinese Exclusion Act of 1882, the first race-based anti-immigrant law targeting a specific nationality, prohibited further entry of Chinese laborers, with exceptions for diplomats, merchants, and their families. Discriminatory policies persisted in Portland, and urban expansion destroyed Chinese vegetable gardens in areas such as Tanner Creek, Goose Hollow, Guilds Lake, Albina, and Mount Tabor. However, despite all of this, early Chinatown thrived along the Willamette River, featuring retail shops, restaurants, residential apartments, and temples adorned with ornate balconies and Chinese architectural details. By 1900, Portland's Chinatown was the second largest after San Francisco's. Following the Great Flood of 1894 and the growing desirability of its location, which now encompasses the site of the Pioneer Place shopping area, Chinatown relocated to its current site, creating the New Chinatown/Japantown Historic District.

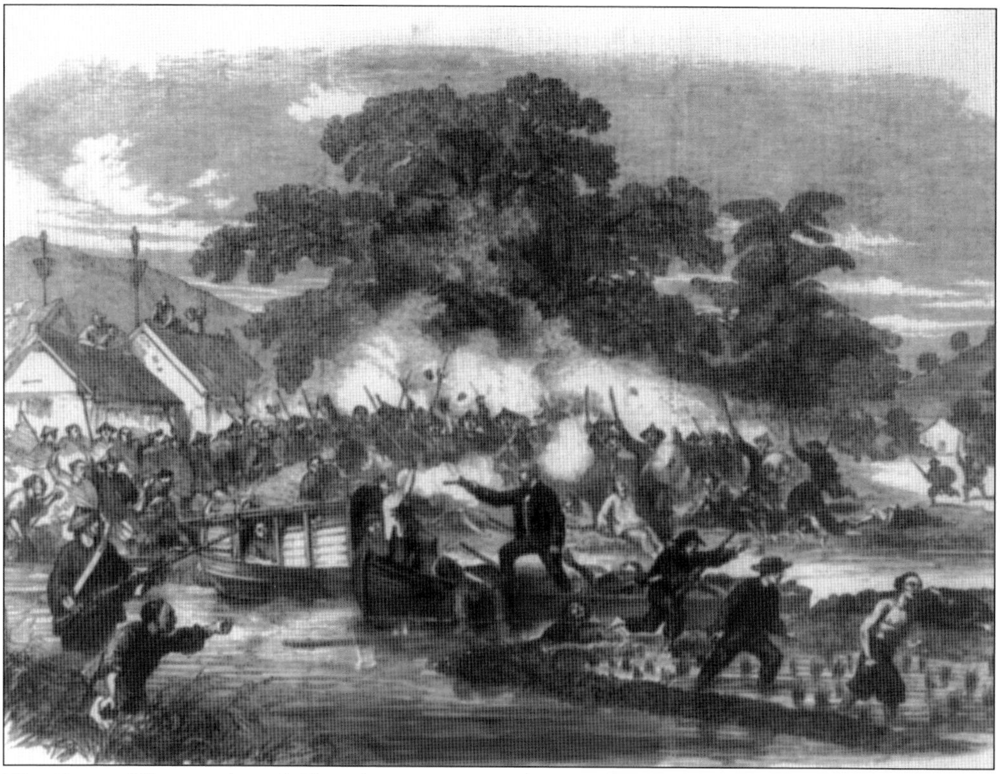

The Opium Wars weakened China's government, disrupted its economy, and expanded Western influence. To address trade deficits, Britain and France smuggled opium into China, causing widespread societal challenges. This instability drove many to seek better opportunities abroad. As a result, Hong Kong was ceded to Britain after the First Opium War, then the Kowloon Peninsula and Stonecutters Island after the Second Opium War. (Prints and Photographs Division, Library of Congress.)

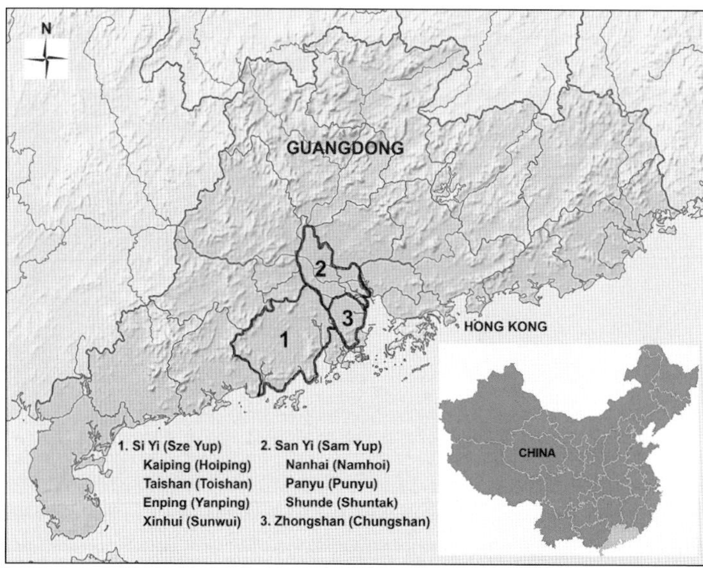

This map of the Pearl River Delta region in Guangdong Province shows the origin of the early Chinese immigrants. They came from areas known as Sze Yup (four counties), Sam Yup (three counties), and Zhongshan (one county), with approximately half from Toishan County alone. Overseas Chinese sent money to their families in China, which helped to improve the local economy and overall prosperity of the region. (Kristin Wong.)

TONG SUNG HOUSE.

Second st., directly in rear of the "Columbian."

MR. SUNGSUNG from China, would inform the public that he has opened a Boarding House and Restaurant, and, having first rate China cooks, can give good board and lodging to those who may favor him with their patronage. Private rooms for gentlemen, and suppers got up to order. A choice variety of liquors constantly on hand.

Portland, Nov. 15, 1851 -tf

An advertisement for the Tong Sung Boarding House and Restaurant first appeared in the November 15, 1851, *Weekly Oregonian*. It was Portland's earliest known Chinese business. It provided accommodations for Chinese laborers, along with introducing Portlanders to Chinese cuisine. Located behind the Columbian Hotel on Second Street near the Morrison Street dock, it was by a key arrival point for immigrants and travelers. This image is from the December 6, 1851, issue of the *Oregonian*. (The *Oregonian*.)

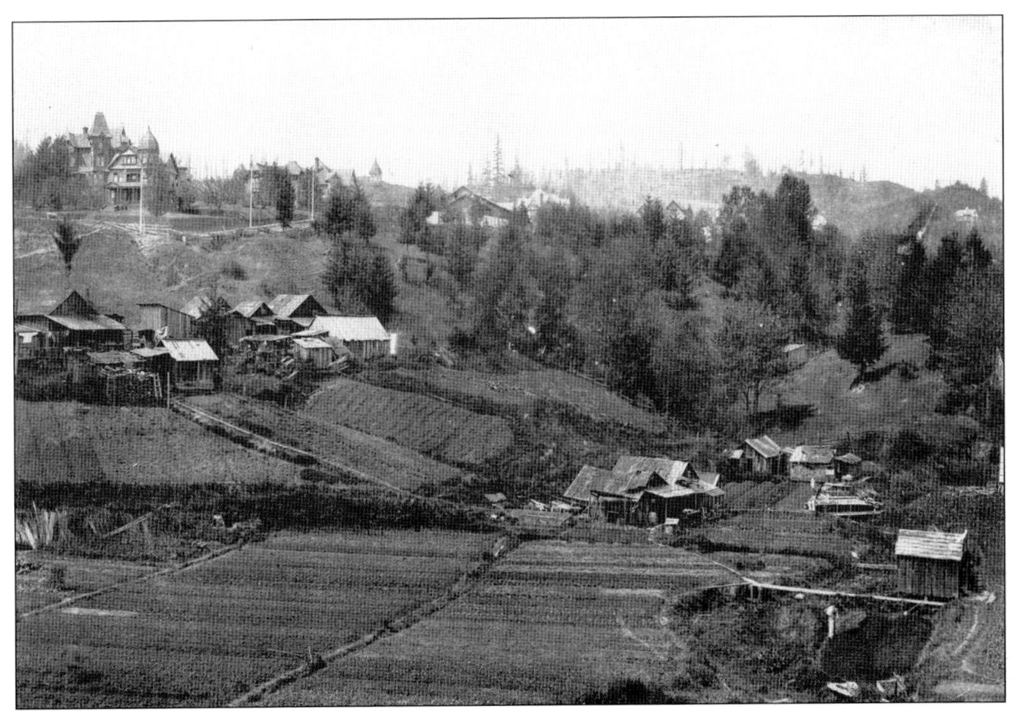

This 1892 photograph shows a Chinese vegetable garden along Tanner Creek, west of Portland's first Chinatown, between Southwest Sixteenth and Twentieth Avenues and Jefferson and Washington Streets. This garden expanded to 20 acres within a decade. Farmers lived in shanties below hilltop mansions but supplied fresh produce to the city. Today, it is the site of the Multnomah Athletic Club, Portland's soccer stadium, and Lincoln High School. (Gholston Collection.)

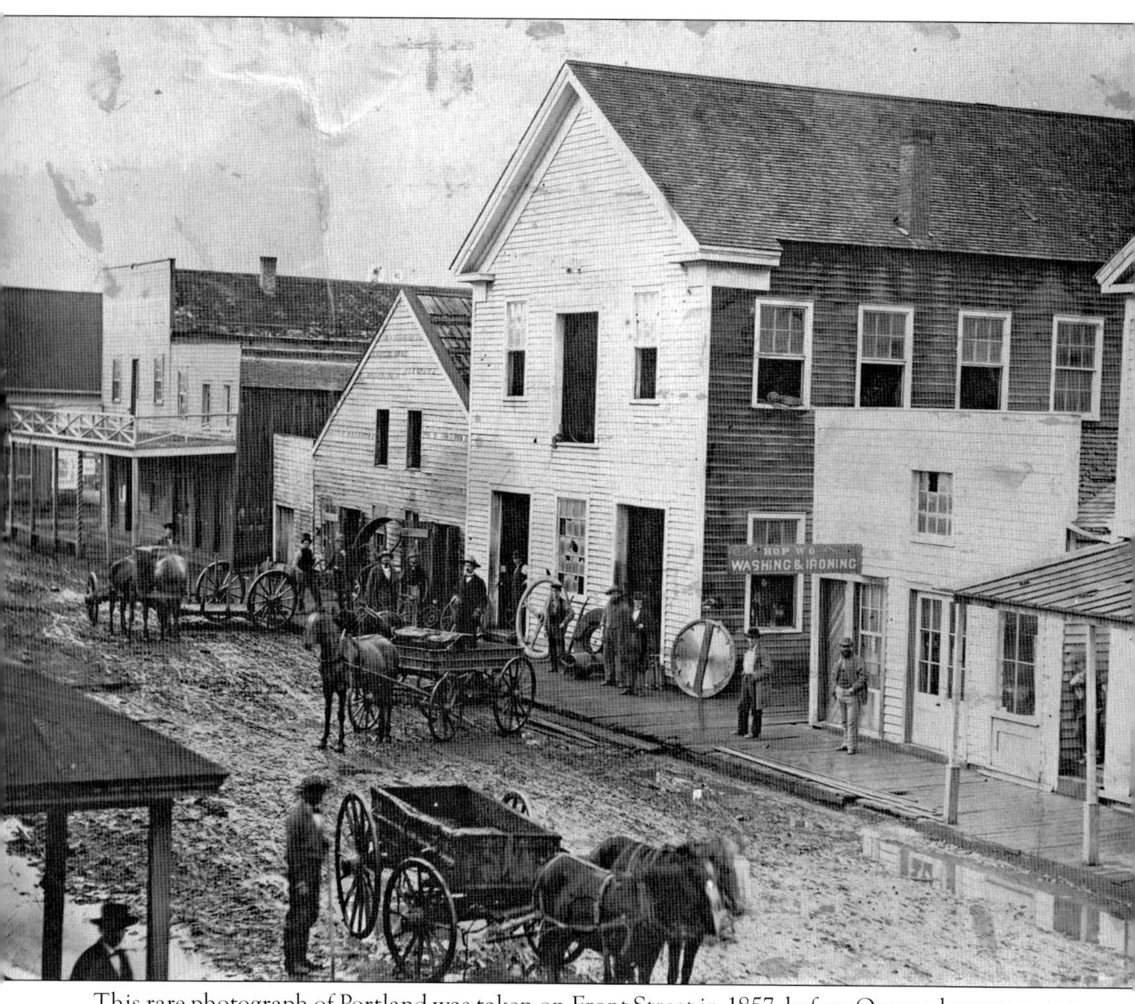

This rare photograph of Portland was taken on Front Street in 1857, before Oregon became a state in 1859. This is the earliest known image of a Chinese business in the city. Hop Wo Washing and Ironing, located at Southwest Front Avenue and Morrison Street, was next to the Monastes and Davis blacksmith shop. In frontier towns where men outnumbered women, early Chinese pioneers saw opportunities in laundries, which faced little competition amidst limited opportunities. They provided essential services to the community, where single men often relied on such businesses for domestic chores. Though grueling, the hand laundry business offered a livelihood for Chinese workers to help provide for their families back in Guangdong. The 1860 US Census was difficult to conduct accurately due to the highly mobile workforce, but it was estimated that there were roughly 20 Chinese individuals in Portland at the time, mostly men and a few women. (Portland Chinatown Museum.)

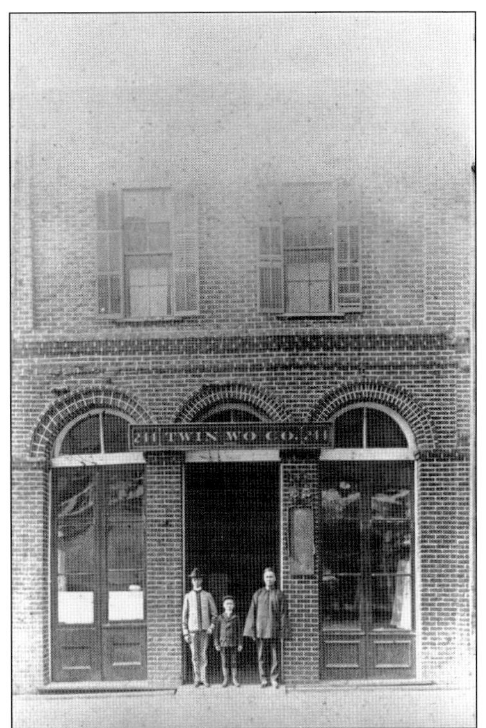

Moy Back Hin was a successful import and export merchant in Chinatown. In the late 1870s, Moy established Twin Wo Company at 244 Yamhill Street, a labor contracting business. He supplied much of the labor for the railroad companies and for the salmon canneries in Oregon and Washington. Inside, the walls were adorned with handwritten calligraphy scrolls bearing good wishes and auspicious phrases, including one that indicated its role as a labor contractor. By providing essential goods and employment, Moy significantly impacted the local community and economy. By the 1890s, Moy's success enabled him to expand and open a second branch in Hope, Idaho, extending his influence beyond Portland. (Both, Portland Chinatown Museum.)

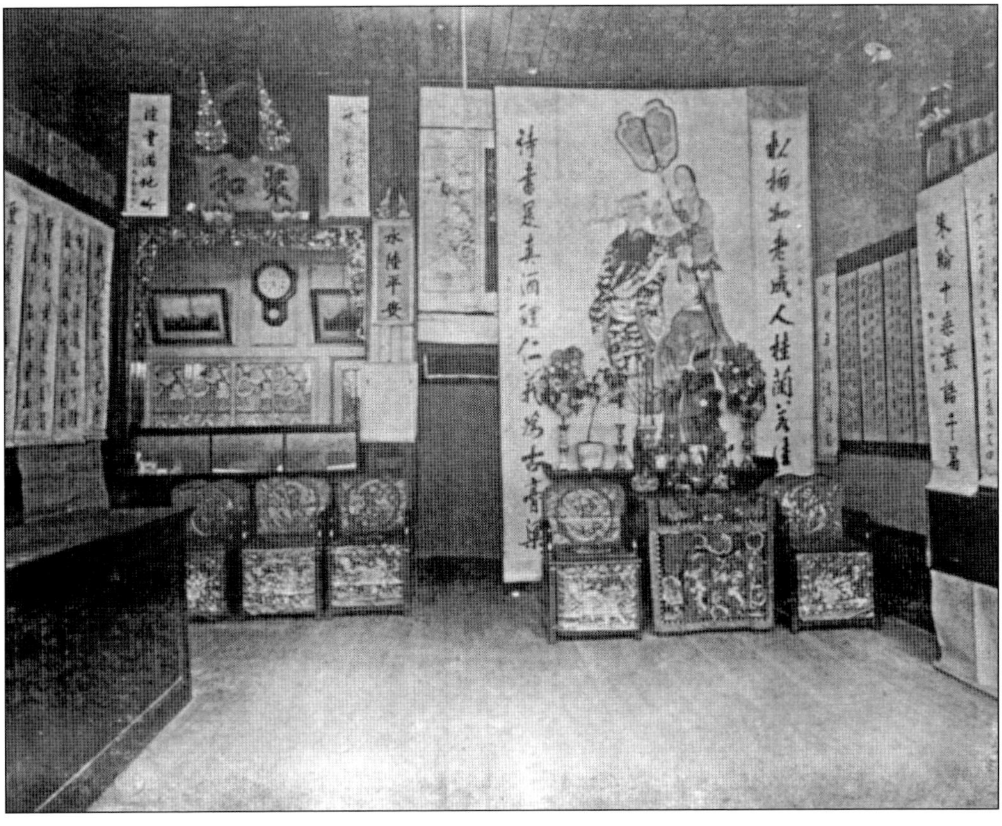

Historic Sites of Chinatown 1890-1901

112 Ling Hing

100 Hop Lee
133 Kim Chung
135 Theater

Sing Ng K

201 Bow Chung
203 Kim Sin Low
203 Lee Sang Lung
205 Kwong Mow Hing

200 Hop Chong
206 Quong Sing Hong
212 Chinese Temple
212 Gee Wa Bing Kee
218 On Hing

300 Lee Sing
303 Fook Hang
303 Hong Yick
305 Kwong Chong
309 Goey Lung
313 Theater
313 Temple
323 Wah Sing

300 On Lee

425 Mission

520 Empress Bazaar

521 Hang Far Low
523 Bow Yuen
523 See Lung
527 Hang Wo
535 Theater

334 Tong
125 Fook Sang

605 Yuen Wa
611 Kwong Sang
615 Chung Sag
621 Joss House
631 Sung Lee

604 On Chung Wa
608 Hong Fook Tong
612 Temple
612 Chew Chong
616 Wing Sing Lung Kee

215 Sun Soon

710 Gee Wo

327 Bing Kee

210 Twin
813 Kwon
827 Lee Sang Wa
837 Hop Sing Wo
837 Pow Chung Lung
838 Yee Chung Lun Kee
839 Ye Chung Lun Kee

819 Kwong Tai

This is a street map of historic sites in Portland's first Chinatown from 1890 to 1901. This was adapted by Staci Wong and compiled by Harlan Luck for the Portland Chinatown History and

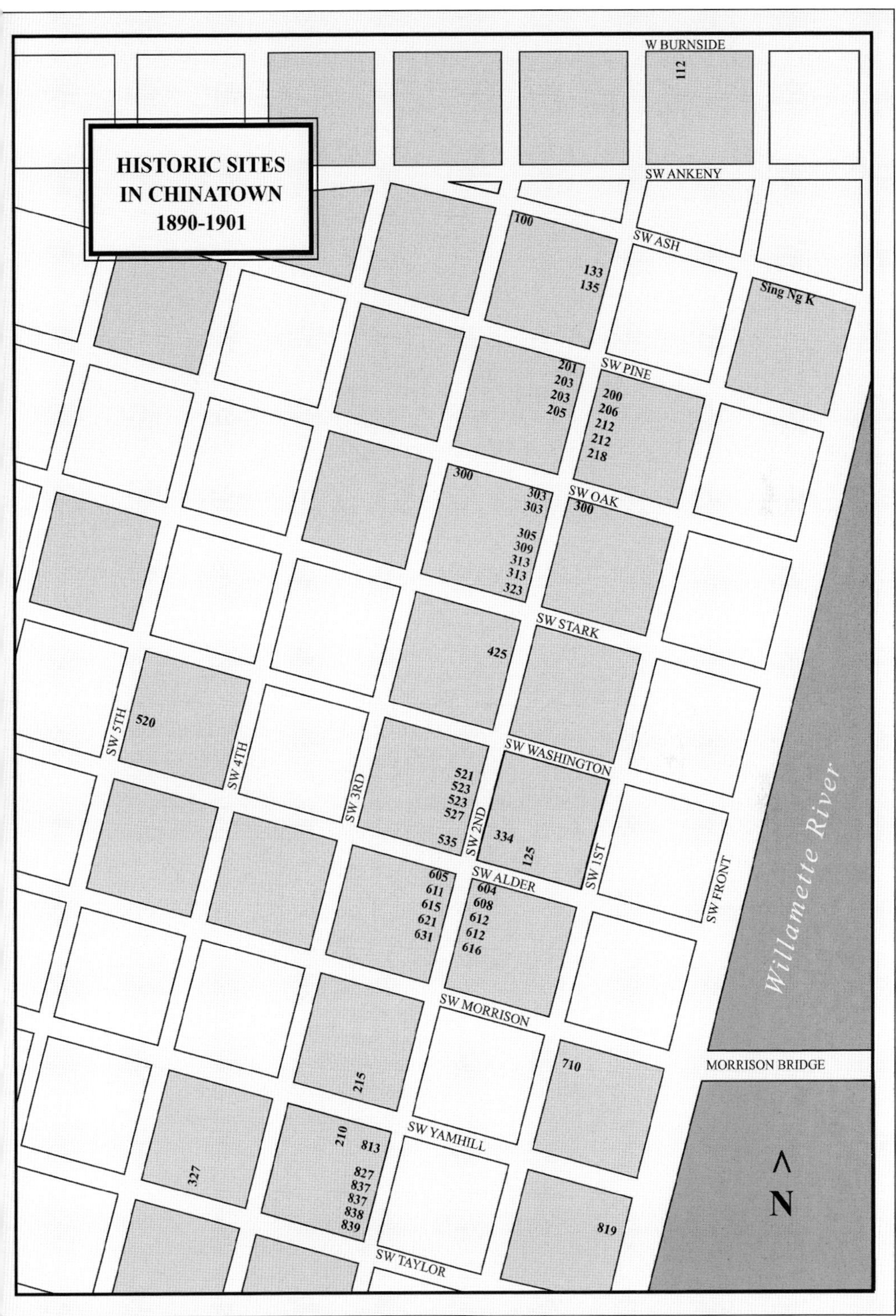

Museum Foundation. (Portland Chinatown Museum.)

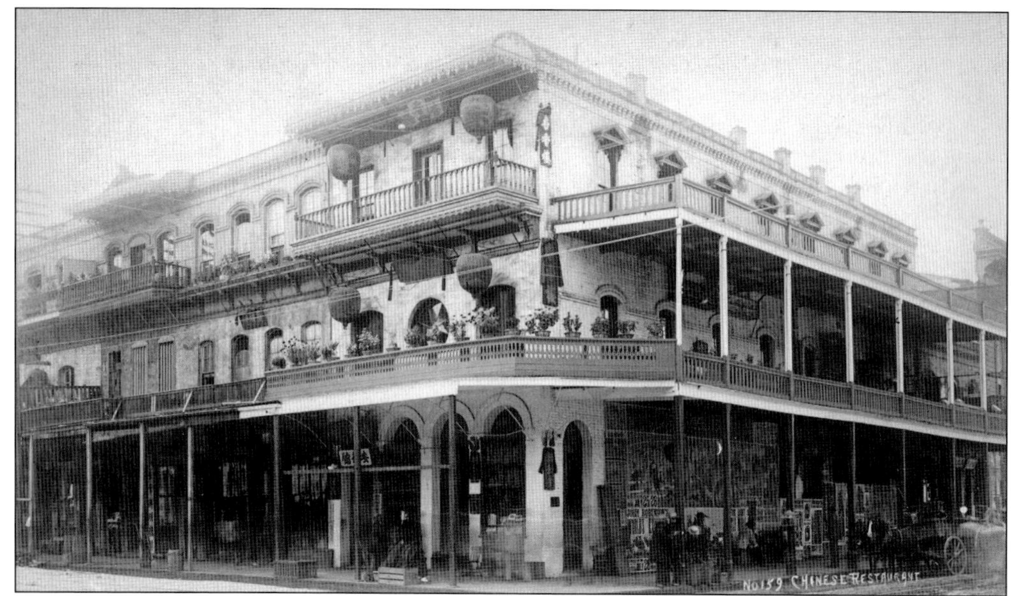

These photographs from 1890 show the building at Southwest Second Avenue and Alder Street in the heart of Portland's first Chinatown. The ground floor included grocery stores Yuen Wo and Company and Hop Tai Wo and general merchandise stores Wing Ching Lung and Hop Chong. According to the 1882 Wells Fargo Chinese Business Directory, Jung Wah Company was also located here; it later became known as the Chinese Consolidated Benevolent Association. Above is Hung Far Low restaurant, along with other spaces for social and cultural activities. This layout efficiently utilized space while supporting the needs of the community. This style of building, with its ornate architecture and wooden structure, was common at the time. (Both, Gholston Collection.)

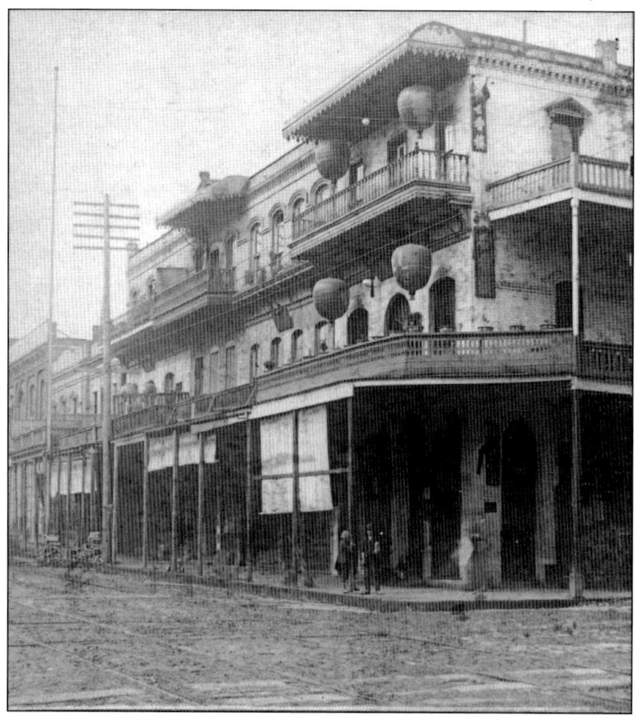

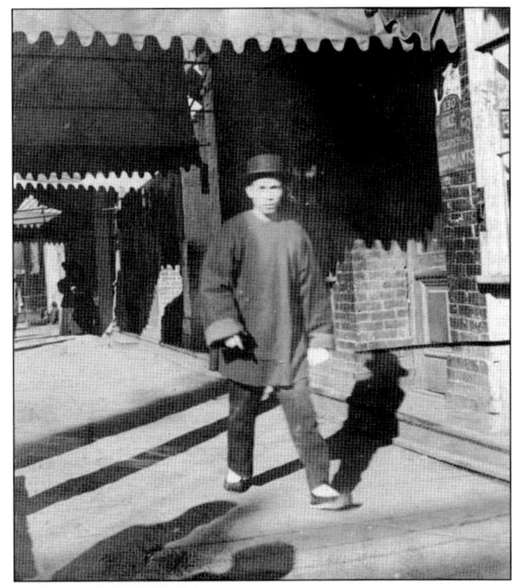

The Chinese Exclusion Act of 1882 barred most Chinese laborers from immigrating, except for merchants, teachers, students, travelers, and diplomats. This federal law intentionally resulted in a predominantly bachelor society. Many Chinese men earned money and sent it back to their families, hoping to return home later. The law also prevented Chinese immigrants from becoming US citizens. (City of Portland Archives, 4633.)

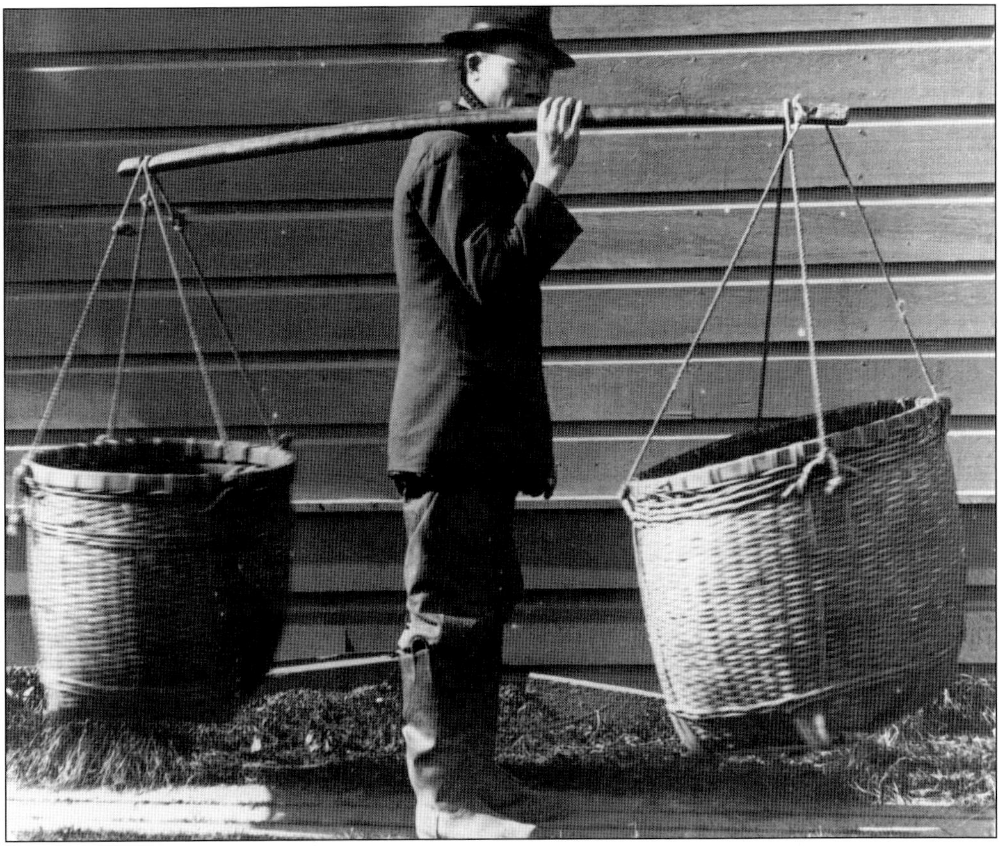

Farming offered a way to earn money as early as 1879, when Chinese vegetable gardens first appeared in Southwest Portland. Fresh produce was sold to Chinatown businesses and markets, as well as in the West Hills, using wicker baskets hung from a pole for transport. Some also provided door-to-door hand laundry services and sold firewood. (Portland Chinatown Museum.)

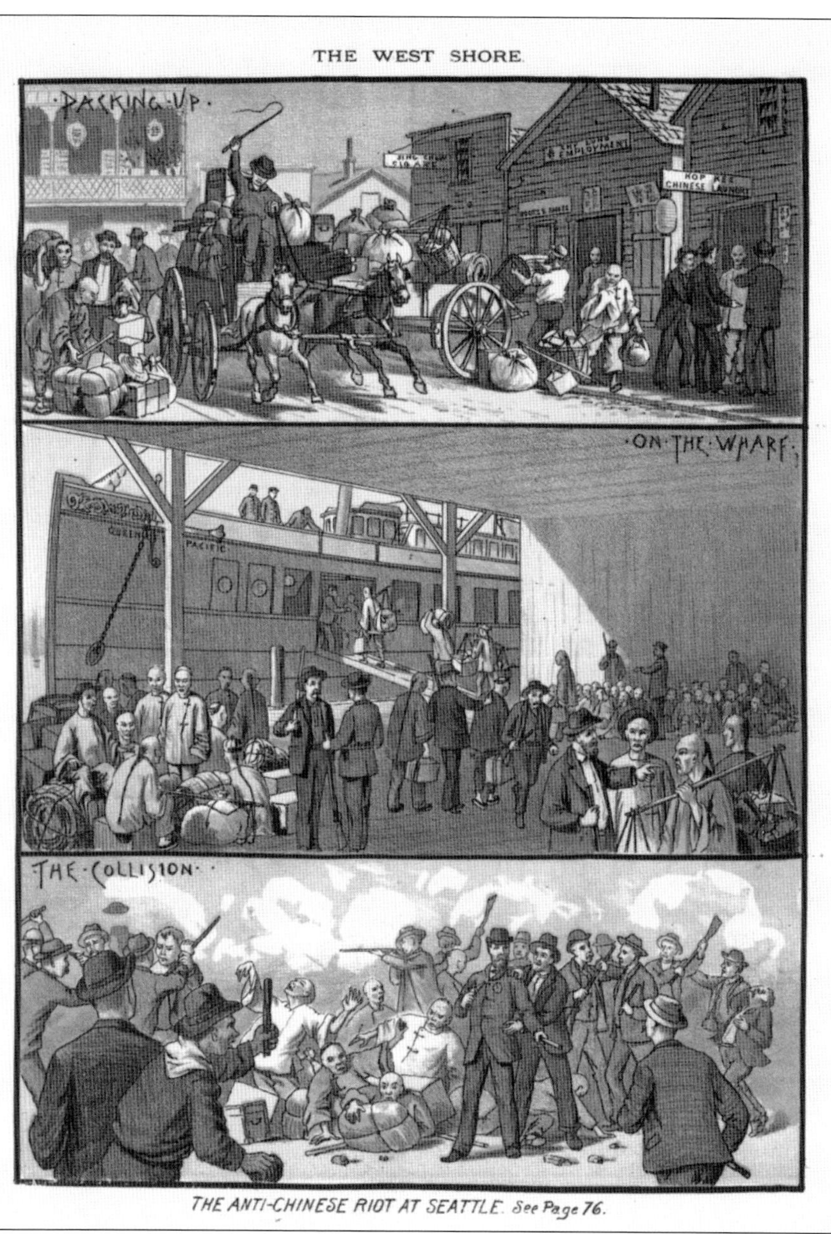

Following the passage of the Chinese Exclusion Act, rampant racism surged on the West Coast amid an economic downturn, which was part of the depression of 1882 to 1885. There was a significant decline in railroad construction and related industries, such as iron and steel, leading to bank failures. This culminated in widespread unemployment and economic hardship. Chinese workers had developed a reputation for being more efficient and accepting lower wages than their white counterparts. This hostility resulted in a racially motivated riot in Tacoma in 1885, when about 200 Chinese residents were beaten and forced out. A prominent businessman in Portland's Chinatown, Moy Back Hin, rescued and relocated them via trains bound for Portland. Another riot in Seattle took place in 1886, as depicted in this *West Shore* magazine article. While Portland did experience discrimination and racism, the city was largely spared from the violence, partly due to the efforts of prominent Chinese leaders and merchants in Chinatown. (Gholston Collection.)

Albertine Mitchell, a committed Baptist missionary, worked with Portland's Chinese community, offering English classes and spiritual guidance. In 1871, she traveled to Guangdong with local men to establish a mission. Her work bridged cultural gaps, helping immigrants learn English while managing demanding jobs. Missionaries like Mitchell were instrumental in Chinatown, providing education and support while sharing Christianity during a pivotal time in Portland's history. (Gholston Collection.)

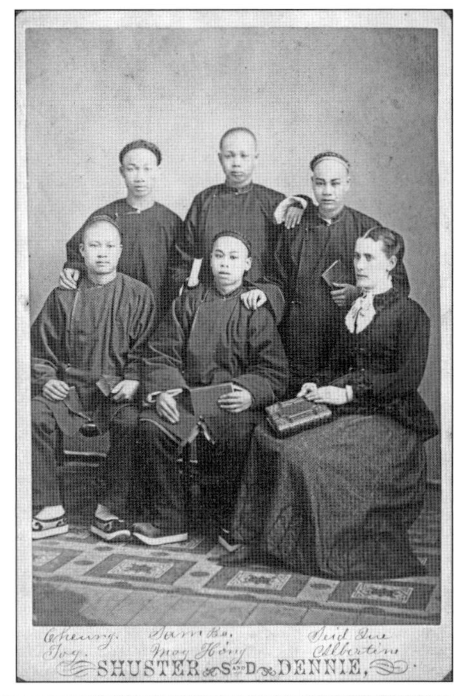

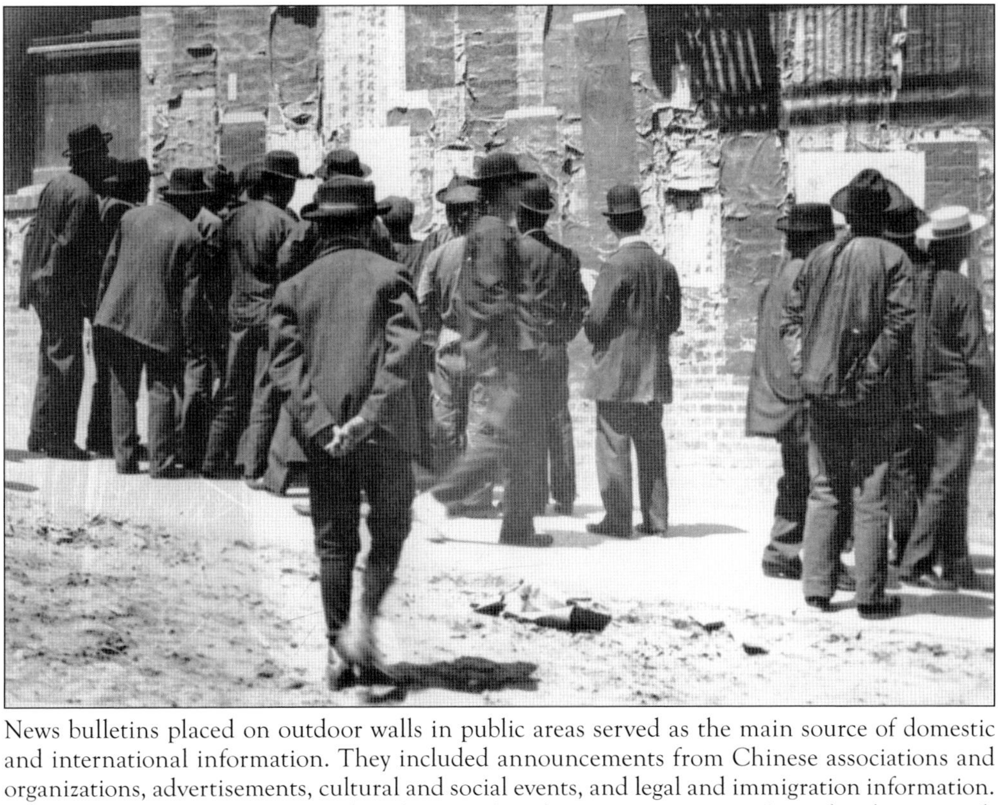

News bulletins placed on outdoor walls in public areas served as the main source of domestic and international information. They included announcements from Chinese associations and organizations, advertisements, cultural and social events, and legal and immigration information. These bulletins played a crucial role in keeping the Chinese community informed and connected. (Portland Chinatown Museum.)

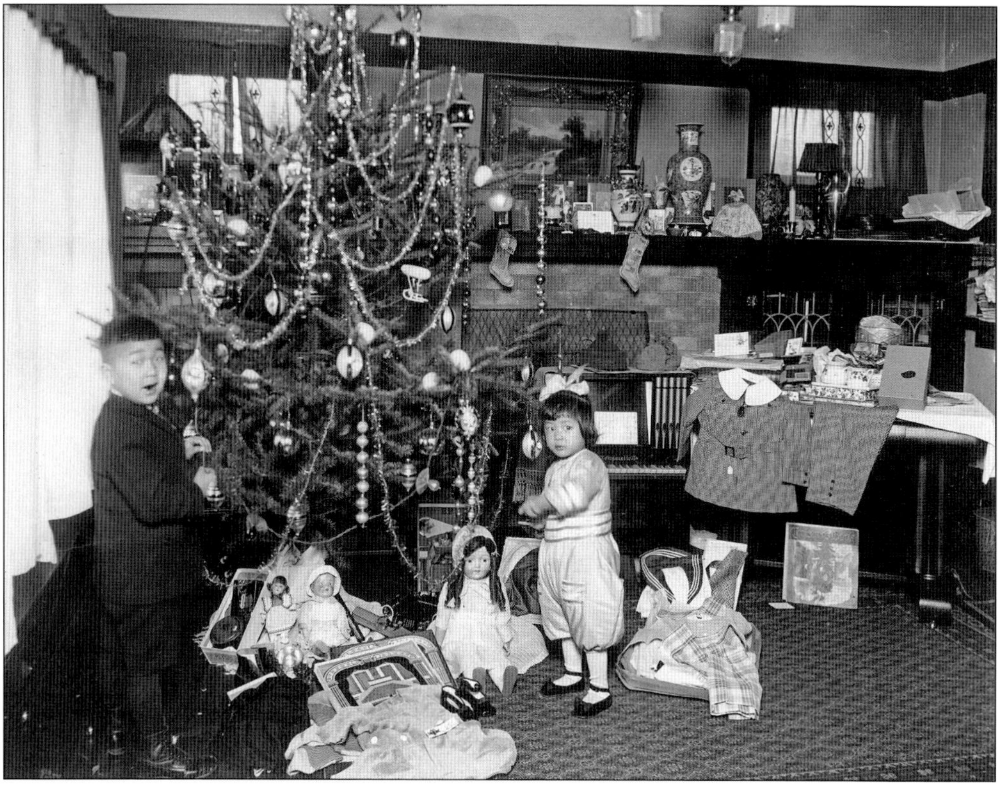

Seid Back was a prominent merchant, labor contractor, and community leader. After the death of his wife, Back married Ching Wan, and they adopted two white children, Daniel and George, from an orphanage. Back's son Seid Gain, also known as Seid Back Jr., and an unidentified girl are in this c. 1886 photograph during Christmas. Many Chinese converted to Christianity through the efforts of missionaries in Chinatown. (Portland Chinatown Museum.)

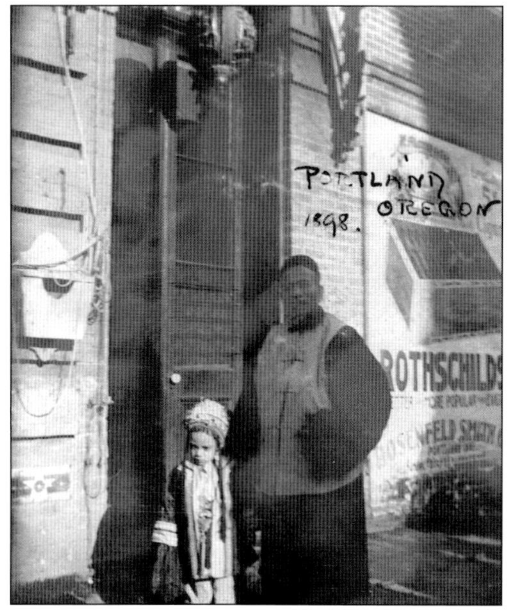

This photograph from 1898 shows a man and a child wearing special occasion Chinese clothing of the time. The child's hat was believed to offer protection from illness and evil spirits, and it symbolized health, courage, wealth, and happiness. A diverse array of amulets with different meanings adorned children to offer protection from evil or represented a long and prosperous life. (City of Portland Archives, 4634.)

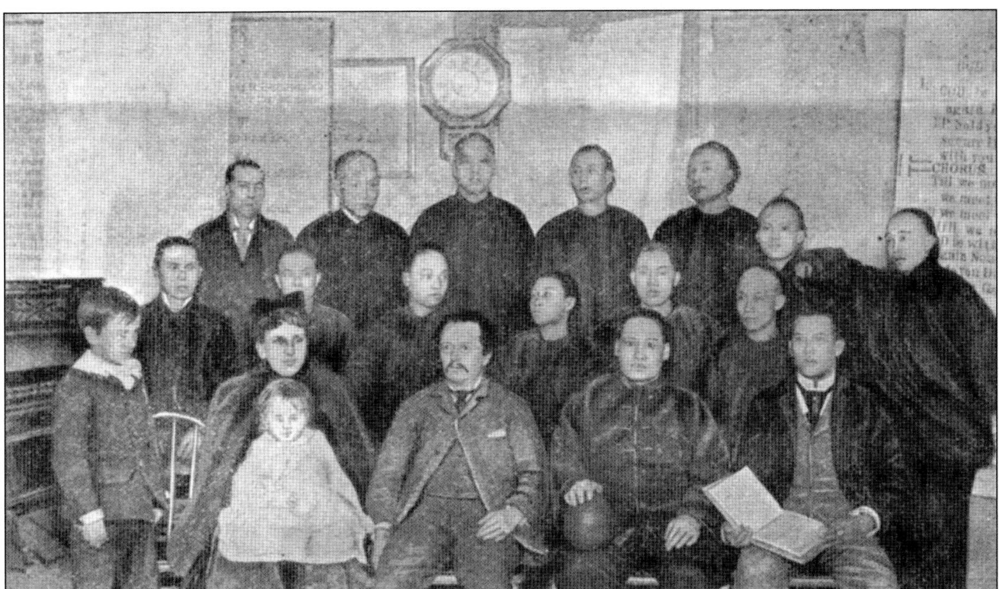

After beginning missionary work in Shanghai in 1873, Rev. William and France Holt returned in 1885 to Portland, where they founded a night mission school. The school focused on teaching English and Christianity to immigrants. This 1895 photograph captures them with their children (at the forefront) and students at Mission Chapel, highlighting their unwavering dedication to education and spiritual guidance for this community. (Gholston Collection.)

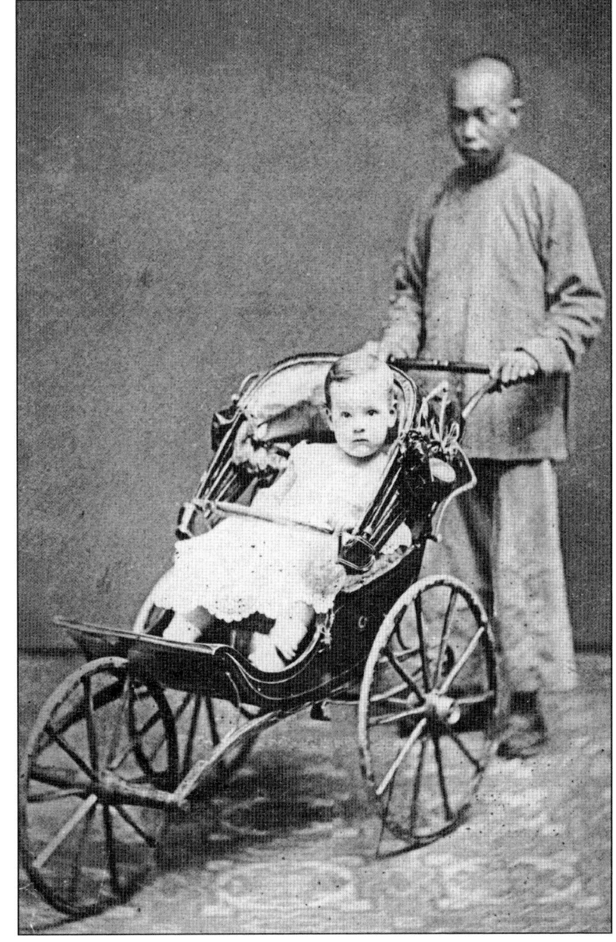

Early Chinese immigrants found work in industries that required minimal formal education and English proficiency, allowing them to quickly learn the necessary skills. Although these jobs were low-paying and often involved hard labor, they provided opportunities to earn a living. Some immigrants went on to become successful entrepreneurs, opening stores, laundries, and restaurants. (Gholston Collection.)

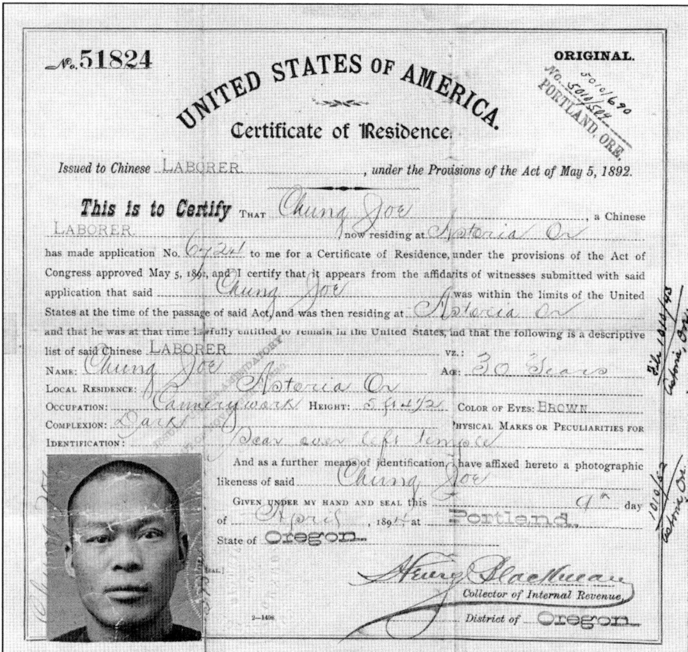

No. 51824 ORIGINAL.

UNITED STATES OF AMERICA.

Certificate of Residence.

Issued to Chinese LABORER, under the Provisions of the Act of May 5, 1892.

This is to Certify THAT Chung Joe, a Chinese LABORER now residing at Astoria Or has made application No. 6724 to me for a Certificate of Residence, under the provisions of the Act of Congress approved May 5, 1892, and I certify that it appears from the affidavits of witnesses submitted with said application that said Chung Joe was within the limits of the United States at the time of the passage of said Act, and was then residing at Astoria Or and that he was at that time lawfully entitled to remain in the United States, and that the following is a descriptive list of said Chinese LABORER viz.:

NAME: Chung Joe AGE: 30 Years

LOCAL RESIDENCE: Astoria Or

OCCUPATION: Cannerywork HEIGHT: 5 ft 4 1/2 COLOR OF EYES: BROWN

COMPLEXION: Dark PHYSICAL MARKS OR PECULIARITIES FOR IDENTIFICATION: Scar over left temple

And as a further means of identification, I have affixed hereto a photographic likeness of said Chung Joe

GIVEN UNDER MY HAND AND SEAL this 9th day of April, 1894 at Portland State of Oregon.

[SEAL.]

Henry Blackman
Collector of Internal Revenue,
District of Oregon.

The Geary Act of 1892 extended the Chinese Exclusion Act's ban on immigration for another 10 years and later made it permanent until 1943. The act required Chinese immigrants to carry a special certificate of residence issued by the Internal Revenue Service. Those found without this certificate faced hard labor and deportation. (Portland Chinatown Museum.)

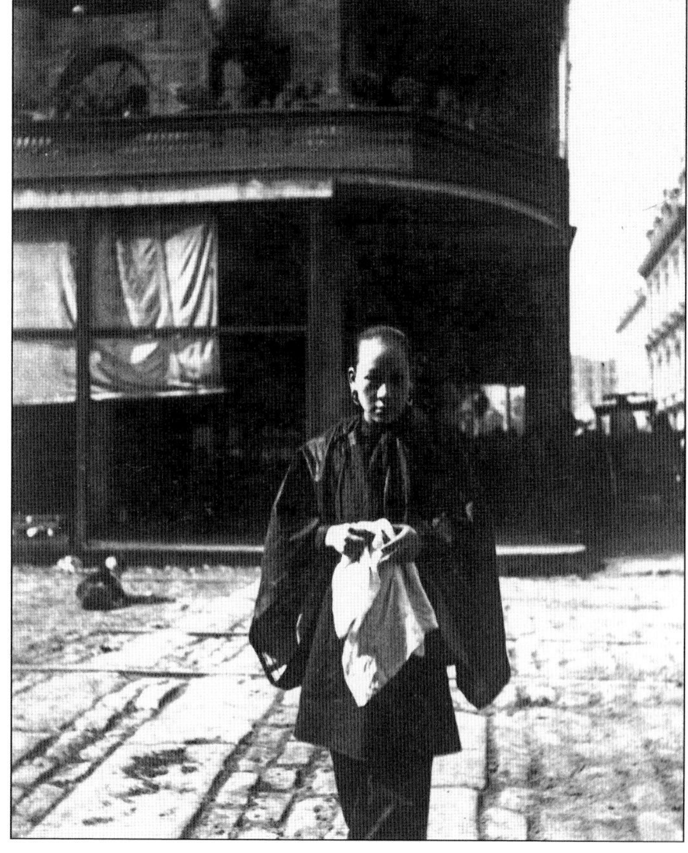

In 1890, Chinese women constituted only 5 percent of the Chinese population in America. The Page Act of 1875 severely restricted their immigration, allowing only those from the merchant or diplomat class to enter. This law aimed to curb the influx of Chinese women, who were often perceived by the white community as a threat to moral and social order. Consequently, Chinese communities in the US became predominantly male. (Gholston Collection.)

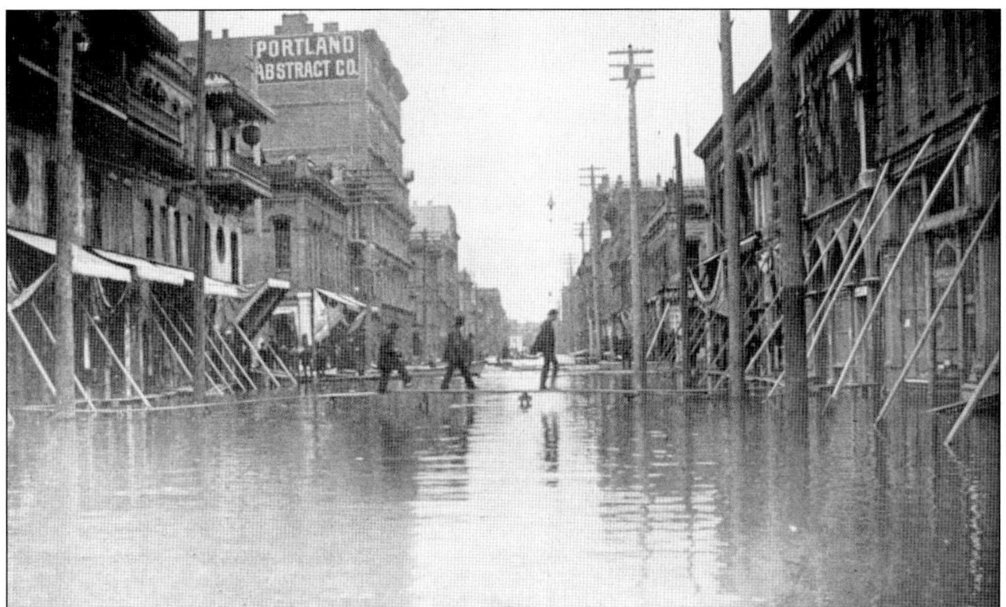

The Great Flood of 1894 impacted the downtown and Chinatown areas. Wooden planks served as temporary sidewalks, as shown at Northwest Second and Morrison Streets in Chinatown. Before the seawall was built along the Willamette River in the late 1920s, the area was prone to flooding. The 1894 flood, along with the growing commercial desirability of the area, led to Chinatown's relocation starting in the late 1890s. (City of Portland Archives, AP/4930.)

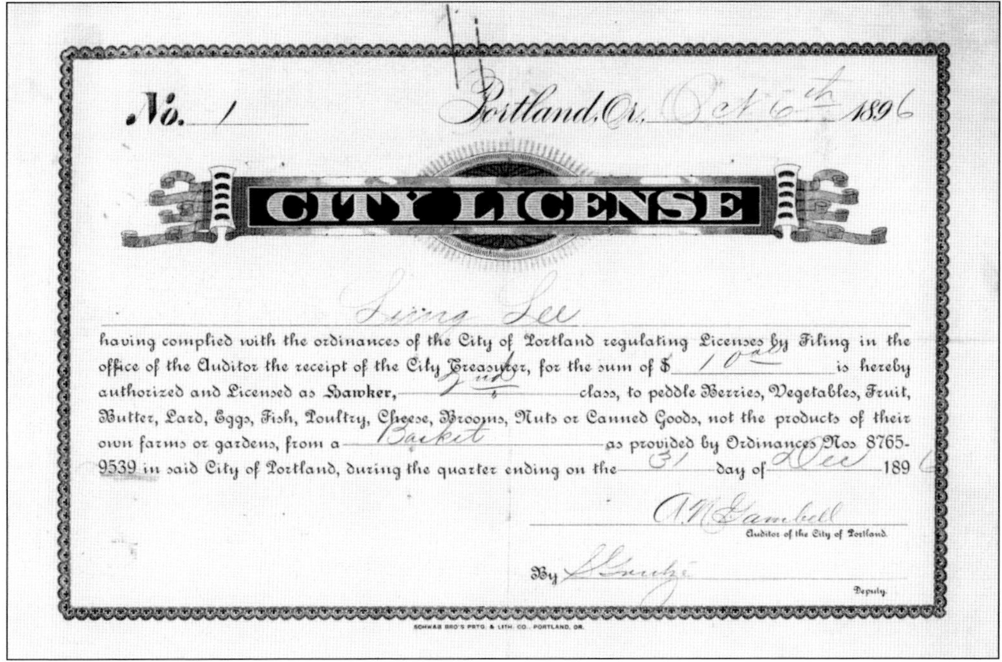

No. 1 Portland, Or. Oct 6th 1896

CITY LICENSE

Ling Lee

having complied with the ordinances of the City of Portland regulating Licenses by Filing in the office of the Auditor the receipt of the City Treasurer, for the sum of $ 10 00/100 is hereby authorized and Licensed as Hawker, 2nd class, to peddle Berries, Vegetables, Fruit, Butter, Lard, Eggs, Fish, Poultry, Cheese, Brooms, Nuts or Canned Goods, not the products of their own farms or gardens, from a Basket as provided by Ordinances Nos 8765-9539 in said City of Portland, during the quarter ending on the 31 day of Dec 1896

A N Gambell
Auditor of the City of Portland.

By [illegible]
Deputy.

SCHWAB BRO'S PRTG. & LITH. CO. PORTLAND, OR.

In 1896, Lee Ling was issued a $10 license to sell items not from his own garden, which included produce, butter, eggs, fish, and more. Street peddlers were banned in 1910 as part of discriminatory practices against Chinese immigrants. Despite these challenges, the community remained resilient, finding other ways to earn a living. (City of Portland Archives, AP/15985.)

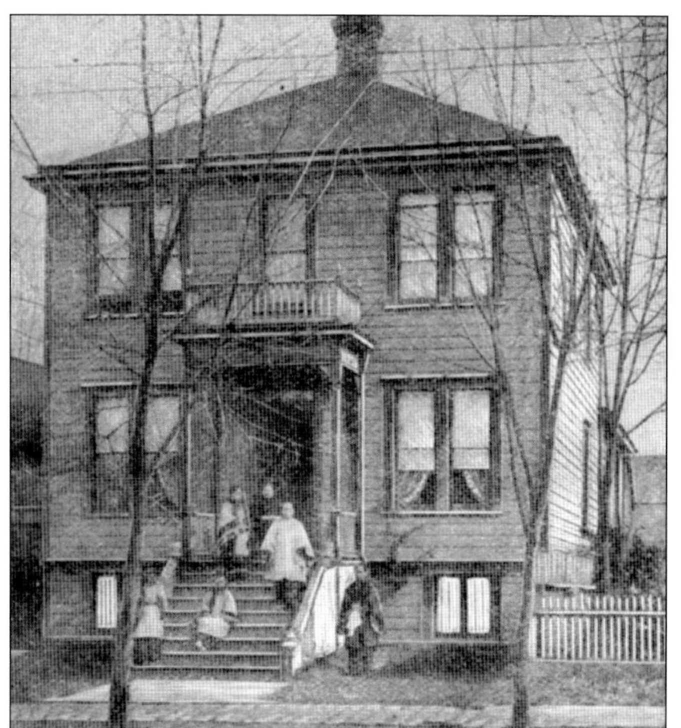

After starting their missionary work, France Holt established the Chinese Women's Home, where by 1895, she had rescued 37 women and girls, offering them safety, support, and education. This initiative transformed lives, providing a path toward dignity and a more hopeful future. France and her husband, Rev. William Holt, became outspoken advocates for Portland's Chinese community, urging other churches to join them in offering protection and solidarity. (Gholston Collection.)

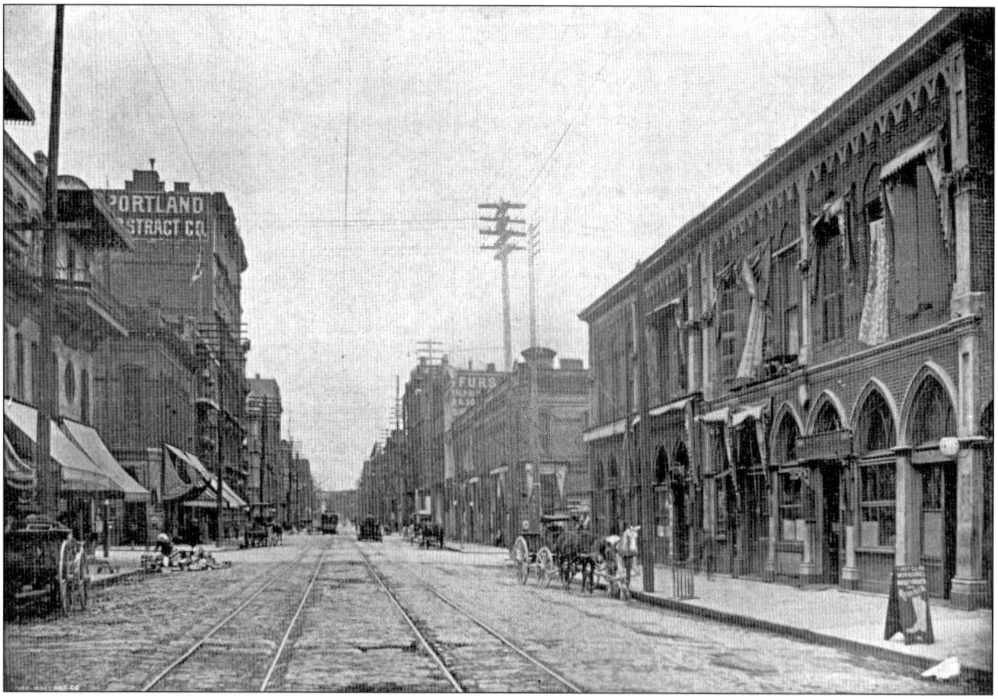

This street view of Chinatown on Second Street in 1899 shows Portland's streetcar system, which began in the 1870s and grew into one of the largest in the country. It was a vital part of the city's transportation network, connecting downtown Portland to various neighborhoods, including Chinatown. (City of Portland Archives, AP/57643.)

Before 1900, Chinatown's streets were bustling with peddlers and artisans offering repair services for shoes, umbrellas, and more, alongside skilled tinsmiths and jewelers. These tradesmen provided affordable services to the Chinese residents and other locals in the Portland community while creating a vital source of income. (Portland Chinatown Museum.)

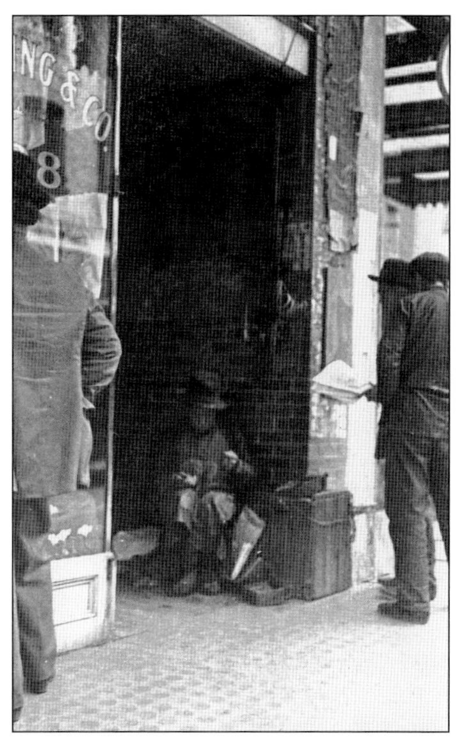

This photograph depicts a Chinese home at Southwest Fourteenth Avenue and Mill Street. Women played a vital role in maintaining cultural traditions and supporting family businesses like boardinghouses, tailoring, and herbal shops. Despite facing restrictive immigration laws and social prejudices, their contributions were crucial to the community's resilience and cultural preservation. Their efforts fostered a sense of home and belonging for Chinese immigrants in a new land. (Portland Chinatown Museum.)

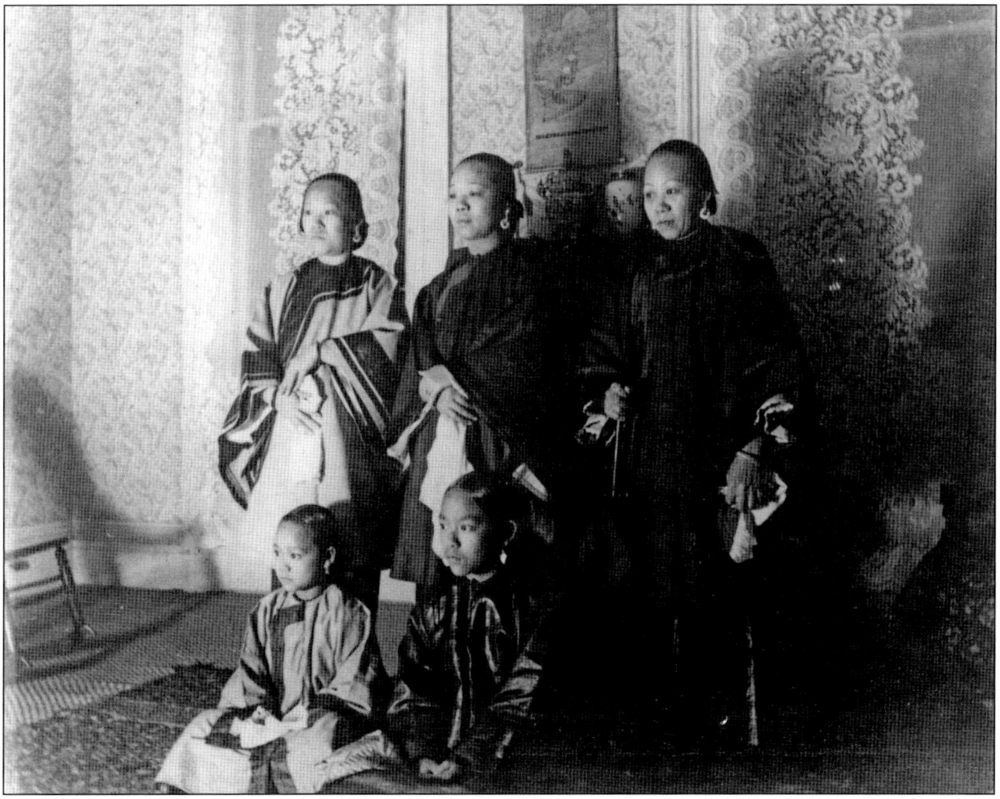

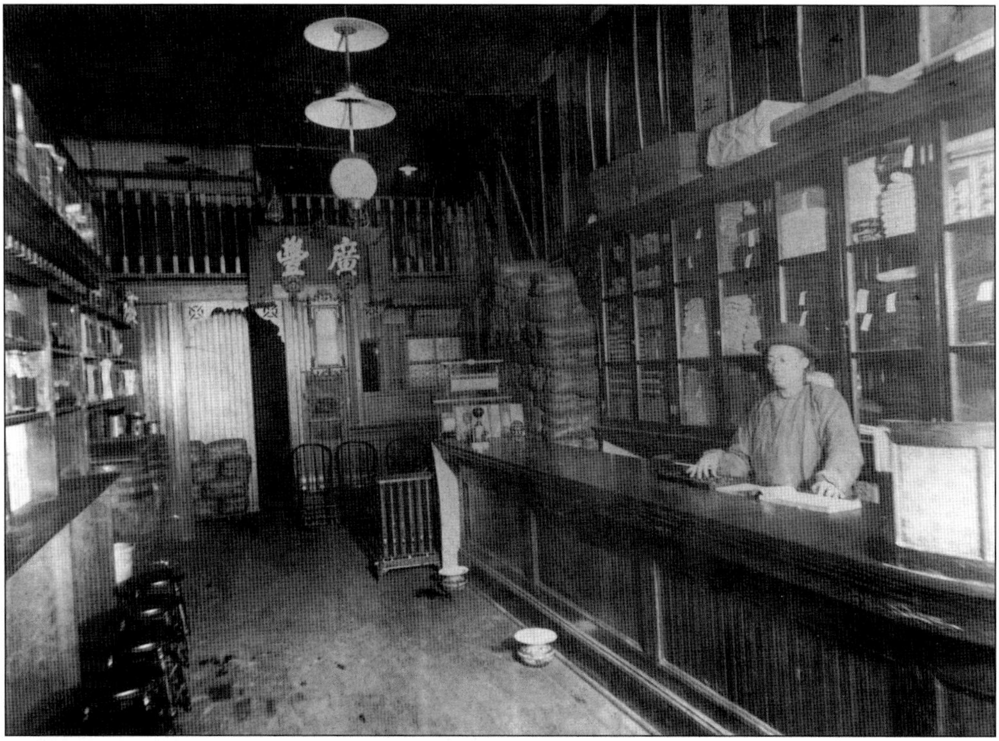

Merchants like Kwong Fung received merchandise packed in wooden crates and barrels for protection during the long journey from China. Textile goods were wrapped in cloth or burlap sacks and secured with rope, while fragile items were cushioned with straw or sawdust. The man in the photograph is using an abacus, a traditional counting tool. The abacus was important in daily operations, helping merchants maintain accurate records. (Portland Chinatown Museum.)

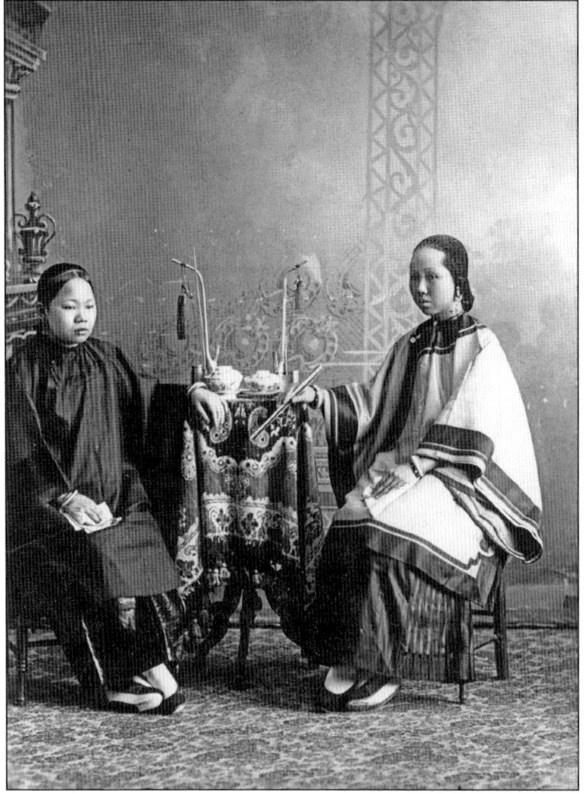

Under the Qing Dynasty, bound feet were associated with higher social status, elegance, and refinement. This painful practice also limited women's mobility and often caused lifelong disabilities. This was banned in China in 1912 following the fall of the Qing Dynasty. This professional photograph shows two women, which was rare to see in Portland due to the limitation on immigration. (Portland Chinatown Museum.)

Many Chinese men became entrepreneurs, pooling resources to start businesses. This collaborative approach allowed them to share financial risks and benefits, making it easier to establish and sustain ventures. Partnerships facilitated access to a broader network of contacts and resources, enhancing their ability to navigate challenges and contributing significantly to the economic development of Chinatown. (Portland Chinatown Museum.)

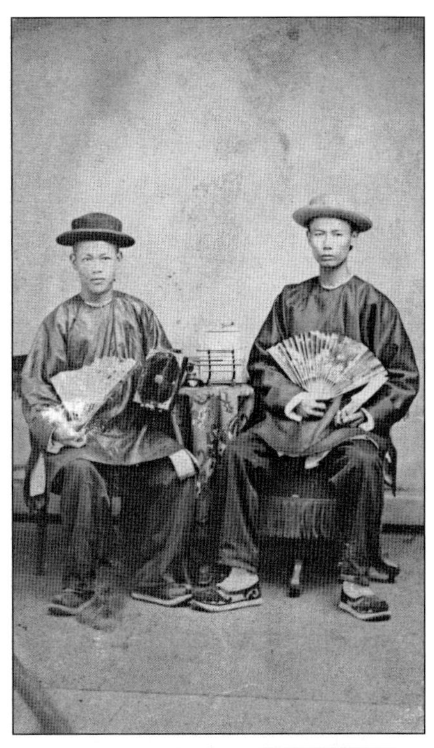

Andrew Kan and Company was known for its high-quality imports, catering to both the Chinese and Japanese communities as well as Portland's broader population. The store played a significant role in the city's Chinatown economy, offering luxury items like silk, porcelain, rugs, and furniture, reflecting the tastes and cultural influences of the time. (Portland Chinatown Museum.)

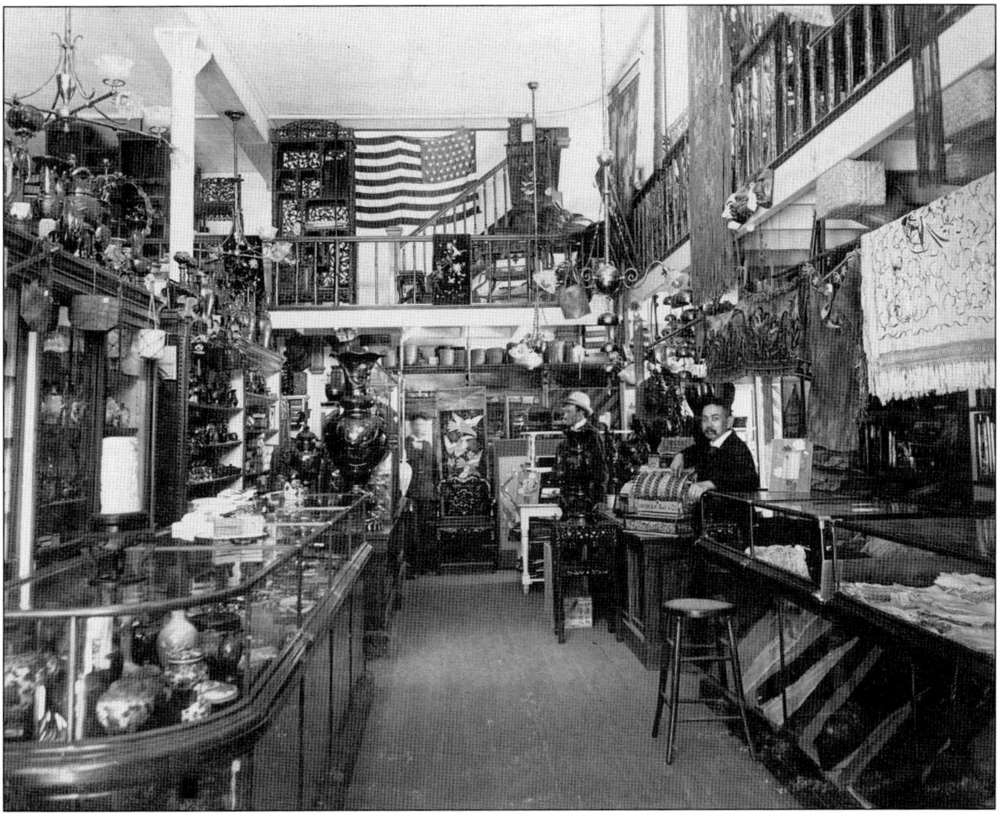

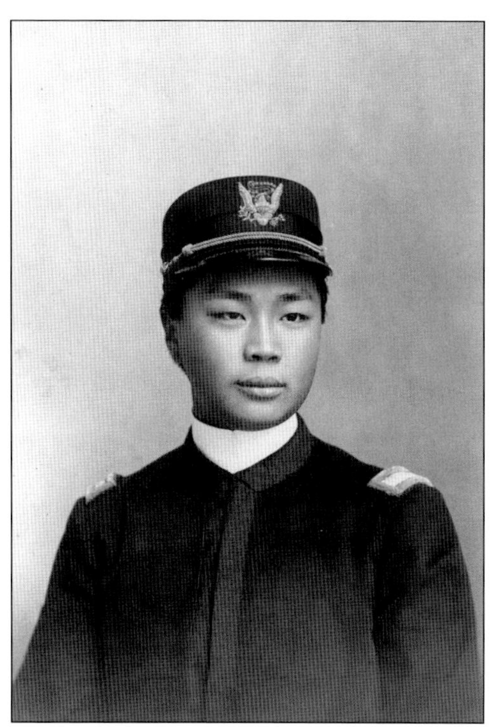

Seid Gain attended Portland's Bishop Scott Academy and the University of Oregon. Gain was the first Chinese American to practice law in Oregon in 1907. He was an interpreter for the US Immigration Bureau and was the founder of the American Born Chinese Association and the American Born Chinese Brigade. Born in Portland in 1878, he supported the social advancement of American-born Chinese and patriotism toward the United States. (Gholston Collection.)

In 1898, during the Spanish-American War, Seid Gain formed the American Born Chinese Brigade and served as captain. This was the first of its kind in the country. Volunteers served to demonstrate their patriotism and commitment to their country despite the discrimination they faced. The first lieutenant, Moy Bow Wing, was the son of renowned merchant and community leader Moy Back Hin. (Portland Chinatown Museum.)

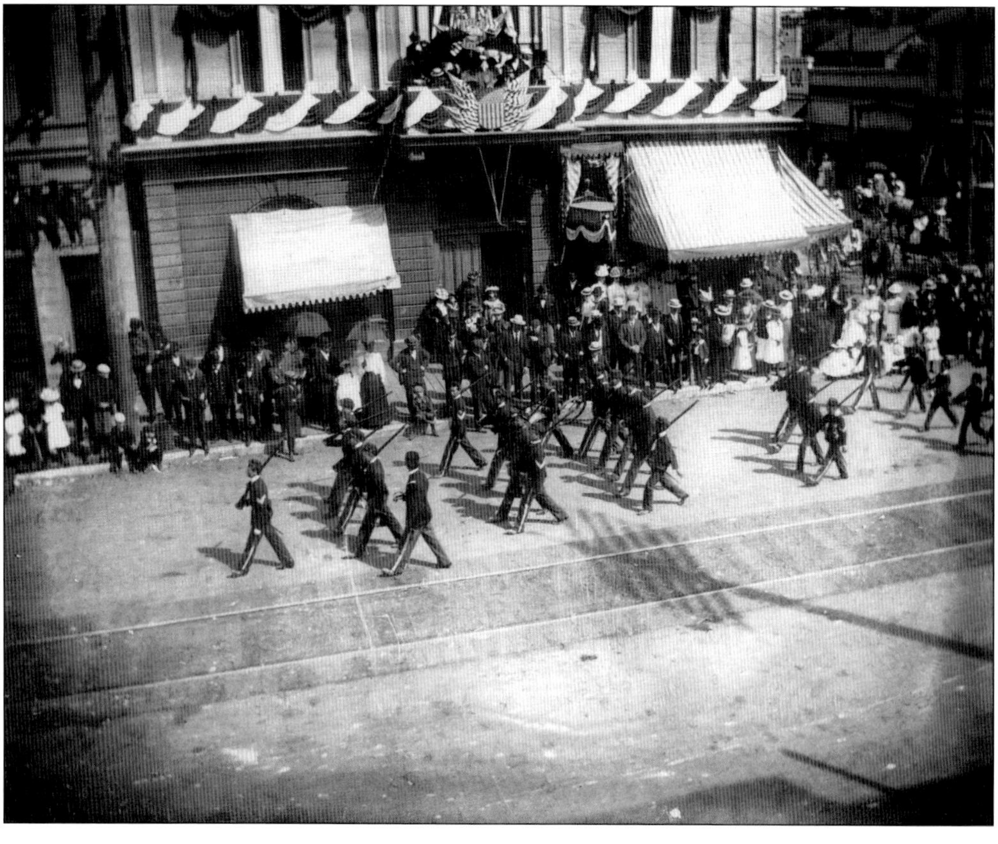

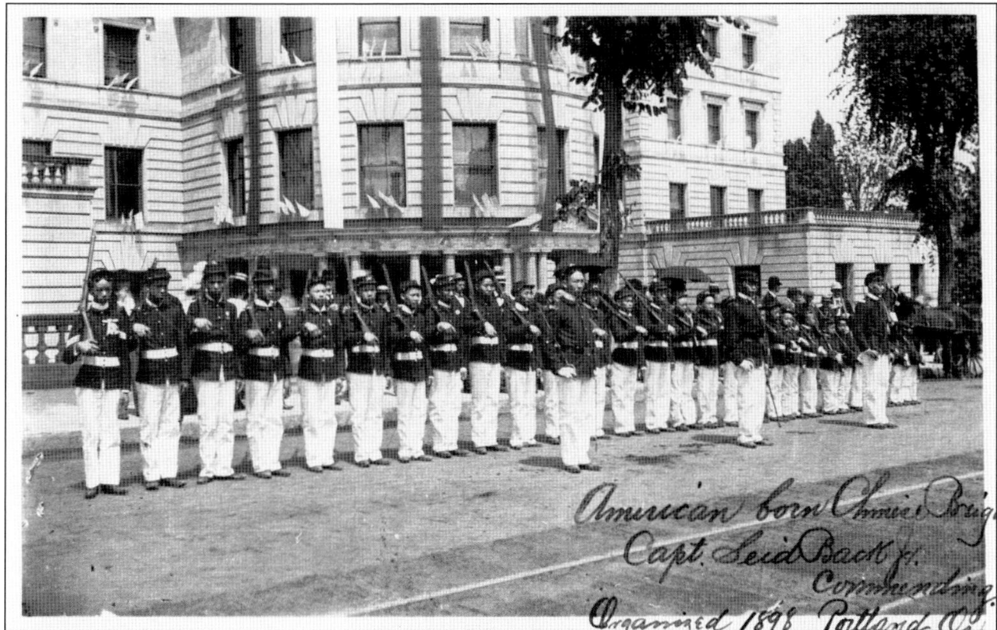

The American Born Chinese Brigade was a paramilitary organization from 1898 to 1905 that supported the social, mental, and physical advancement of American-born Chinese children during a time when immigrants faced considerable discrimination. It disbanded as racial tensions began to ease and the Chinese American community found other ways to advocate for their rights and safety through various organizations and community efforts in Chinatown. The image above shows the brigade standing in front of city hall in 1901. This American Born Chinese Association certificate was awarded to John Sing Ho and signed by president Seid Back Jr. (Above, Oregon Historical Society, OrHi_370; below, US National Archives.)

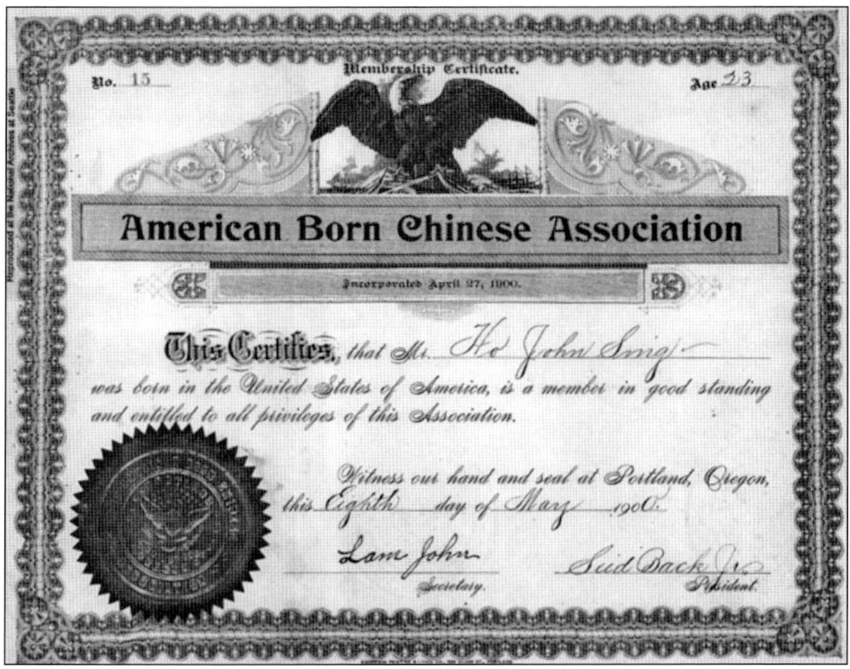
Membership Certificate.

No. 15 Age 23

American Born Chinese Association

Incorporated April 27, 1900.

This Certifies, that Mr. Ho John Sing was born in the United States of America, is a member in good standing and entitled to all privileges of this Association.

Witness our hand and seal at Portland, Oregon, this Eighth day of May 1900.

Lam John, Secretary.

Seid Back Jr., President.

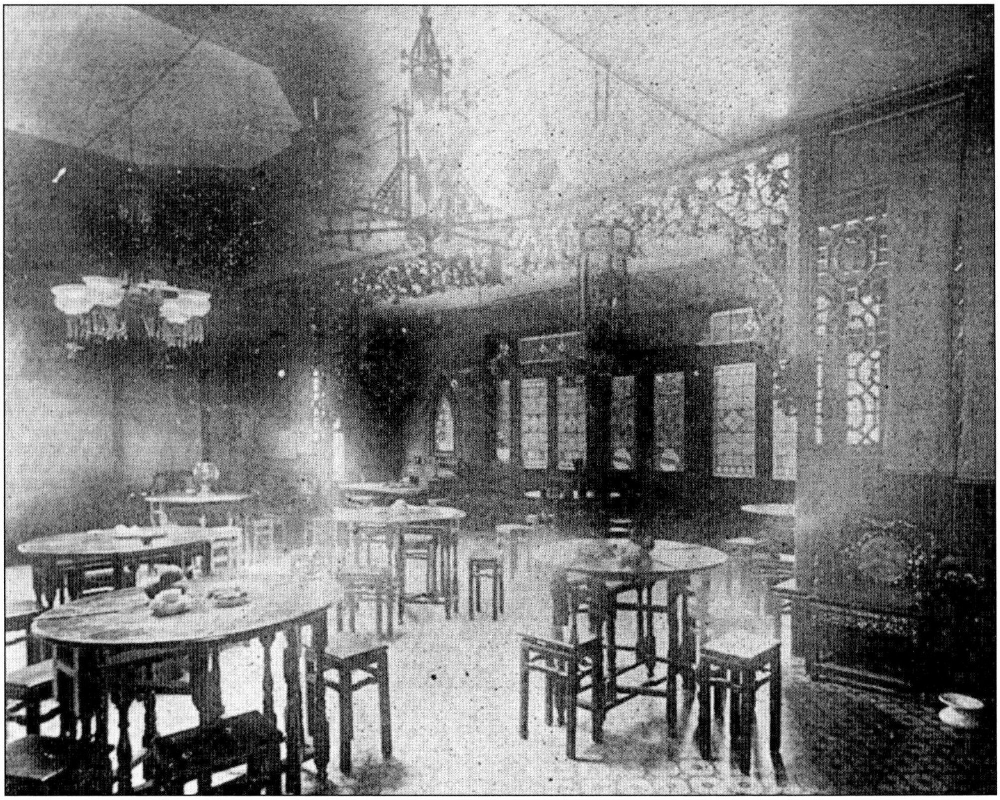

This 1899 photograph shows the interior of a Chinese restaurant at Second Avenue and Pine Street. Restaurants were more than places to enjoy traditional Chinese food. These establishments also served as a social and cultural gathering spot, fostering a sense of community for the early Chinese pioneers. (City of Portland Archives, AP/57656.)

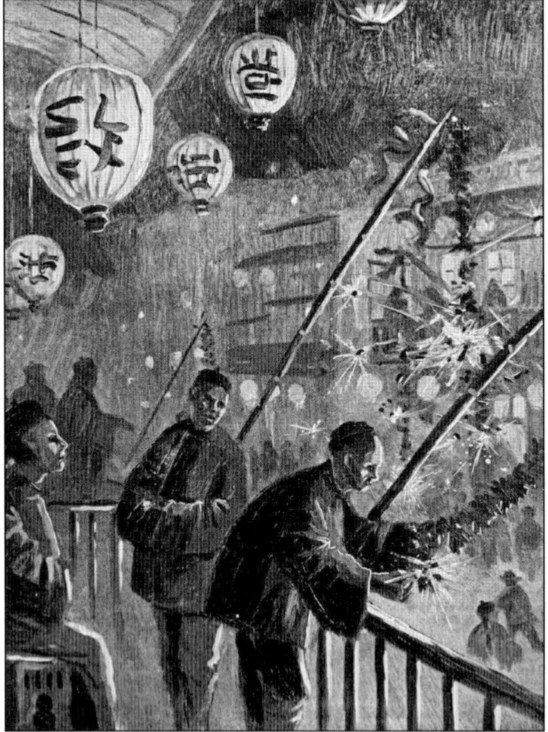

Chinese New Year, or Lunar New Year, is one of the most important holidays in Chinese culture. It is celebrated in other cultures, such as in Tibet, Vietnam, South Korea, and the Ryukyu Islands in Japan, although customs and holiday durations differ. Firecrackers ward off evil spirits, red envelopes are given for good luck, and participants honor ancestors and deities. These traditions continue in various forms today. (Portland Chinatown Museum.)

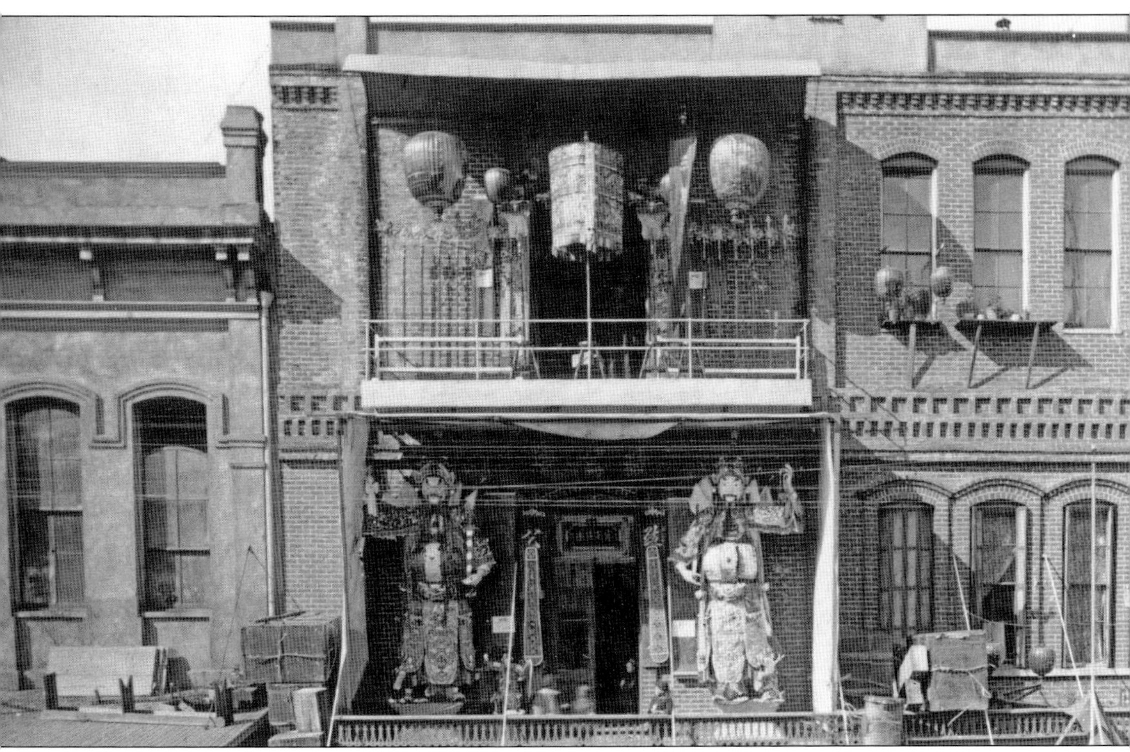

This temple, also called a joss house, was at Chee Kung Tong at 131 Second Street between Alder and Washington Streets in the 1890s. Chee Kung Tong was one of the many tongs, or Chinese fraternal organizations, sometimes referred to as "Chinese Freemasons." Members paid dues in exchange for assistance in disputes, mutual aid, protection, and a strong support network. The joss house served as a religious and cultural center where community members could worship and participate in important cultural traditions. This image shows the Hungry Ghost Festival, which is a Buddhist and Taoist holiday that falls on the 15th day of the seventh month in the lunar calendar or in July or August in the Gregorian calendar. This festival is a time when offerings are made to appease the spirits of the deceased and ensure their well-being in the afterlife. Tongs still exist today, focusing on community services and cultural preservation. On the ground level (not shown) was Kwong Tai, a Chinese merchandise store. (Portland Chinatown Museum.)

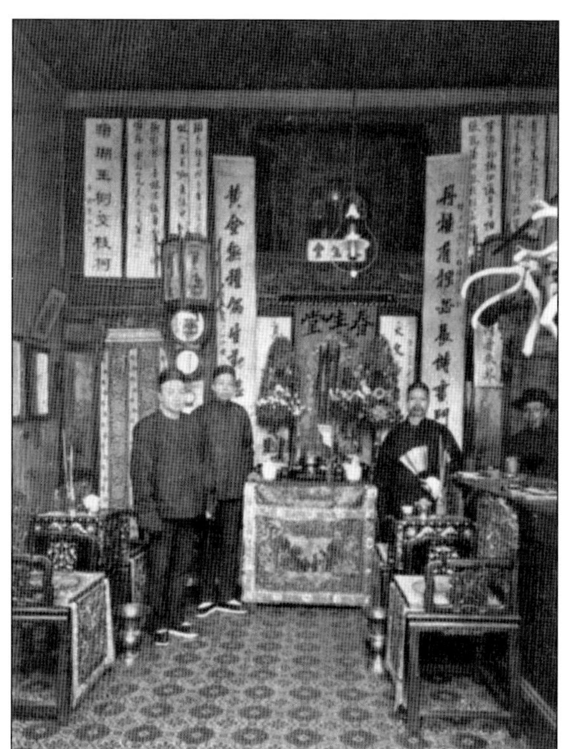

Cheun Sang Tong was at 141 Second Street. The inspiring scrolls on the walls emphasized the importance of education and the belief that diligent effort leads to prosperity. These messages not only encouraged knowledge and hard work but also reflected the core values in the community. This made it a place where individuals could find both motivation and support in their pursuit of a better future. (City of Portland Archives, AP/19831.)

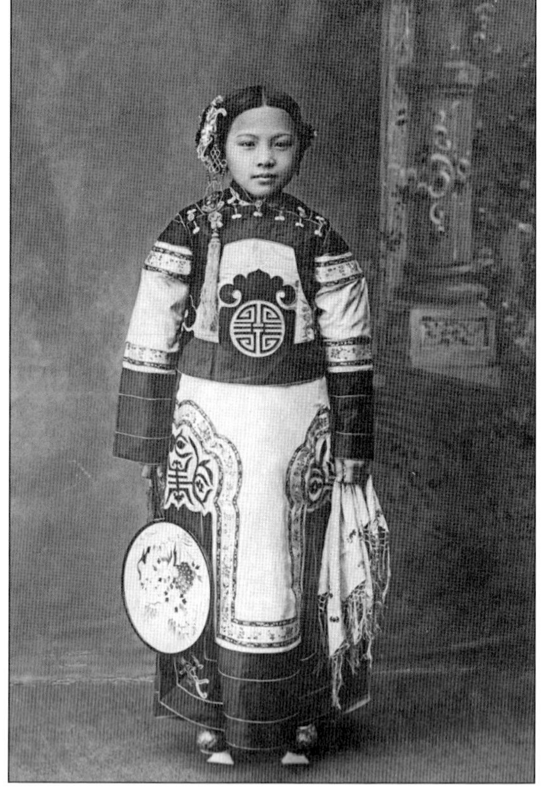

This young girl, a member of the Seid Back family, is captured in a professional photograph from around 1895. Taken during a festival or celebration, the image highlights the cultural importance of such events in Chinese American communities, showcasing traditional attire and the joy of community gatherings. This photograph offers a glimpse into the heritage and social life of the time. (Gholston Collection.)

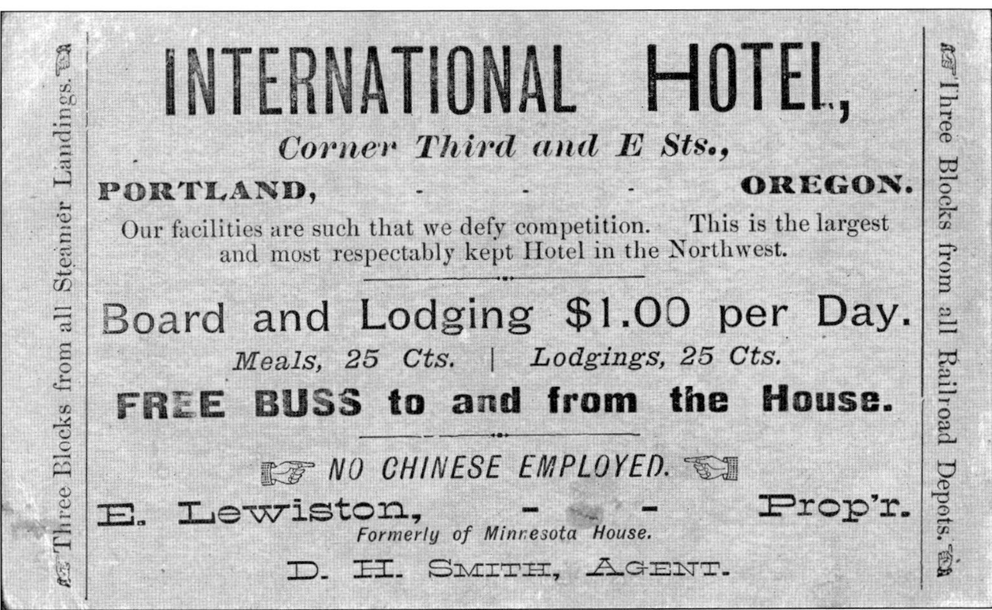

In 1895, the International Hotel provided lodging for travelers arriving by regional and transcontinental trains and overseas via steamer ships. The advertisement, however, openly promoted discrimination, reflecting the prevalent biases of the time. This practice underscored the harsh realities faced by certain groups during that era, contrasting sharply with the hotel's role as a welcoming haven for travelers from diverse backgrounds. (Gholston Collection.)

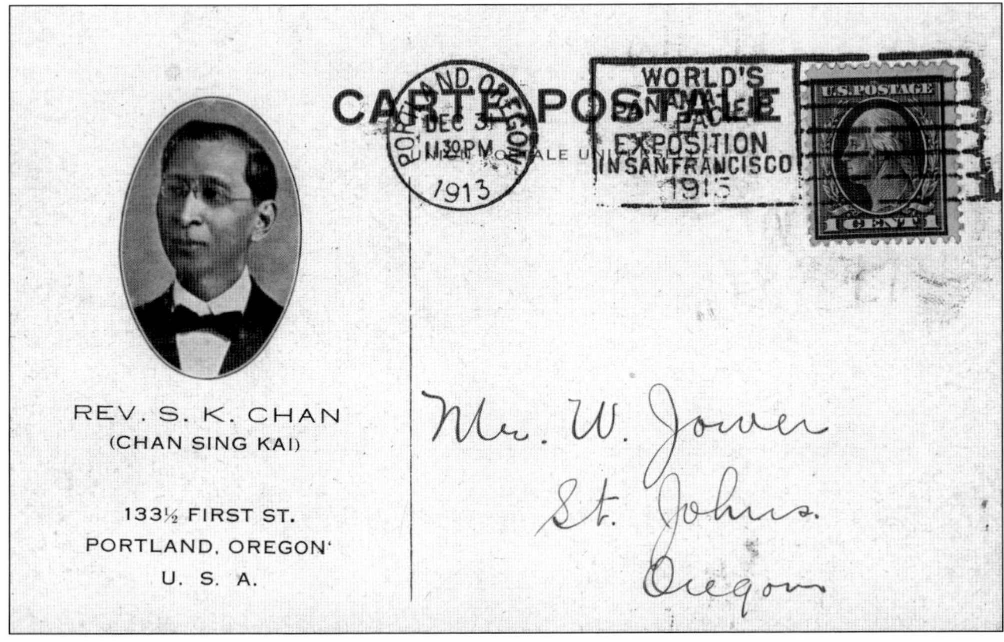

Rev. Sing Kai Chan and his wife, Dr. Kate Chee Chow, a midwife, immigrated to Vancouver, Canada, from Guangzhou in 1885. He founded the first Chinese Methodist Church. In 1900, they moved to Portland, where he became minister of the Chinese Methodist Mission. Dr. Chow, the first female Chinese doctor, opened a traditional Chinese medicine practice and founded the Equal Suffrage Society for Chinese women. (Portland Chinatown Museum.)

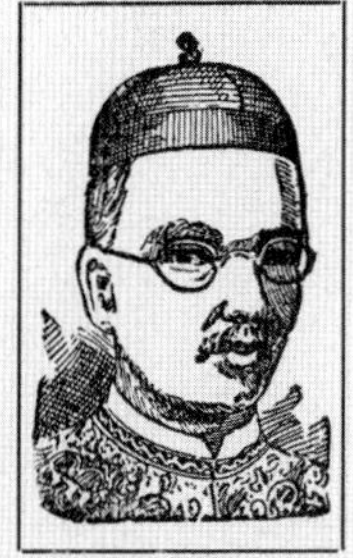

WHY DO YOU SUFFER?

When the Great Chinese Doctor

C. GEE WO

can cure you of any ailment by his powerful and harmless Chinese herbs and roots, which are unknown to medical science of this country. His wonderful cures throughout the U. S. alone tell the story. Thousands of people are thankful to him for saving their lives from OPERATIONS

Then why let yourself suffer? This famous doctor knows the action of over 500 different remedies that he has successfully used in different diseases.

The following Testimonials from well-Known people tell of the wonderful curative powers of nature's own herbs and roots:

Thomas Walsh, Tenth and Everett street, City, cured of stomach trouble two years' standing.

Miss Helene Enberg, 506 Vancouver avenue, city, suffered many years with dyspepsia of the stomach and lung trouble, and was said by doctors to have incurable consumption. I am thankful to say, after five months' treatment of Dr. C. Gee Wo's remedies, I have fully regained my health and strength. I recommend all that are sick to go and see him.

Saved from operation: Mrs. Theresa George, 705 Fourth street, city—I had suffered from inflammation of the womb and ovaries and female weakness, and tried many doctors, but all said I would die if I did not have an operation. I tried Dr. C. Gee Wo's remedies as my last resource, and am thankful to say that after four months' treatment I was entirely cured.

He guarantees to cure Catarrh, Asthma, Liver, Kidney, Lung Trouble, Rheumatism, Nervousness, Stomach, Female Trouble and all private diseases. Hundreds of testimonials. Charges moderate. If you are sick with any of the above ailments then call and see him. Consultation free. Patients out of the city write for blank and circulars. Inclose stamp. Address

The C. Gee Wo Medicine Co. 253 Alder St., Cor. 3rd Portland, Oregon

City of Portland (OR) Archives, AP/292

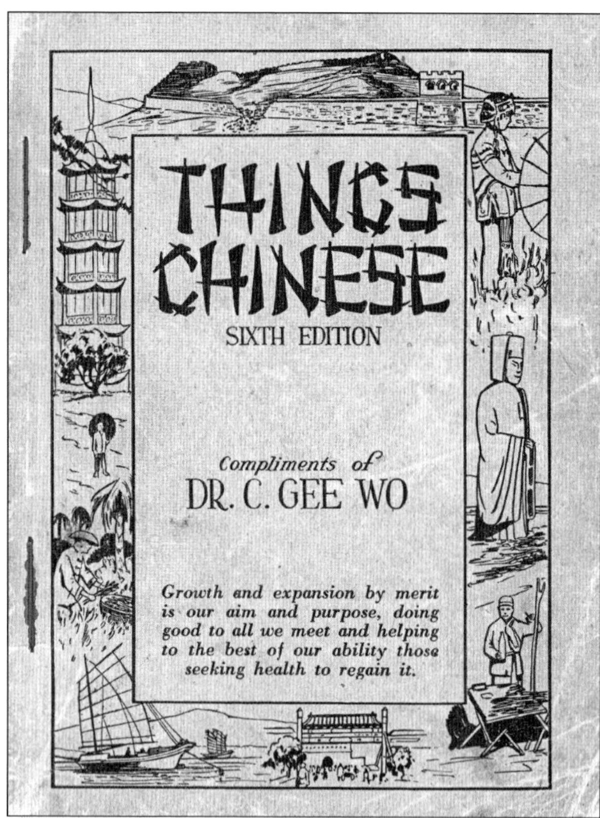

Chequong Gee Leo Wo gained prominence as a doctor of traditional Chinese herbal medicine. He cosponsored the Chinese Village exhibit at the 1893 Chicago World's Fair, investing $90,000. After running a successful practice in Omaha, Nebraska, he moved to Portland in 1900 with his wife, Sarah Starbuck, whom he met through her physician father. Dr. Wo treated Portland's Chinatown and the broader community, bridging cultures through his practice. In his 1905 advertisement above, he emphasized his expertise in traditional healing. Shown to the left is his booklet, which includes patient testimonials. The Dr. C. Gee Wo House at 23 Northeast San Rafael Street features Chinese design elements, reflecting his heritage. He and Sarah are buried at Lone Fir Cemetery, leaving a legacy of cultural and medical contributions. (Above, City of Portland Archives, AP/292; left, Gholston Collection.)

In these 1905 Chinatown scenes, a woman and child are seen returning from the market, capturing the everyday activities of the community. Typical grocery stores featured an array of produce, often displayed on sidewalks or elegantly hung in windows. This arrangement not only offered convenience for shoppers but also contributed to the vibrant and lively street ambiance, showcasing the bustling spirit of Chinatown's close-knit community. (City of Portland Archives, AP/4645.)

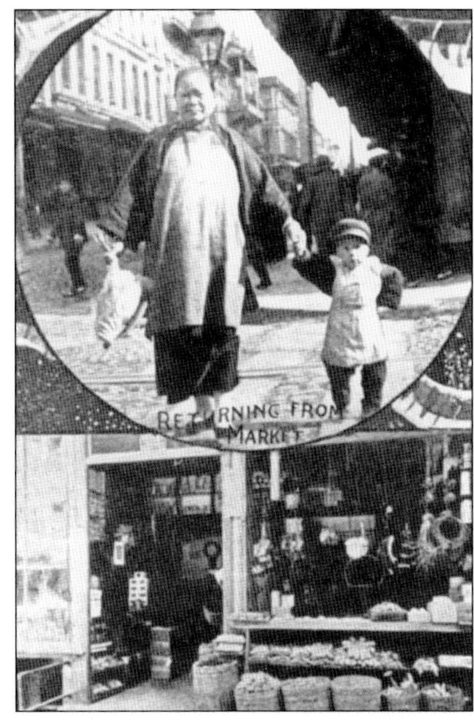

In the late 19th century, several organizations were established with distinct goals such as civic improvement, political support, and charitable fundraising. These groups adopted Westernized systems of governance to further their objectives. Notable examples included the Chinese Empire Reform Association (Baohuanghui), the Chinese Peace Society, and the Chinese Nationalist Party (Kuomintang). These organizations fulfilled specific needs for Chinese immigrants who were establishing roots in Portland. (Carey Wong.)

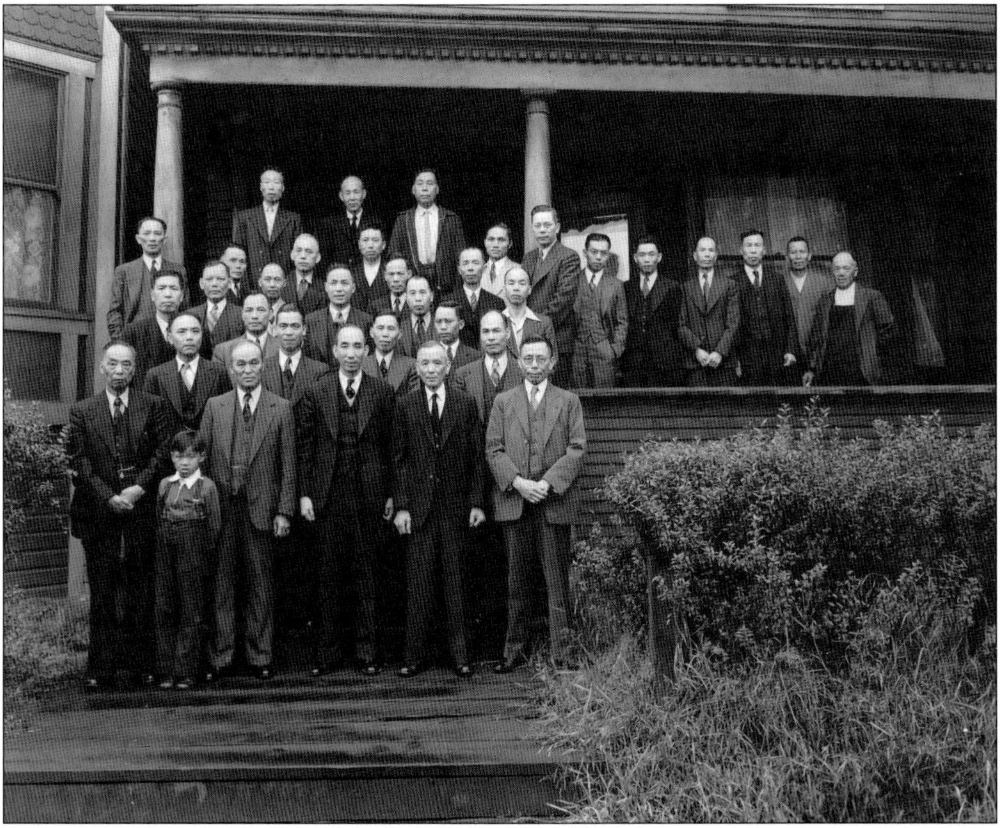

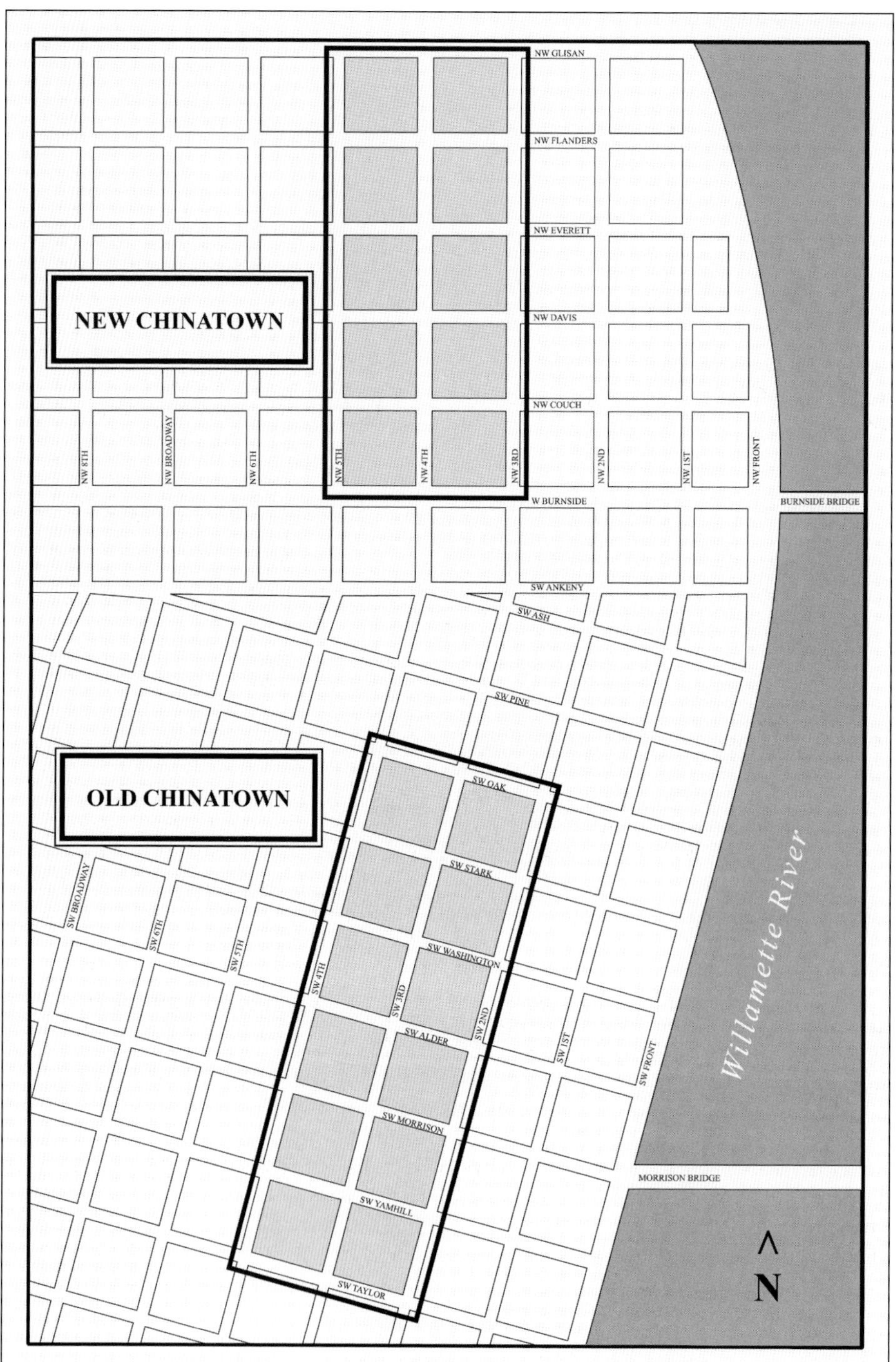

This map illustrates the two Chinatown locations, showing the heart of the first enclave. Unlike cities with rigid boundaries, such as San Francisco and New York, Portland's old Chinatown stretched from Front Avenue to Broadway and Market to Burnside Streets, integrating Chinese and non-Chinese businesses, reflecting an integrated urban layout. This image was adapted by Staci Wong from *Sweet Cakes, Long Journey*, by Marie Rose Wong, PhD. (Staci Wong.)

Two

Second Chinatown and Becoming American 1906–1945

Approximately 50 years after the first Chinese immigrants arrived, Chinatown's businesses and residents were forced to relocate due to increasing pressures from the city. The transition from Portland's first Chinatown to the New Chinatown area was a gradual process that unfolded over several decades. Chinatown started to migrate north across Burnside Street into the existing Japantown area due to its close proximity, and the Japanese were also facing similar discrimination and restrictive laws. During this time, Chinatown witnessed shifts in political views and national identity. The Chinese Empire Reform Association (Baohuanghui) had a chapter in Portland, advocating for constitutional monarchy reforms in China. However, the 1911 Revolution, led by Dr. Sun Yat-sen, overthrew the Qing Dynasty and established the Republic of China, transforming overseas Chinese perspectives. While some returned to China to support modernization, most stayed in Portland due to established livelihoods and the restrictive Chinese Exclusion Act, which limited reentry. Beginning with the second generation, American-born Chinese were less connected to China's political changes, embracing American life while preserving cultural traditions passed down by their parents. During the Second Sino-Japanese War (1937–1945), Portland's Chinatown united to fundraise and train aviators to support China against the Japanese invasion. Both citizens and noncitizens contributed by serving in World War I (1914–1918) and World War II (1939–1945). Chinatown's diverse community included Japanese, Greeks, Jewish, African Americans, and Filipinos. This fostered cultural exchange and enriched Portland's culinary scene. Cantonese cuisine adapted to American tastes, introducing dishes like chop suey and egg foo young. Before the civil rights movement, African Americans frequently patronized Chinese restaurants, which provided nondiscriminatory spaces. For Jewish Americans, dining at Chinese restaurants became a tradition, particularly on Christmas when other establishments were closed. World War II reshaped Chinatown and Japantown following Executive Order 9066, which relocated all Japanese to internment camps, regardless of citizenship. As a result, Chinese businesses expanded into over 100 abandoned businesses left by Japanese tenants. With the repeal of the Chinese Exclusion Act in 1943, Chinese immigrants gained citizenship and property ownership rights, further prompting an exodus from Chinatown. The transformation of Portland's Chinatown during this time reflects a story of resilience, unity, and cultural evolution, contributing significantly to Portland's diverse history.

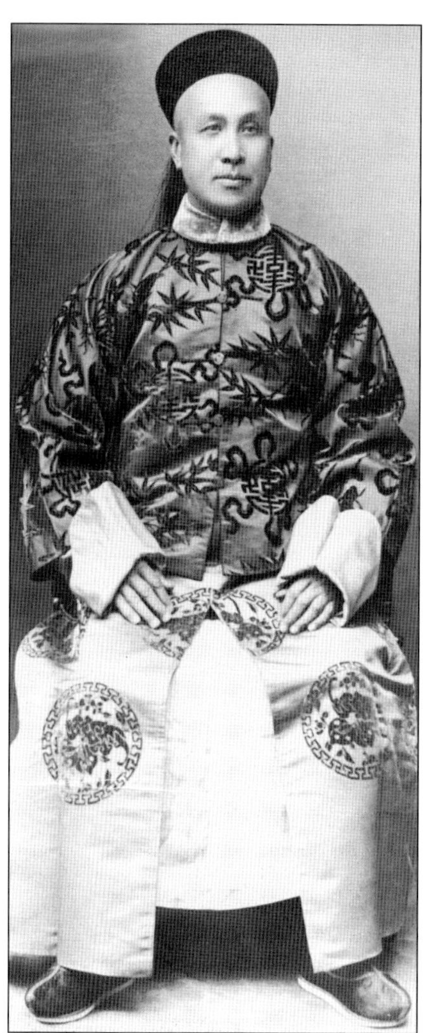

Moy Back Hin immigrated in 1868 and worked as a servant for Judge Matthew Deady's family, earning $6 per month. Moy later became a successful merchant in Chinatown. He assisted those fleeing anti-Chinese riots in Tacoma and became one of the first Chinese millionaires in Portland. Moy was also appointed honorary vice Chinese consul in 1906, then full consul in 1933, reflecting his significant contributions to the community. (Oregon Historical Society, 0095P019.)

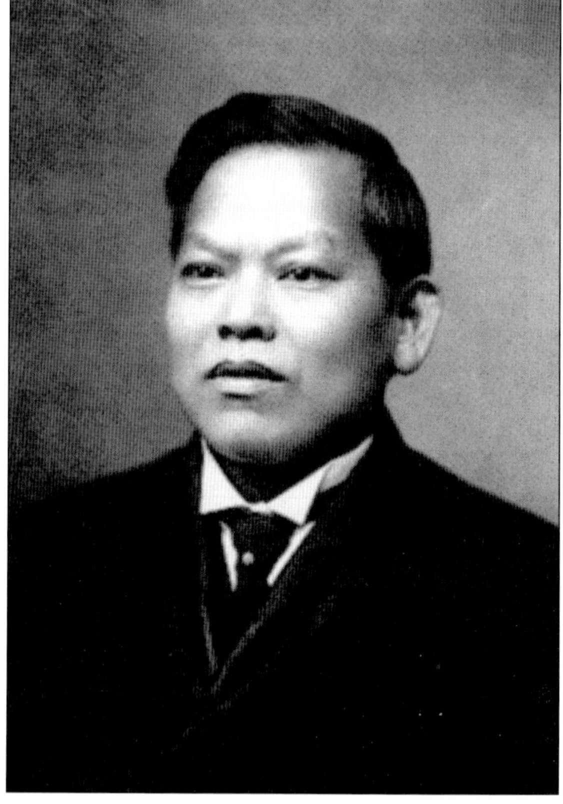

Goon Dip began his journey as a domestic worker for the Samuel McBride family and rose to become a prominent entrepreneur and community leader in Portland and Seattle. In the 1880s, he worked for Moy Back Hin before establishing multiple businesses himself. Goon was a labor contractor for salmon canneries and, in 1909, was appointed the Chinese government's consul in Seattle, highlighting his contributions. (CCBA Museum.)

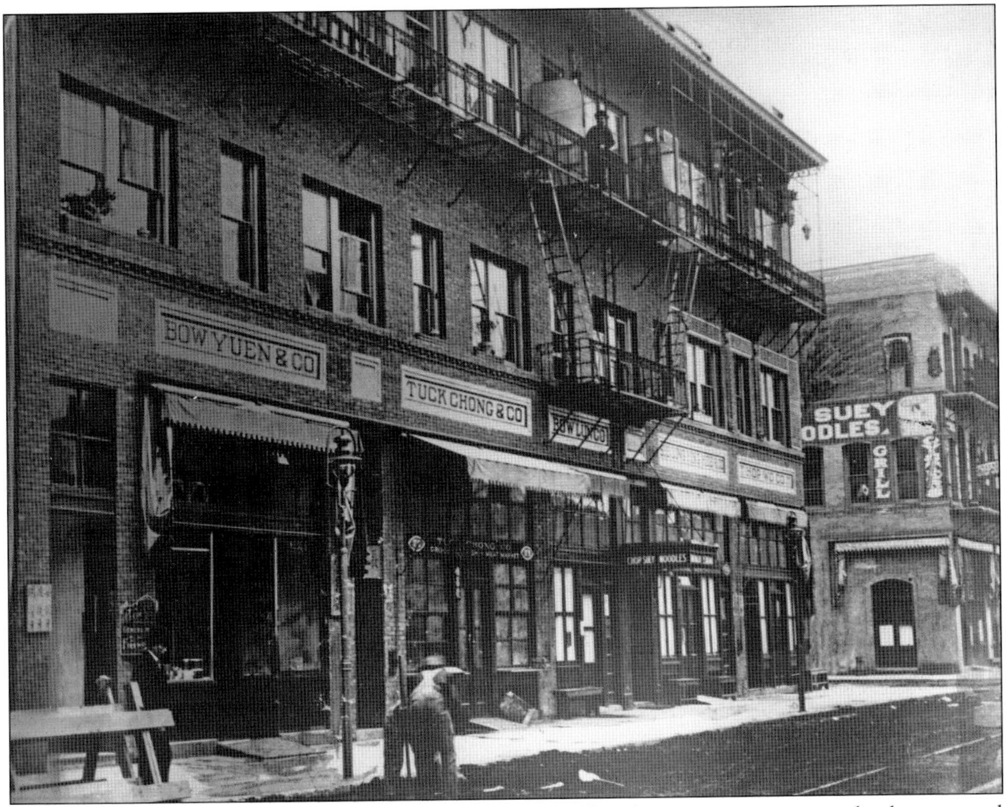

Bow Yuen and Company was a cornerstone of Portland's Chinatown, serving as both a general merchandise store and a vital community establishment. Initially located on Second Street in the first Chinatown, it later relocated to 69 North Fourth Street, which was eventually renamed Northwest Fourth Avenue. Established with $500 investments each by Lee Lung, his brother Lee Hong, and another sibling, along with his son Henry Lee, the store stocked Chinese merchandise, fireworks, and American flags, serving the local community's cultural and daily needs. More than a business, Bow Yuen played a key role in fostering connections and preserving Chinatown's identity during a period of significant growth and transformation. The image below captures the store's interior, featuring an unidentified employee. (Above, Portland Chinatown Museum; below, Oregon Historical Society, OrHi_28938.)

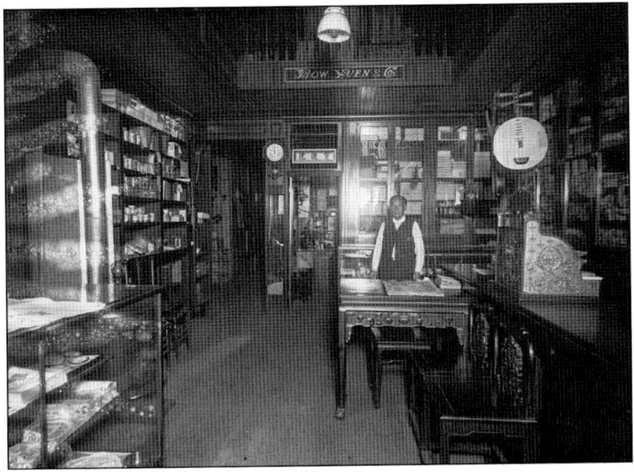

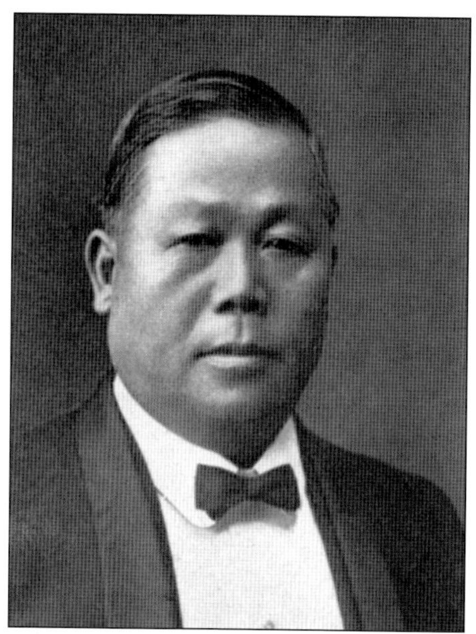

Seid Back immigrated in 1868 at the age of 17 and worked as a cook. With $3,000 that he saved, he opened Seid Back and Company, a general merchandise store, and Wing Sing Long Kee Company, a labor contracting business, which supplied labor for railroad construction and salmon canneries. His company provided over 1,600 railroad workers per season. He became a prominent businessman, philanthropist, and community leader. (City of Portland Archives, AP/12657.)

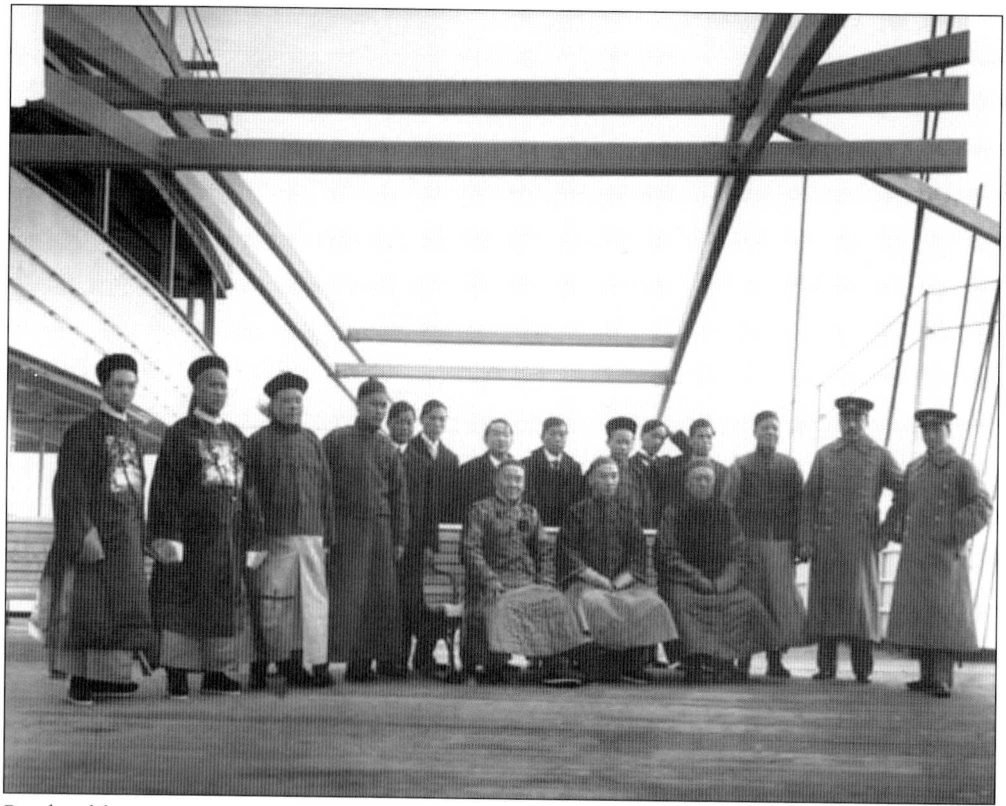

Portland businessmen met with the Chinese Trade Commission in 1906 in Port Townsend, Washington. From left to right are (seated) Li Shengte, Prince Tsai Tseh, and Shang Chi Hong; (standing) Moy Bow Wing, Moy Back Hin, Seid Back, two unidentified, Chin Lem, Lew King, two unidentified, Lew Kay, and the rest are unidentified. (PEMCO Webster and Stevens Collection, Museum of History and Industry, Seattle.)

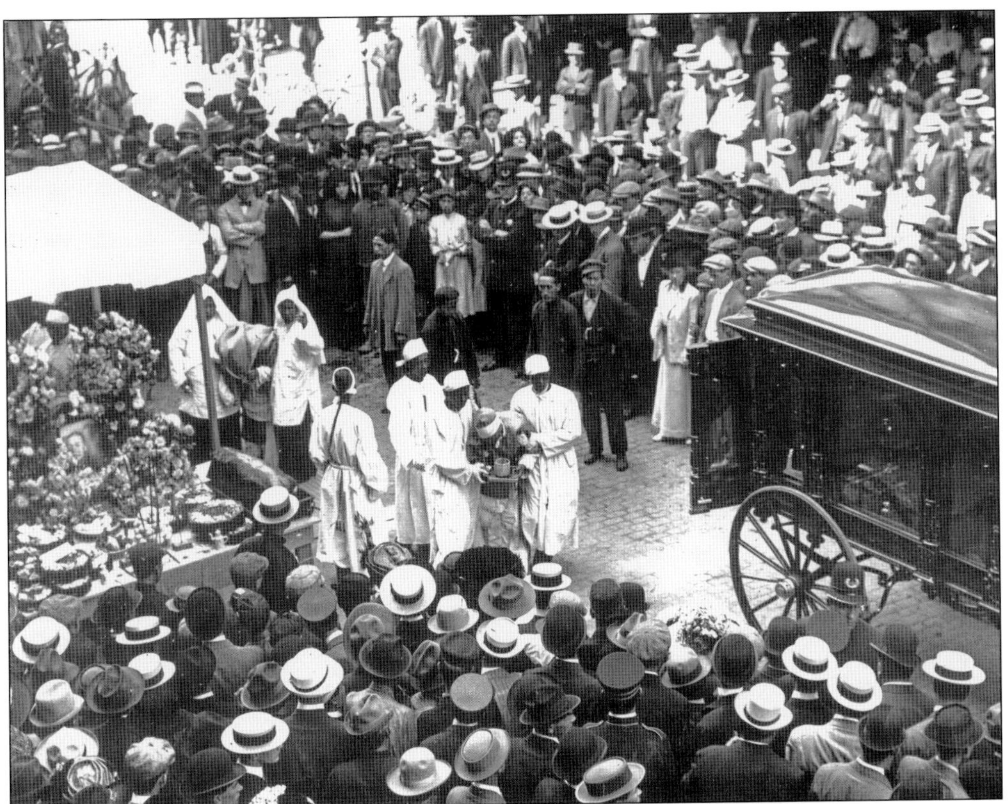

Traditional funeral ceremonies span seven days, with mourners dressed according to their relation to the deceased. White, symbolizing death, is worn, while red, associated with celebrations and weddings, is avoided. These rituals emphasized respect and mourning, reflecting cultural beliefs about death and the afterlife, ensuring the deceased's peaceful transition, and honoring their memory. (Portland Chinatown Museum.)

Lee Mee Gin, known as Portland's "Mayor of Chinatown," was a prominent figure and a key member of the Lee Family Association. Lee owned multiple businesses, including Kwong Lun Tai and Company, a general merchandise store and labor contracting company for Alaska's salmon canneries. As president of the Chinese Empire Reform Association and the Chinese Peace Society, he played a significant role in addressing tong disputes and promoting community welfare. (CCBA Museum.)

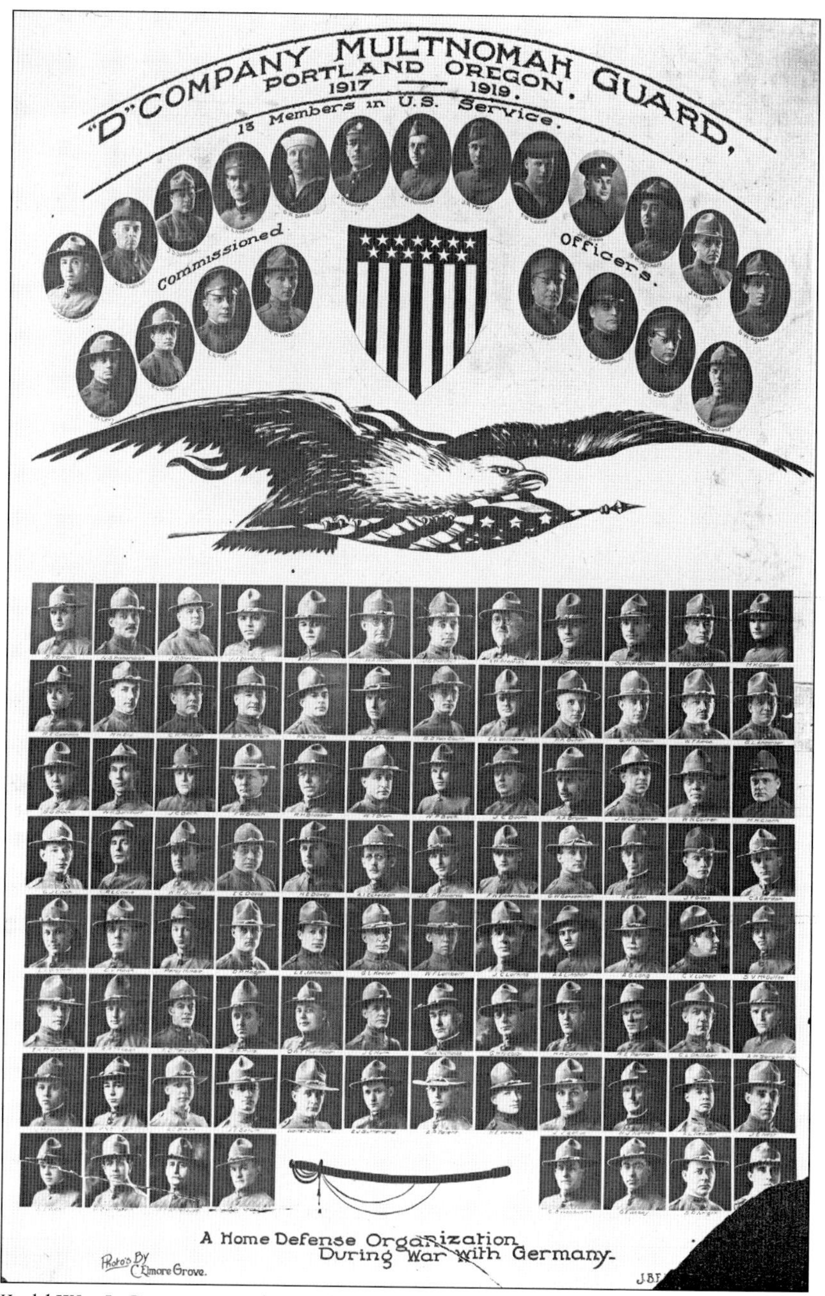

During World War I, German attacks on the US East Coast raised concerns about potential threats to the West Coast, prompting Portland to take defensive measures. In response, the Multnomah Guard was formed as a civilian home defense force from 1917 to 1919, mirroring the structure of the National Guard of Oregon. Comprised of civilians who retained their regular jobs, the Multnomah Guard focused on protecting vital infrastructure such as shipyards, warehouses, grain elevators, canneries, and food depots. Their efforts helped maintain Portland's security and supported wartime stability. This historical image features Seid Gain, an active member, identified in the third row down on the left. This highlights the contribution of Portland's Chinese American community to the city's safety during a challenging time in US history. (Gholston Collection.)

DESCRIPTION

Name: Wong Shee
Age: 30 Height: 5 ft. 2 1/2 in.
Occupation: Housewife, Tualatin, Oregon.
Admitted as wife of Lee Jip, native. Ex ss "Princess Charlotte," November 3, 1918. No. 36157/4-1.
Physical marks and peculiarities: Deep pit near inner end left eyebrow; four pits over right eyebrow.
Issued at the port of Seattle, Wash.
this 17th day of January 1919
John H. Sargent
Immigration Official in Charge

This certificate of identity, issued on January 17, 1919, at the Port of Seattle, belonged to Wong Shee, the wife of Lee Jip (or Jyp). It was designed to distinguish legal immigrants following the enactment of the Chinese Exclusion Act. The 1882 act was repealed in 1943 by the Magnuson Act during World War II, allowing Chinese nationals in the United States to become naturalized citizens. The annual quota of 105 Chinese immigrants was later eliminated by the Immigration and Nationality Act of 1965, which implemented a preference system based on skills and family relationships. (Both, George W. and Mary N. Leong family.)

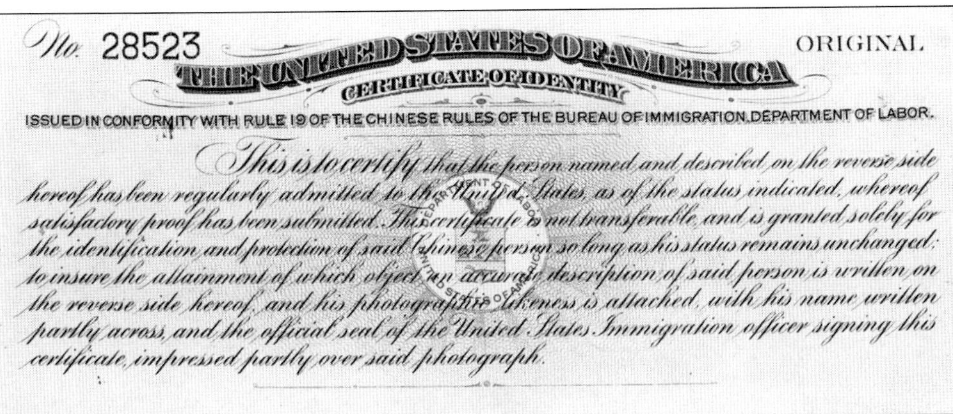

No. 28523 ORIGINAL

THE UNITED STATES OF AMERICA

CERTIFICATE OF IDENTITY

ISSUED IN CONFORMITY WITH RULE 19 OF THE CHINESE RULES OF THE BUREAU OF IMMIGRATION, DEPARTMENT OF LABOR.

This is to certify that the person named and described on the reverse side hereof has been regularly admitted to the United States, as of the status indicated, whereof satisfactory proof has been submitted. This certificate is not transferable, and is granted solely for the identification and protection of said Chinese person so long as his status remains unchanged: to insure the attainment of which object an accurate description of said person is written on the reverse side hereof, and his photographic likeness is attached, with his name written partly across, and the official seal of the United States Immigration officer signing this certificate, impressed partly over said photograph.

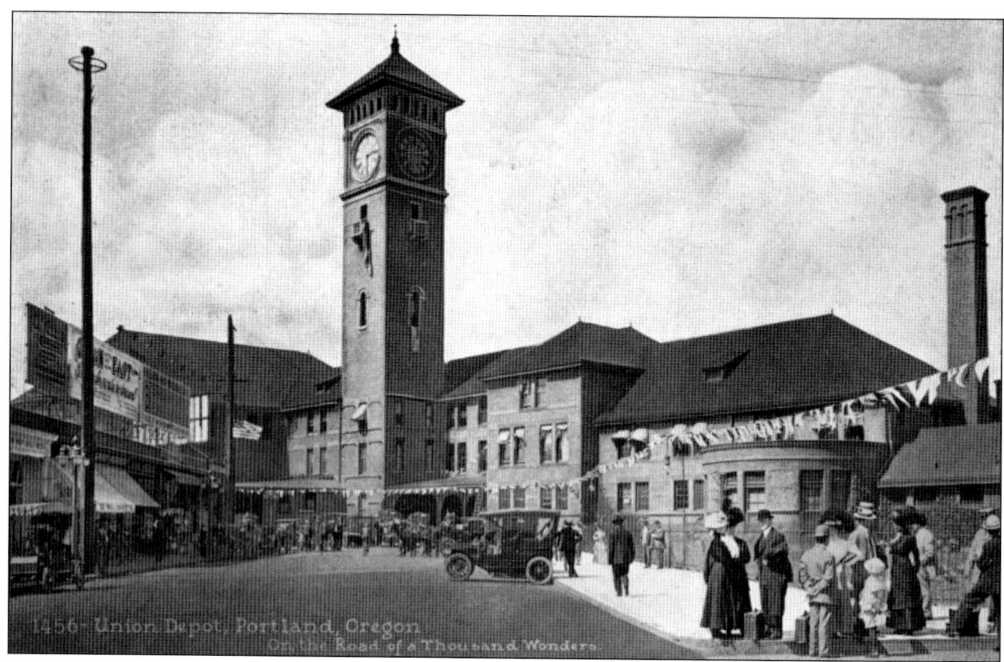

In the 1940s, Oregon exclusion laws impacted both Chinese and African Americans. Union Station, near the Chinatown/Japantown areas, offered jobs to African Americans in the service industry, including railways and hotels. Due to widespread discrimination, it was one of the few areas where they could live. They frequently patronized Chinese restaurants, as segregation often barred them from other establishments, creating a unique dynamic community. (Portland City Archives, AP-32678.)

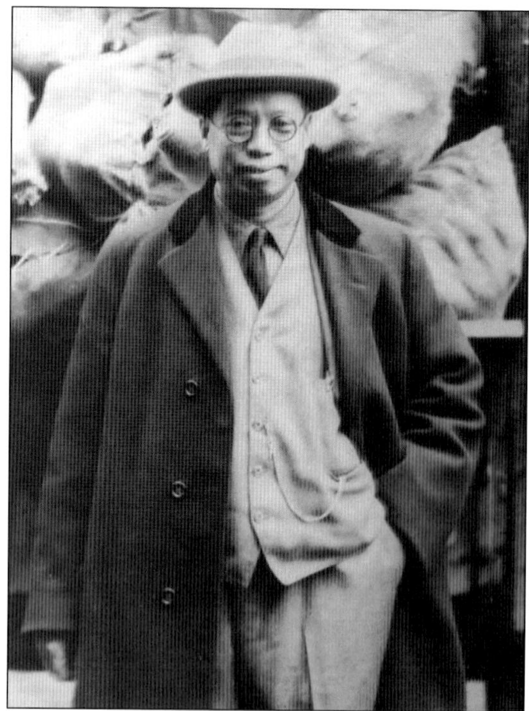

Louie Chung immigrated to Oregon in 1892 and worked as a railroad laborer before becoming a prominent Portland businessman. He managed On Wo Tong, a Chinese medicine shop, and then became a shareholder. He also became a partner at Goey Hing jewelry and clock store and Canton Low restaurant. Chung was a community leader, involved in Bing Kung Tong, the Chinese Peace Society, and the CCBA, significantly shaping Portland's Chinatown. (CCBA Museum.)

Lee Lung played a significant role in Portland's Chinatown, co-owning Bow Yuen and Company while solely operating Nom Kin Low and Company. Nom Kin Low in the first Chinatown initially featured a grocery store on the ground floor and a restaurant above, reflecting the layered functionality of Chinese businesses. As Chinatown developed, it relocated to the New Chinatown at 231 Fourth Avenue, expanding with a third-floor banquet hall, fostering communal gatherings. Lee's business thrived for nearly four decades, bolstering Chinatown's economic foundation. A dedicated community leader, he served on the CCBA's board, cofounded its new building in 1911, and donated $100 toward the auditorium's construction in 1931, reinforcing his civic commitment. (Right, CCBA Museum; below, Gholston Collection.)

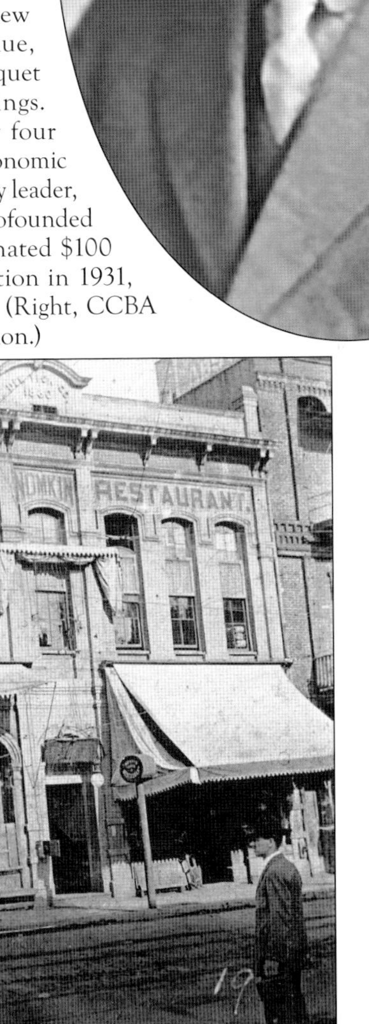

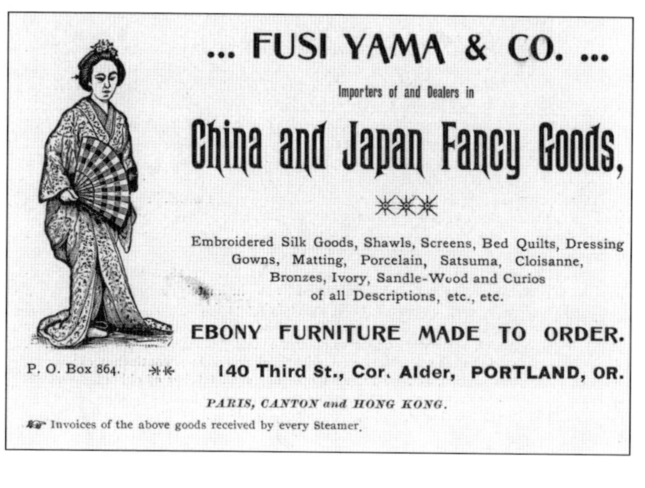

This advertisement from around 1910 highlights Fusi Yama and Company's operations at Southwest Third and Alder Streets. This business specialized in importing a wide variety of goods from China and Japan, offering unique and rare items. This was one of numerous import businesses and was an important part of the community in fostering cultural exchange through commerce. (Portland Chinatown Museum.)

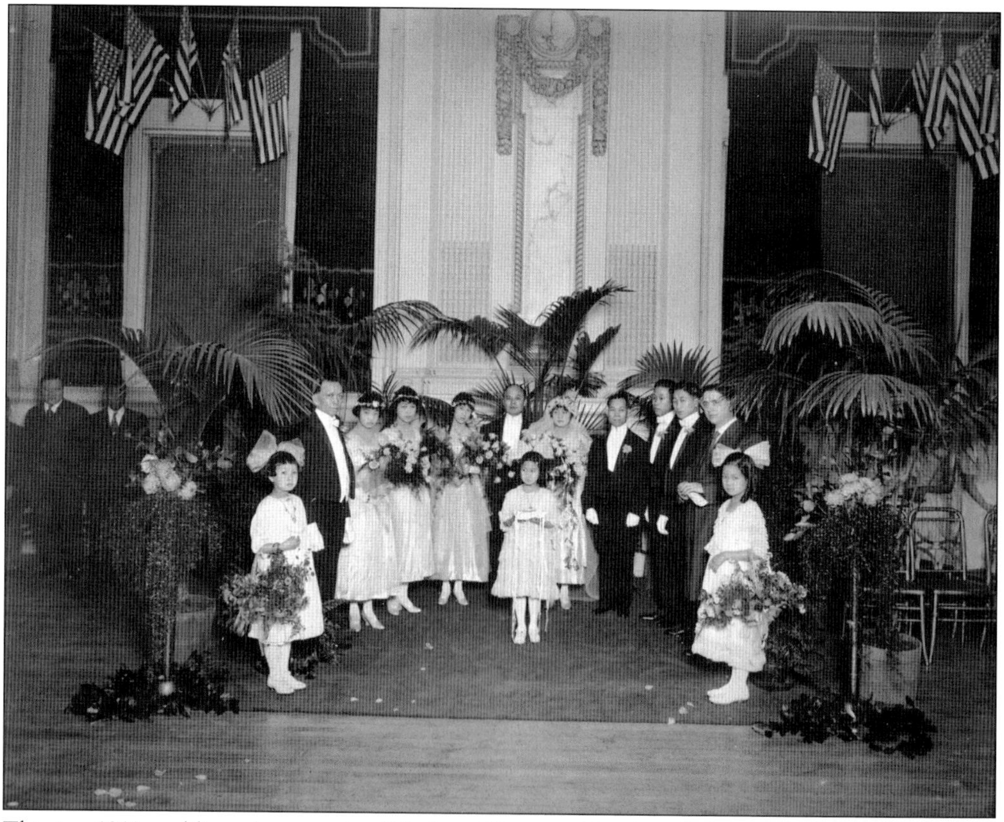

This is a 1918 wedding photograph of Herbert Wong and Violet Chinn at Portland's Multnomah Hotel, now the Embassy Suites Downtown. Their tailored suits and lace-trimmed dresses reflect belonging, respectability, and upward mobility during a time of exclusion. This image stands as a testament to how Chinese Americans forged hybrid identities, rooted in tradition, shaped by adaptation, and expressed through celebration. (Oregon Historical Society, CN_015410.)

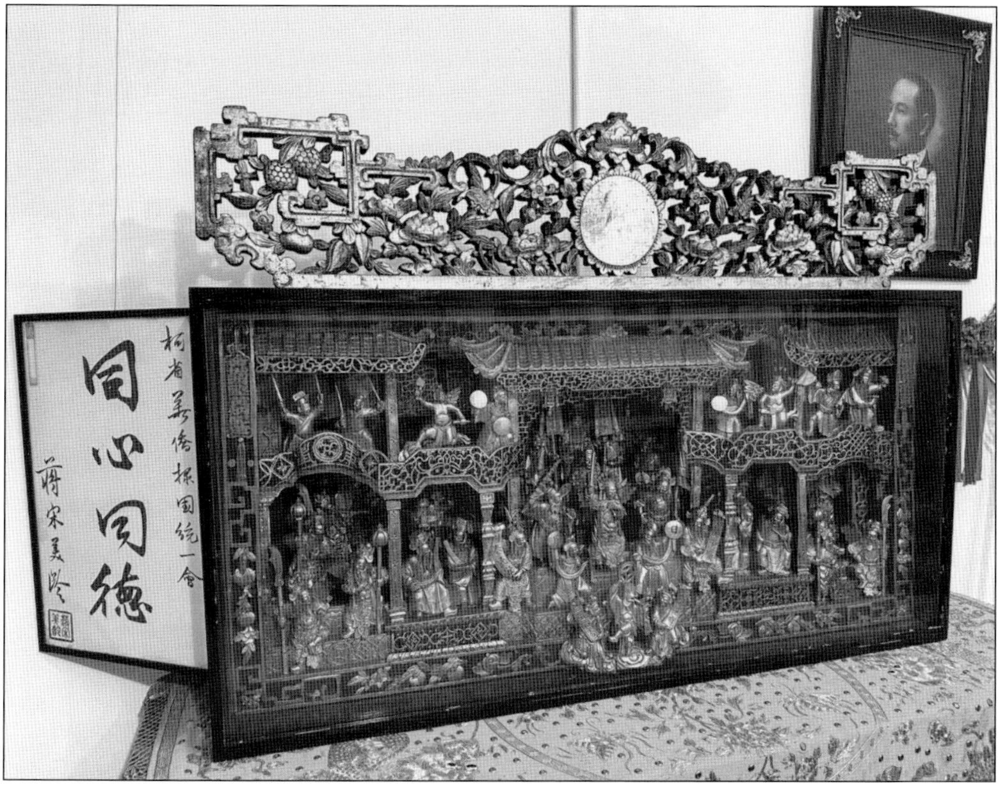

A Chinese restaurant in Salem generously donated an altar to the Chinese Consolidated Benevolent Association building in Portland, reinforcing the organization's cultural and spiritual significance within the community. The presence of the altar enabled the CCBA to classify itself as a nonprofit entity, providing a designated space for worship, fostering spiritual practices, and strengthening its role as a cultural and religious center for Portland's Chinese residents. (CCBA Museum.)

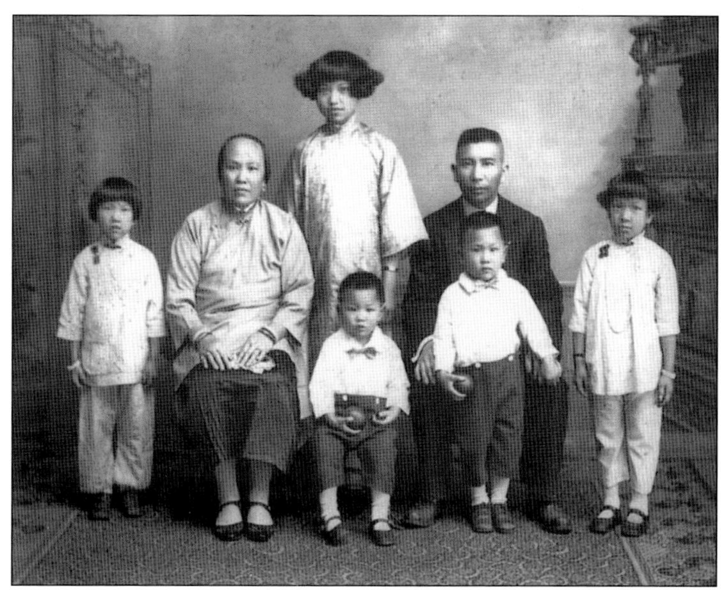

In 1923, the Lee Jyp family relocated from Tualatin to Portland's Chinatown for better opportunities and joined the Chinese community. Lee started a lottery and established the first commercial bean sprout business, supplying local restaurants and stores. From left to right are (first row) Fred Lee and Harold Lee; (second row) Mary N. Leong, Wong Shee Lee, Ruth Mar, Lee Jyp, and Ada Hing. (George W. and Mary N. Leong family.)

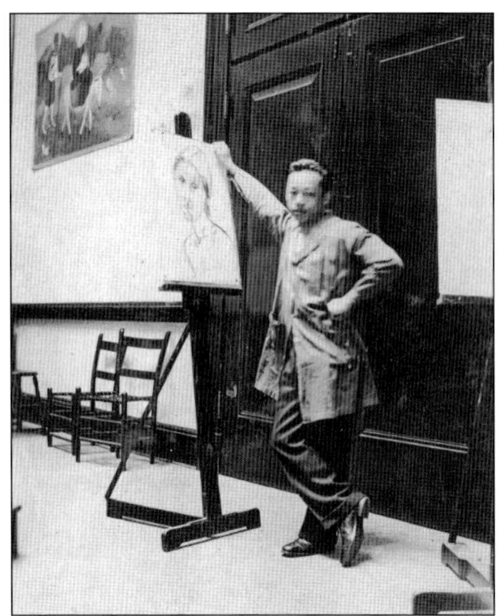

Born in Chinatown in 1893, Bue Kee moved to Clackamas County to help his family manage a hop farm. Returning in 1927, he attended the Museum Art School and became a painter, sculptor, and ceramicist. He worked for the Federal Art Project under the Works Progress Administration, creating notable ceramic centerpieces for Timberline Lodge and Tongue Point Naval Station. (Kee family.)

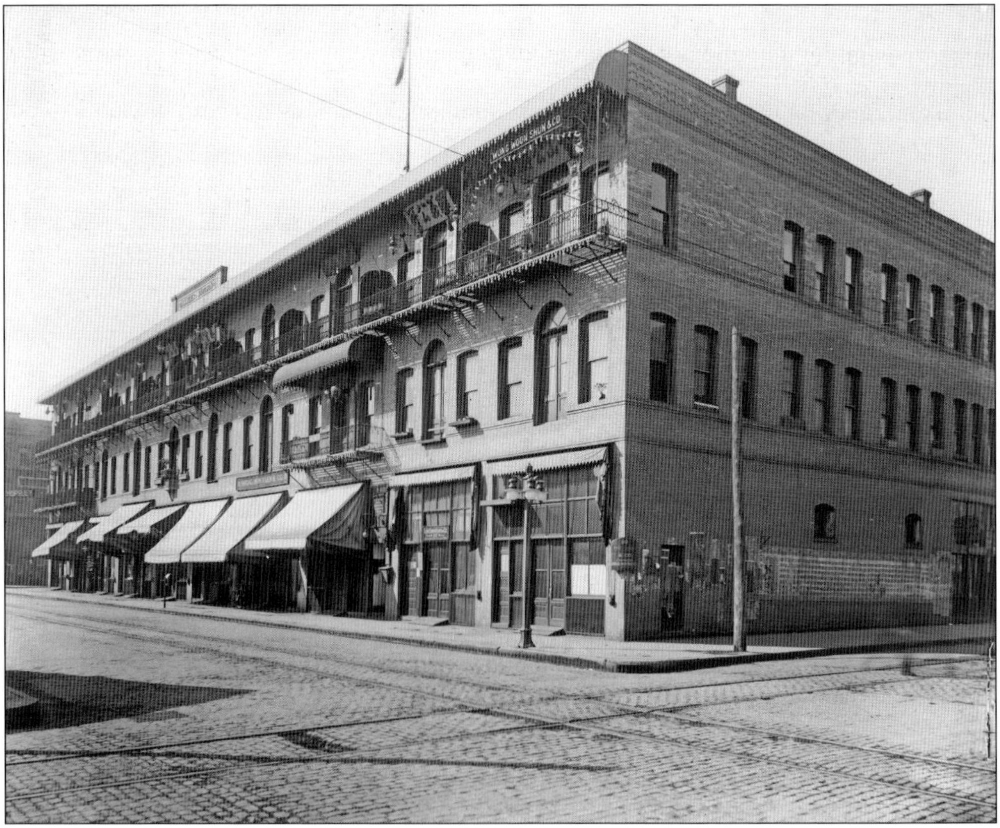

Constructed in 1905, this building at Fourth and Flanders Streets was home to the Hop Sing Tong, a fraternal organization that is still active today. The ground floor housed businesses, including Kwong Mun Yuen and Company, owned by Wong On, along with a jeweler, watchmaker, grocer, and restaurant. In 1932, the Fong Chong Company grocery and restaurant opened there on the corner. In 1979, a fire reduced the building to one story. (Gholston Collection.)

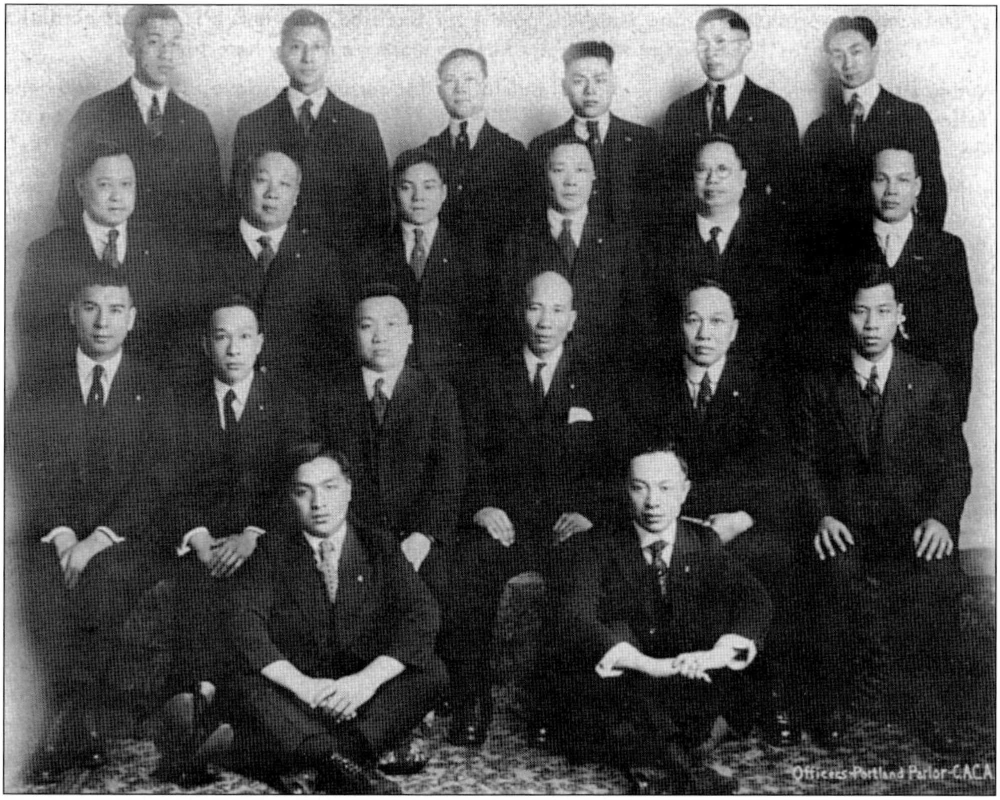

Chartered in 1921, the Portland Chinese American Citizens Alliance (CACA) swiftly established itself as a cornerstone of civic engagement. It was led by president Lee Hing and Woo Lai Sun, the first Chinese American civil engineering graduate from the University of Oregon. Mayor George Baker and District Attorney Walter Evans attended its open house, underscoring its significant community impact. Above are founding members, from left to right, (first row) Kie Ming Moy and Moy Louie; (second row) Herbert Jue Sue Jewel, Woo Lai Sun, Chuck Wing Moy, Lee Hing, Lee Sue, and Ding Gow; (third row) Moy Chee, Lee Foo, Winge Lee, Seid Back, Louie Chung, and Chin Hing; (fourth row) Dan Goon, Paul Hong, Wong Fook Young, Henry Chan, Harold Lowe, and John Wong. The 1933 image below captures the national convention held at Hung Far Low restaurant. (Both, CACA.)

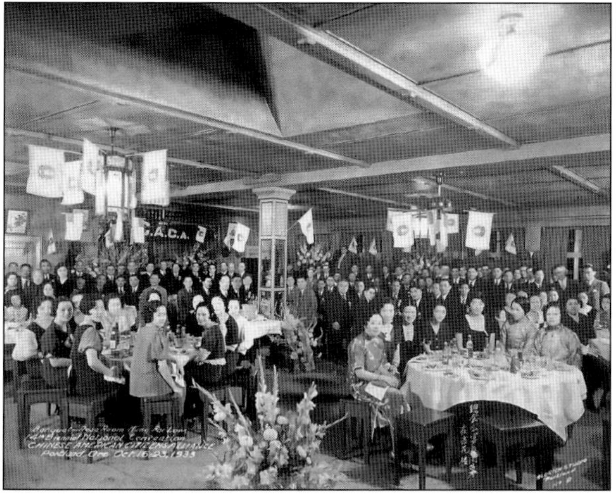

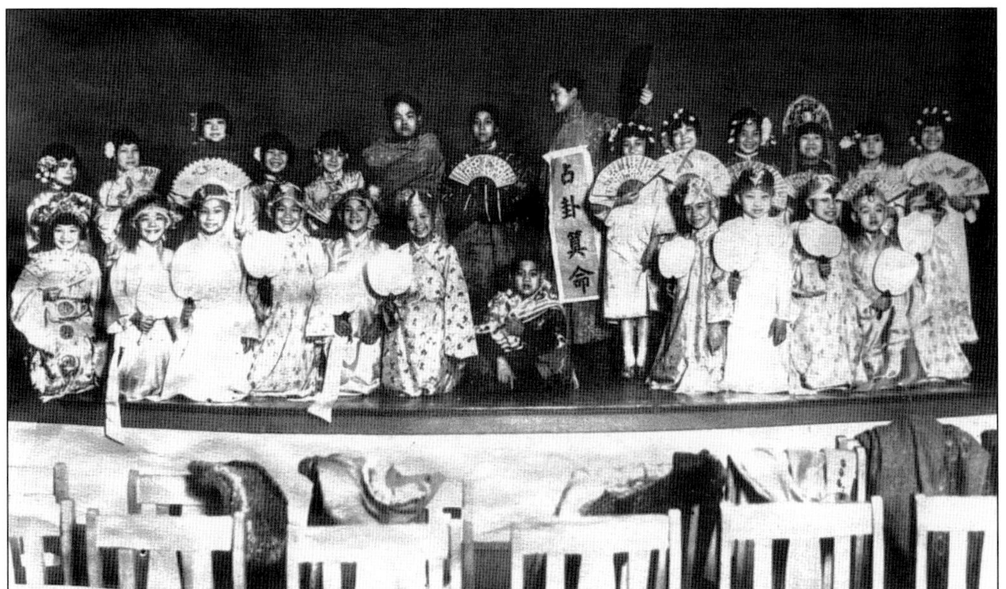

The CCBA Language School was vital in preserving the Cantonese language. From left to right are (first row) Phyllis Wong, Eva Wong Woo, two unidentified, Dorothy Chin, Billy Chin, two unidentified, Eva Goon, Elsie King, Mable Lee, Mary Lee, Dorothy Lee, and Maxine Chu; (second row) Alice Goon, Bryon Lee, unidentified, Howard Lee, James Wong, Billie Moe, Ed King, unidentified, Alice Wong, Richard Chin, Paul Lee, and unidentified. (Harry and Eva Wong Woo family.)

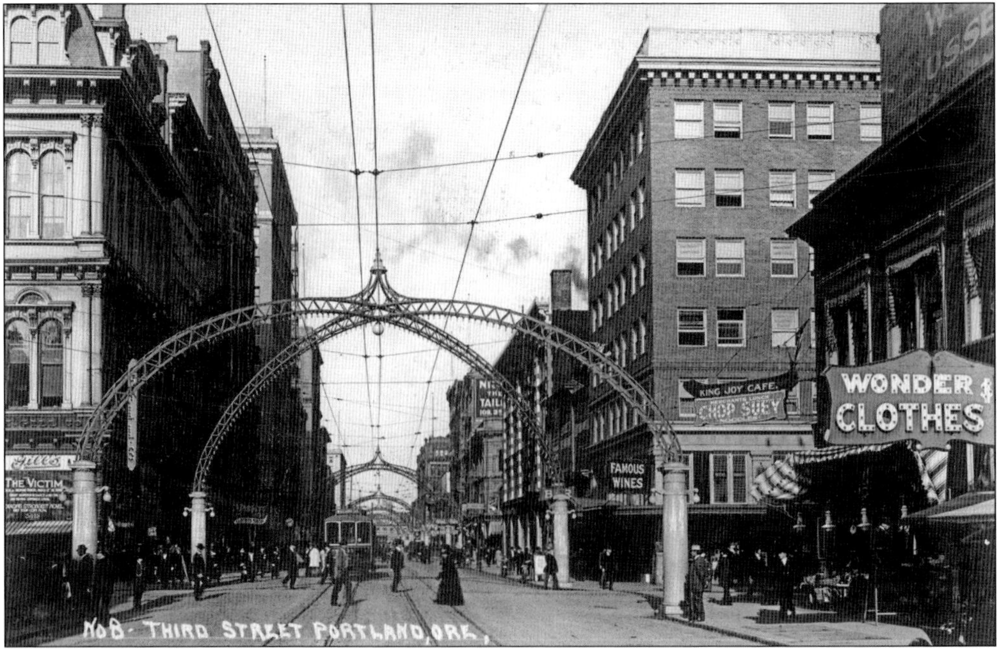

King Joy Café Chop Suey was one of many establishments offering American Chinese cuisine. Chop suey, derived from the Toishan term *tsap seui* (meaning mixed pieces), was introduced by early Chinese immigrants. This dish, a stew made of meat, bean sprouts, mushrooms, and vegetables, gained popularity in America. However, it is not traditionally found in China, highlighting the unique evolution of Cantonese cuisine in the United States. (Portland Chinatown Museum.)

Herbert Wong, a businessman, began as a bookkeeper at Kwong Mun Yuen Company and Hung Far Low for Wong On before partnering with him at Hung Far Low, Republic Café, and Burnside Café, which was acquired after its Japanese owner was sent to Minidoka Relocation Center. He was active in the Chinese community with the Wong Association and the Wong Association lottery, and he also donated $100 to the CCBA's 1931 auditorium remodel. (CCBA Museum.)

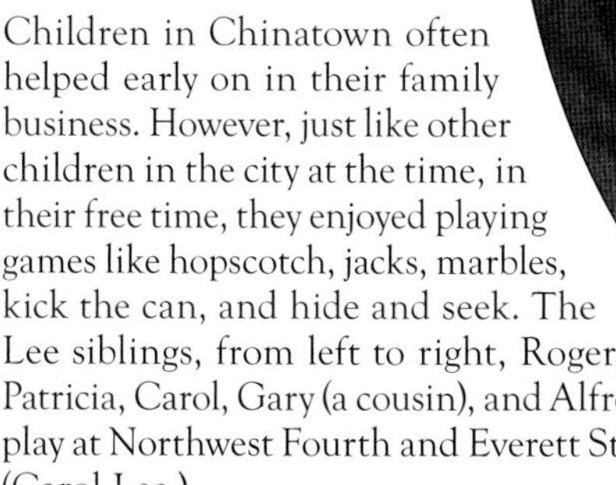

Children in Chinatown often helped early on in their family business. However, just like other children in the city at the time, in their free time, they enjoyed playing games like hopscotch, jacks, marbles, kick the can, and hide and seek. The Lee siblings, from left to right, Roger, Patricia, Carol, Gary (a cousin), and Alfred, play at Northwest Fourth and Everett Streets. (Carol Lee.)

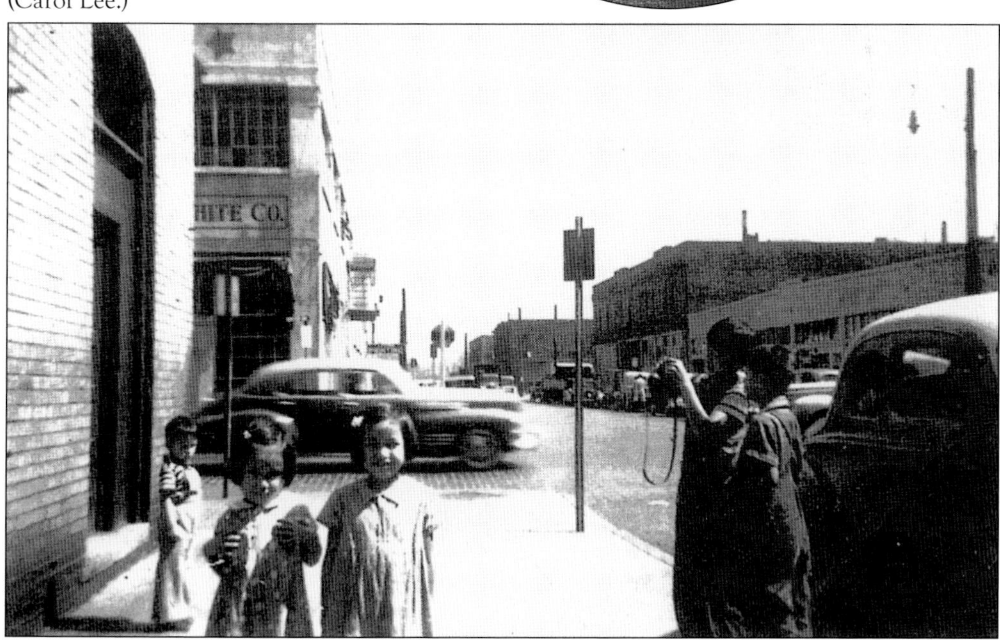

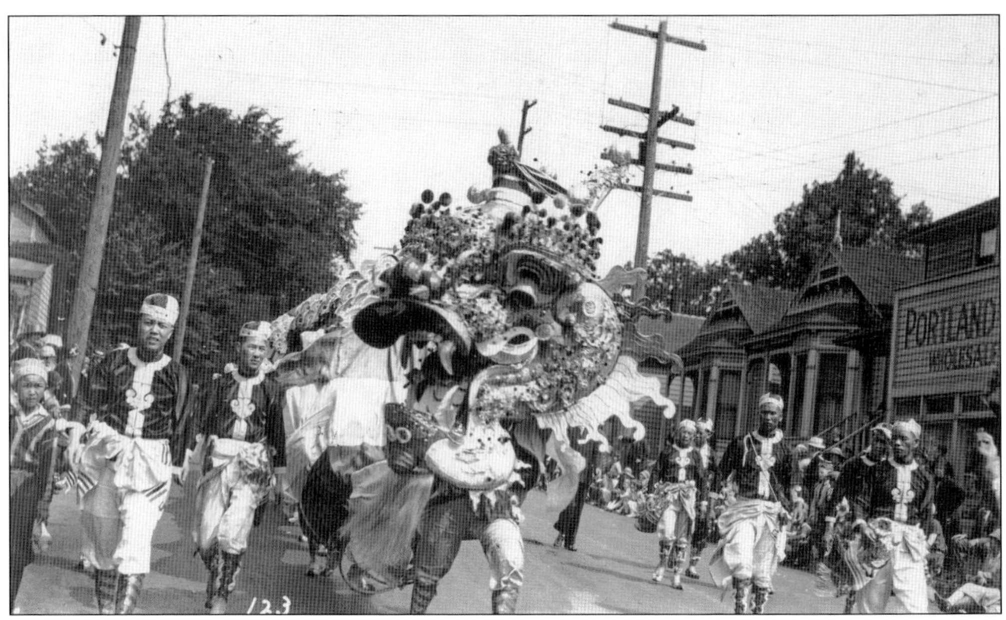

This 1920s photograph captures the highlight of the Rose Festival parade, the mesmerizing dragon dance, which is a symbol of prosperity and good fortune. A dedicated team carried the 100-foot dragon, skillfully maneuvering its segmented body on poles, weaving through the streets to animate its movements and bring it to life. This tradition continues during various celebrations in Portland. (Gholston Collection.)

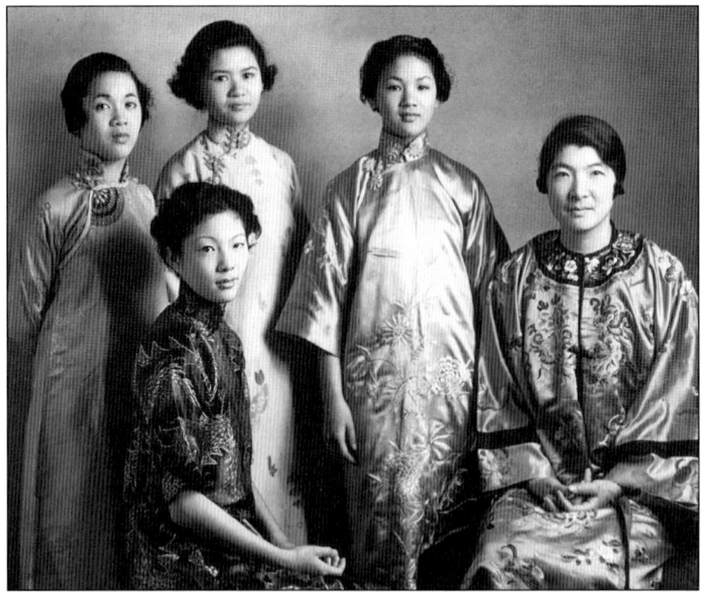

The Chinese Girl Reserve Club, part of the Portland Young Women's Christian Association (YWCA), started in 1918 to foster patriotic war work. In the 1920s and 1930s, thousands of Chinese, Japanese, and African American junior high and high school girls joined the club, which welcomed minorities. From left to right are officers Dorothy Moe, Madeline Chin (sitting), Isabella Lee, Frances Lee, and Lillian Chin. (Oregon Historical Society, 0022P348.)

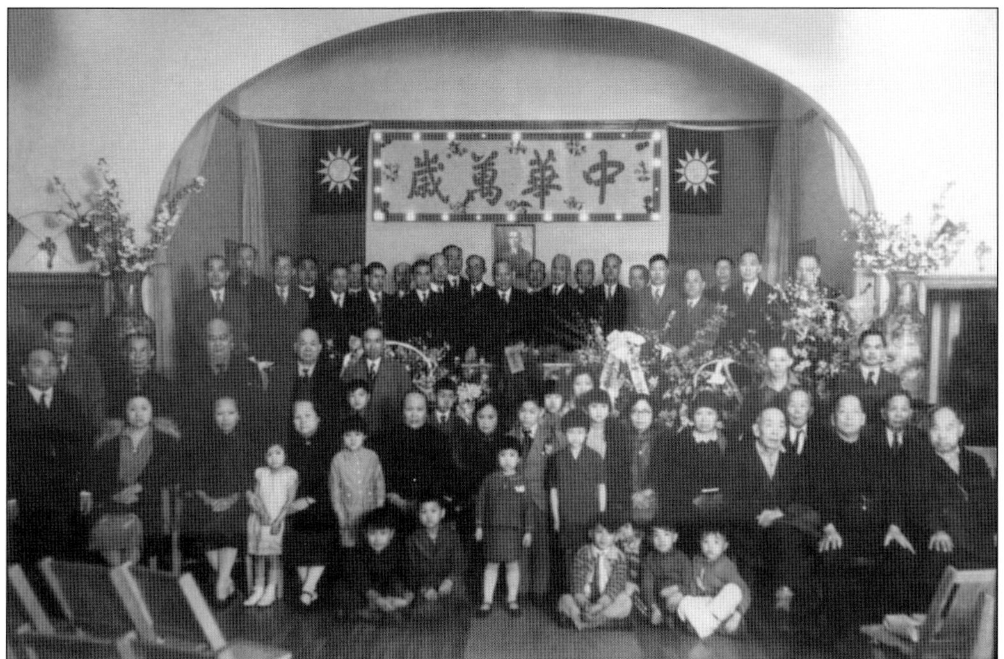

In 1931, members of the CCBA and their families celebrated the grand opening of the remodeled auditorium. Eleven community members, including Herbert Wong, Wong On, and Wong Soon Yook, donated $50 to $100 each for the renovation. This venue became an important community location for celebrations, cultural performances, and Chinese language school performances. (George W. and Mary N. Leong family.)

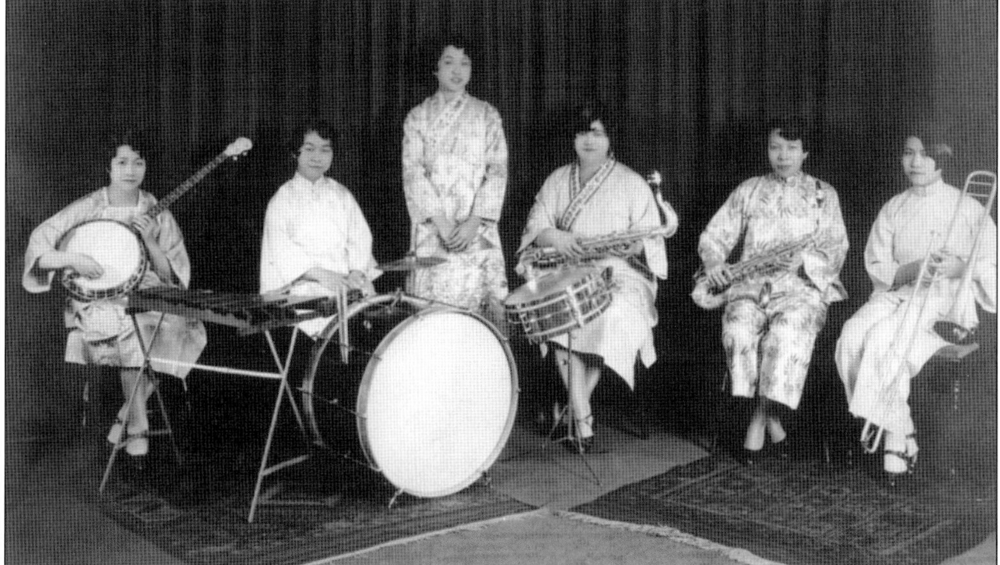

Leah Hing founded the Portland Chinese Girls' Orchestra at Washington High School, touring the United States and Canada with Honorable Wu's Vaudeville Troupe. While working at her family's restaurant, she met Tex Rankin, who offered her flying lessons for $2 each. The orchestra included, from left to right, Mayme Moe, Lillian Lang, Maxine Sun, Lena Lee, Leah Hing, and Virginia Wong. Hing and Wong became pioneering female pilots. (Portland Chinatown Museum.)

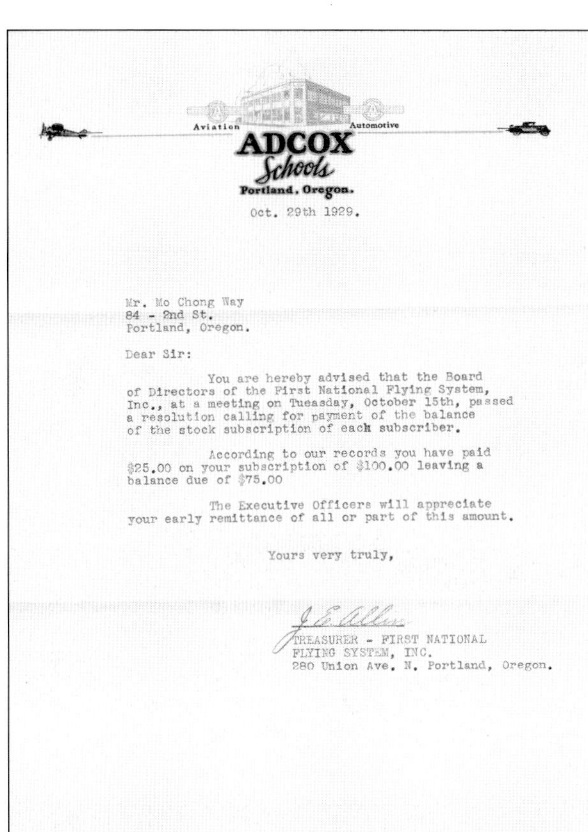

Aviation ADCOX Schools Automotive
Portland, Oregon.

Oct. 29th 1929.

Mr. Mo Chong Way
84 - 2nd St.
Portland, Oregon.

Dear Sir:

You are hereby advised that the Board of Directors of the First National Flying System, Inc., at a meeting on Tueasday, October 15th, passed a resolution calling for payment of the balance of the stock subscription of each subscriber.

According to our records you have paid $25.00 on your subscription of $100.00 leaving a balance due of $75.00

The Executive Officers will appreciate your early remittance of all or part of this amount.

Yours very truly,

J. E. Allen
TREASURER - FIRST NATIONAL
FLYING SYSTEM, INC.
280 Union Ave. N. Portland, Oregon.

The Chinese Flying Club of Portland was the largest club in the US for helping to train Chinese American pilots before World War II. It sponsored 35 students at the Adcox School of Aviation in Portland. Of these, 25 joined the Chinese Air Force during the Sino-Japanese War, playing a crucial role in supporting China's efforts against Japanese aggression. (Portland Chinatown Museum.)

This 1932 image shows graduates of Portland's Al Greenwood Flying School, also known as the Chinese Flying Club. It was founded by prominent Chinese who recruited and trained Chinese Americans during the Sino-Japanese War. From left to right are (first row) Bob Ong, Millard Chung, Sam Chong, Charles Sue, Moy Gee, and Peter Huie; (second row) Arthur Chin, John Wong, Louis Loy, Lim Kwong, Tom Young, and Ralph Chang. (Portland Chinatown Museum.)

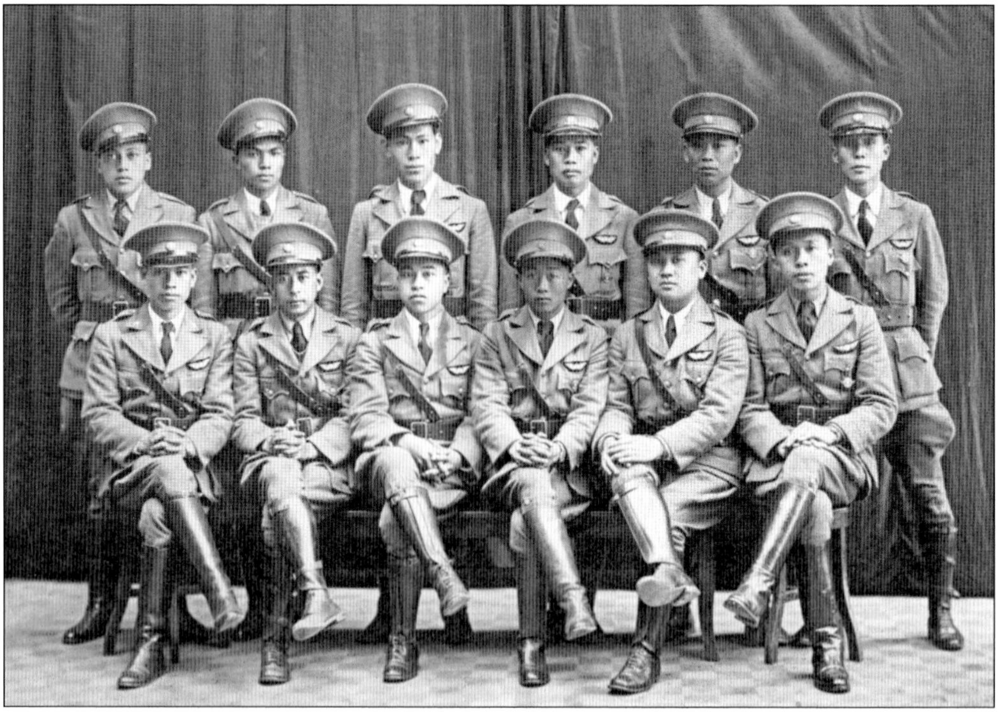

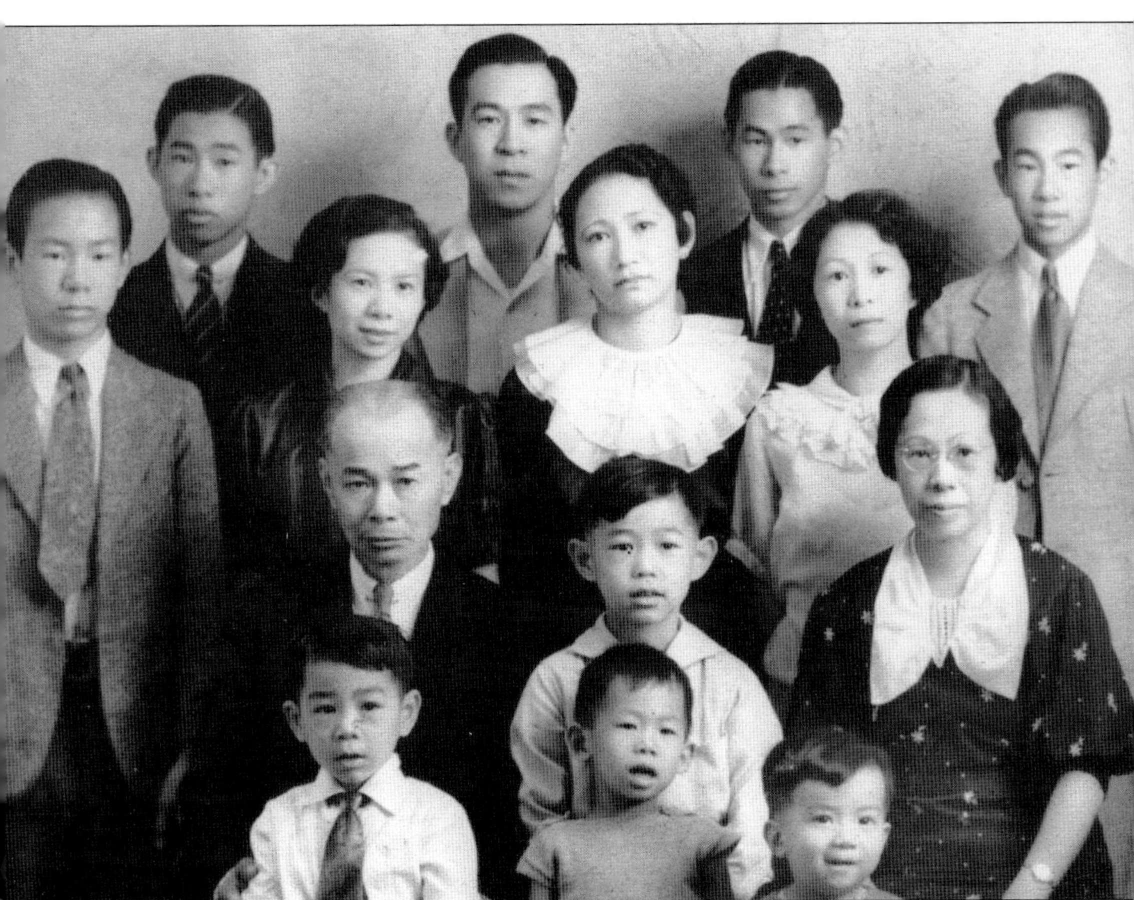

Charles and Eulie Locke immigrated to Oregon in the 1880s; Charles became a rancher and owned several hop farms in Aurora, Oregon. Seeking better opportunities, they moved to Portland's Chinatown. Their son Frank married Agnes Fong in 1954. Agnes's family was a partner in a supper club in Spokane, Washington, where Bing Crosby sang before he became famous. In 1928, their son Norman was born in Portland. For fun, Norman played in the streets with friends and went to late-night movies for 25¢, which included the price of admission, popcorn, candy, and a drink. Three generations of the Locke family are seen in this photograph taken around 1933; from left to right are (first row) Ron Locke, Kenneth Lee (cousin), and Arlen Quan; (second row) Charles Locke, Norman Locke, and Eulie Locke; (third row) Ralph Locke, Jean Locke Quan, Agnes Locke, and Susan Locke; (fourth row) Calvin Locke, Frank Locke, Ed Locke, and Chester Locke. (Norman Locke.)

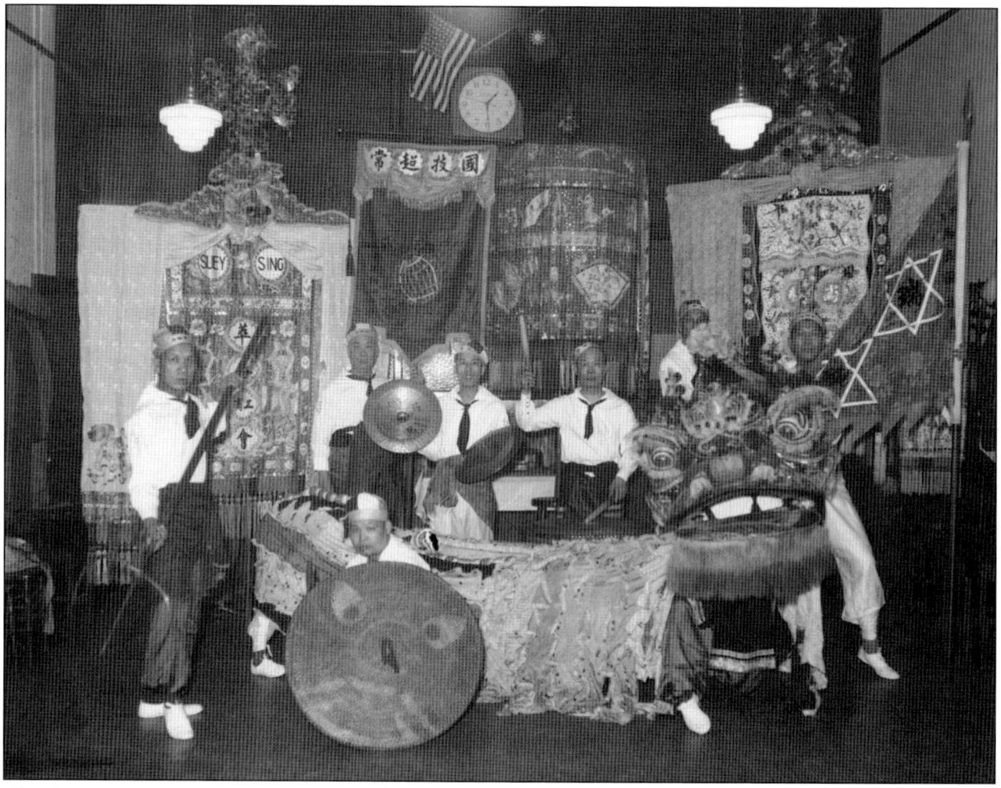

The Suey Sing Association headquarters at Northwest Fourth and Davis Streets provided essential social, cultural, and economic support to its members. As one of Portland's Chinese associations, it played a crucial role in the community. This 1933 photograph captures a performance during the opening of its new headquarters. The association continues to serve the Chinese American community through various social and cultural events. This image is from the December 8, 1933, issue of the *Oregonian*. (The *Oregonian*.)

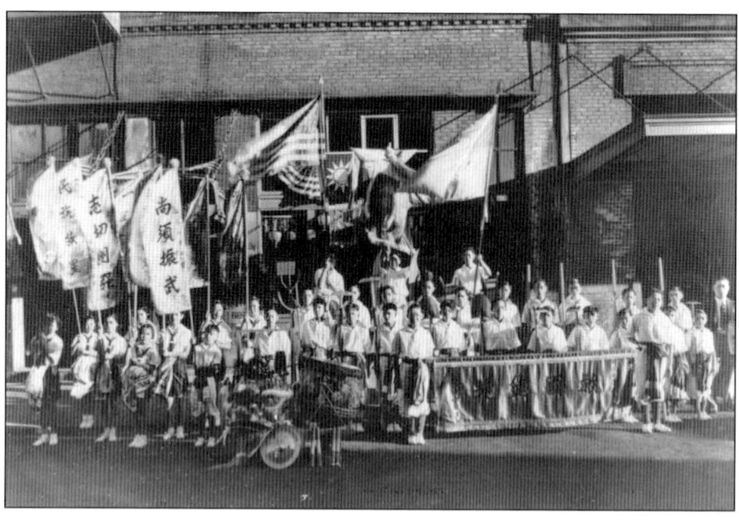

The Shang Gee Shar group gave lion dance and kung fu demonstrations in Chinatown during the Rose Festival parade in 1934. The exhibition was sponsored by Portland's CCBA and the Chinese Peace Society. Eleven-year-old Mary N. Leong is holding a banner, sixth from left. (George W. and Mary N. Leong family.)

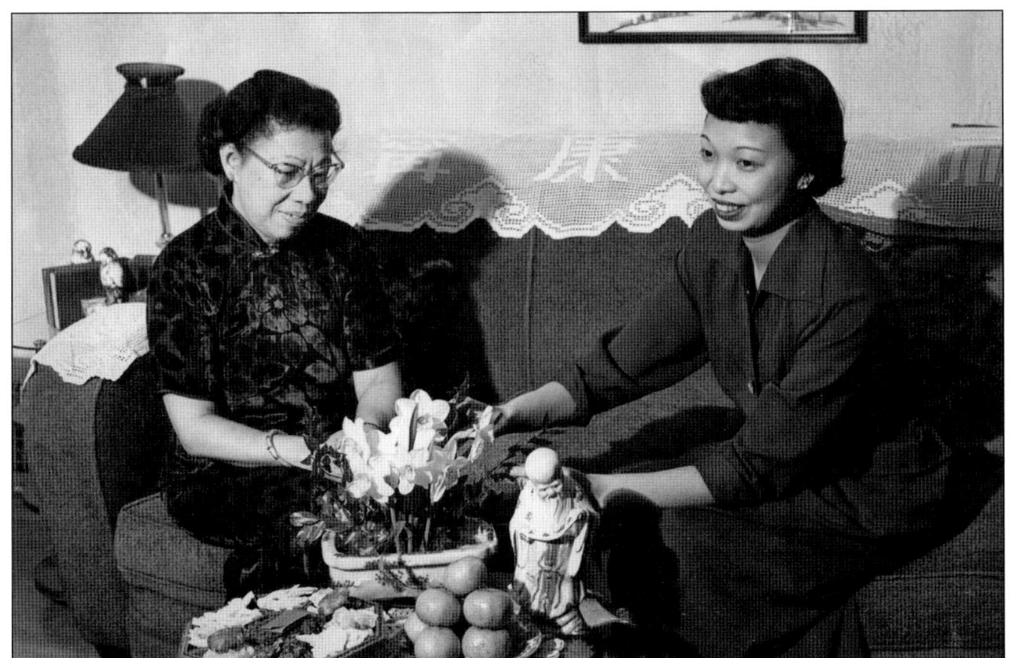

During Chinese New Year, tangerines, candied lotus seeds, winter melon, and kumquats symbolize luck, prosperity, and happiness. The wise old man represents longevity, wisdom, and fortune. This photograph shows Eulie Locke (left) with her daughter-in-law Penny Locke (right) in Eulie's home. The home was purchased for $4,000 in 1935 during the Great Depression, despite laws preventing Chinese land ownership, because the contractor needed to sell the house. (Norman Locke.)

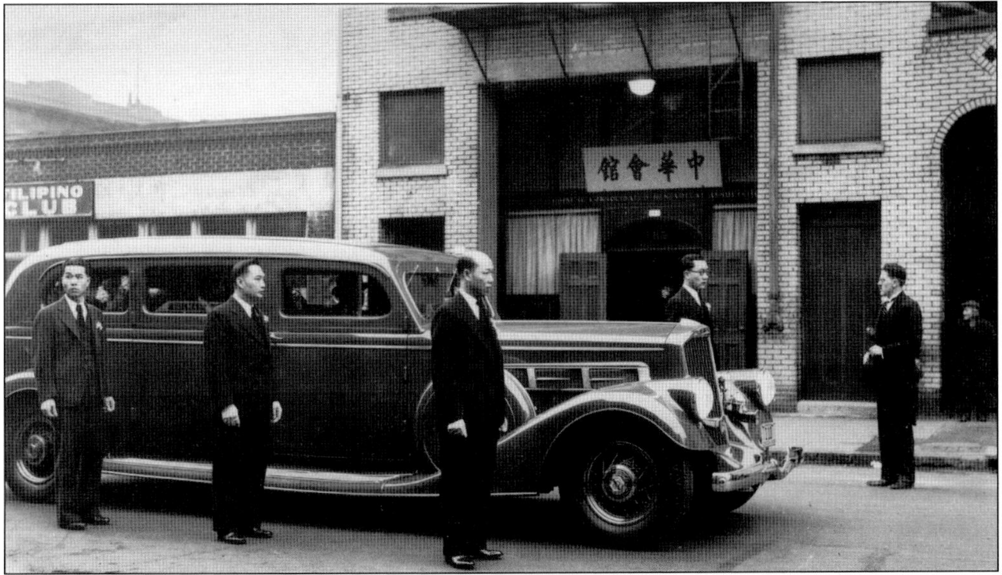

Moy Back Hin's funeral in 1935 attracted a large audience from both Portland's Chinese community and the wider public. Moy's funeral procession through Chinatown passed in front of the CCBA, a key institution representing the local Chinese population. The image captures this solemn moment, highlighting the deep respect and communal support surrounding his passing and the strong presence of Chinatown's cultural traditions. (Portland Chinatown Museum.)

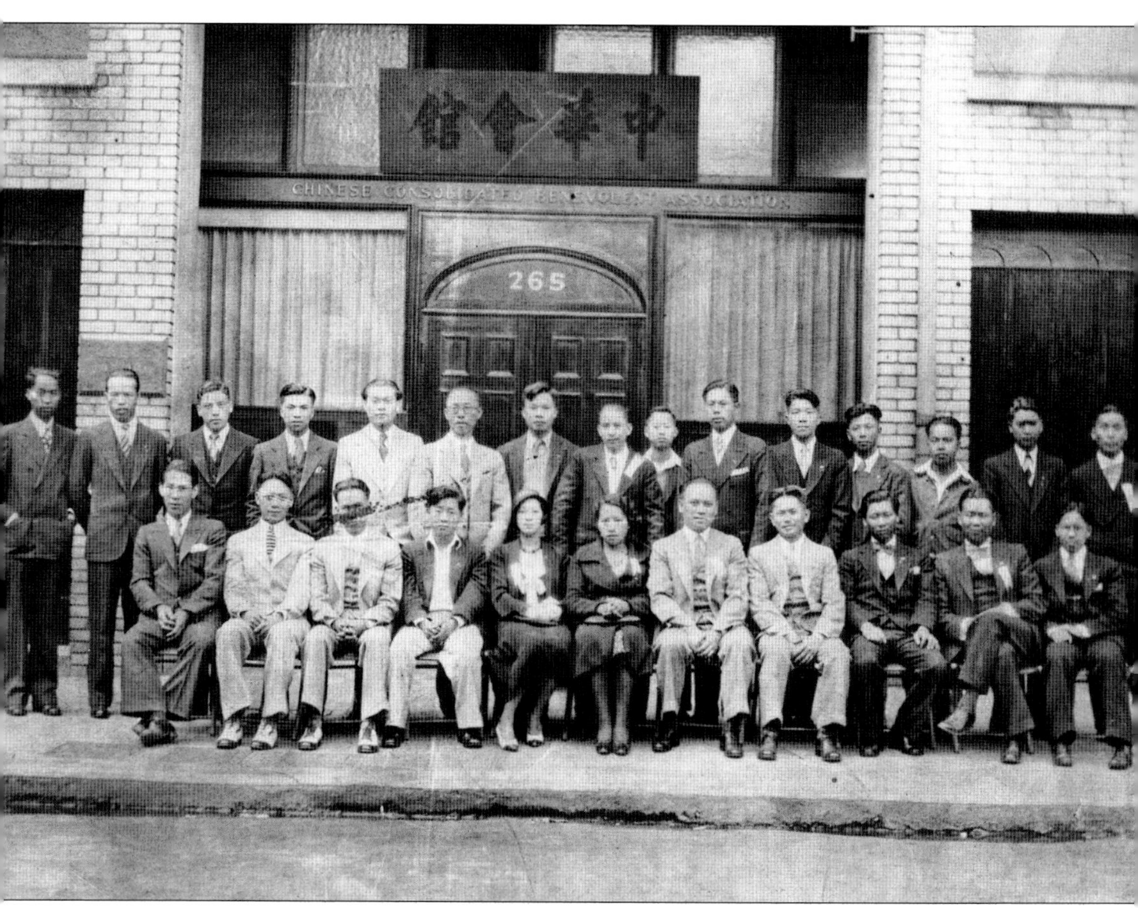

Members of the Portland Flying Club are shown in front of the CCBA building. Every student pledged their willingness to sacrifice their life for China, which highlighted the contributions of these Chinese American pilots. In China, Millard Chung died during bombing practice, and Virginia Wong died of malaria. "Clifford" Louie Yim-qun retired from the military in 1974 and became chief executive officer and then chairman of the board of China Airlines in Taiwan. He married fellow pilot Hazel Ying Lee in 1943. Identified in the image from left to right are (first row) Hazel Ying Lee (fifth) and Virginia Wong (sixth); (second row) Arthur Chin (third), John Wong (fourth), Lim Kwong (seventh), and Thomas Wing Lee (twelfth). (Portland Chinatown Museum.)

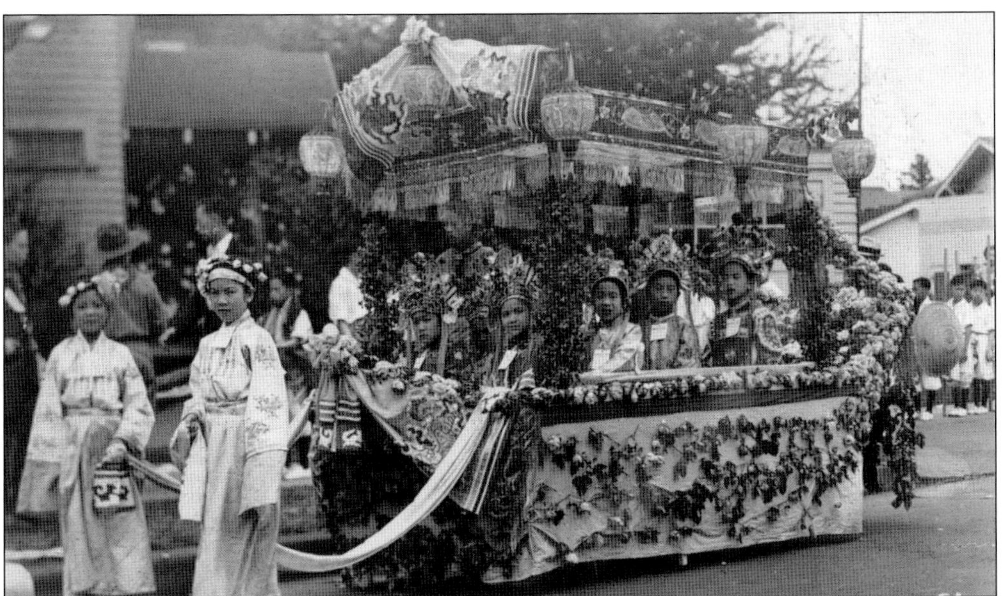

In the 1940s, the Chinese Women's Association in Portland offered crucial social, cultural, and educational support to its members. It organized events, assisted new immigrants, and promoted Chinese culture. The club served as a hub for Chinese women to connect and support each other. Notably, the club had a float in the 1936 Junior Rose Parade, highlighting its community involvement. (George W. and Mary N. Leong family.)

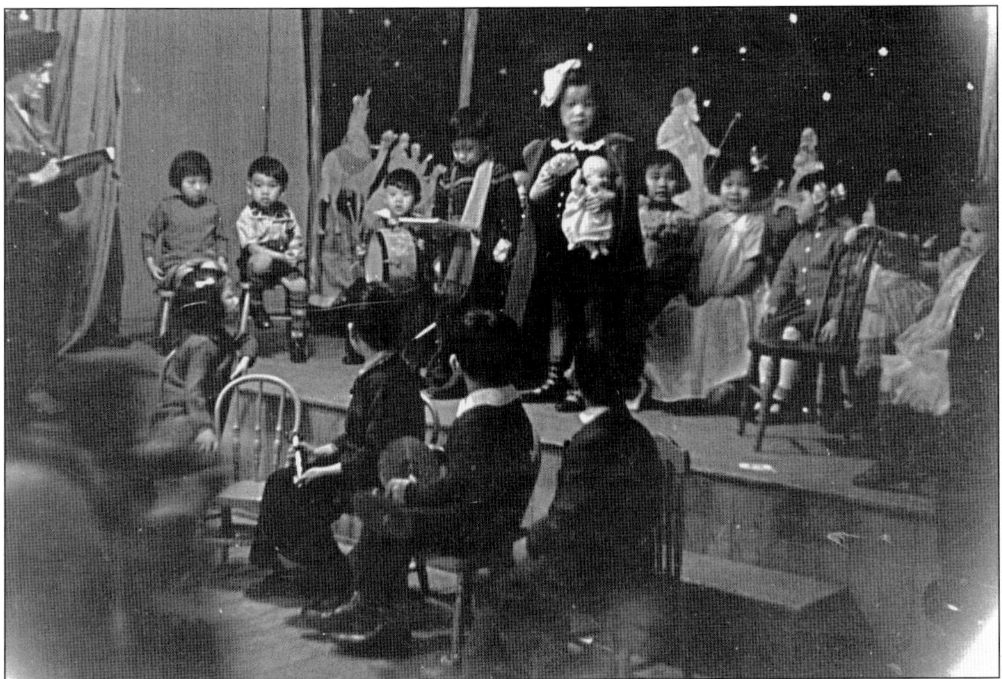

This annual Christmas performance around 1938 was held at Holt Presbyterian Church. The four children sitting in the first row are unidentified, but shown from left to right in the second row are Jeanette Phillips (teacher), Eva Seid, Harvey Leo, Fred M. Wong, Benny Lee, Muriel Lee Wah, Sally Seto, Janet Yut Locke, Gloria Chang, Sherrie Moe, and Verna Lee. (Portland Chinatown Museum.)

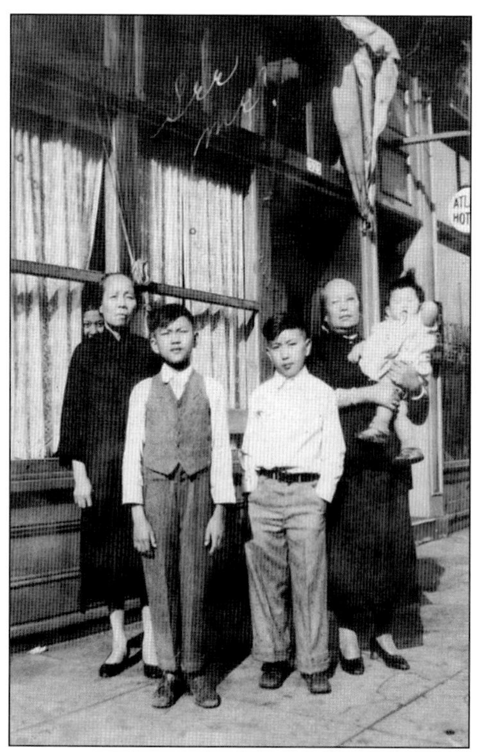

The Lee Jyp family poses in front of their apartment at 525 Northwest Davis Street. This photograph highlights the importance of familial bonds and reflects the shared traditions and resilience that shaped the lives of Chinatown residents. From left to right are Mary N. Leong (peeking out the window), an unidentified aunt, brothers Fred Lee and Harold Lee, mother Wong Shee Lee, and cousin Idabelle Mar. (George W. and Mary N. Leong family.)

In 1939, the CCBA Lion Dance Team performed for the Chinese New Year at the Hong Kong Café, drawing the community together and showcasing cultural pride. Coach Lee Fong (far left) led the team. The lion dance, signifying prosperity, good fortune, and wisdom, is essential to the Chinese New Year and other celebrations. This image is from the February 20, 1939, issue of the *Oregonian*. (The *Oregonian*.)

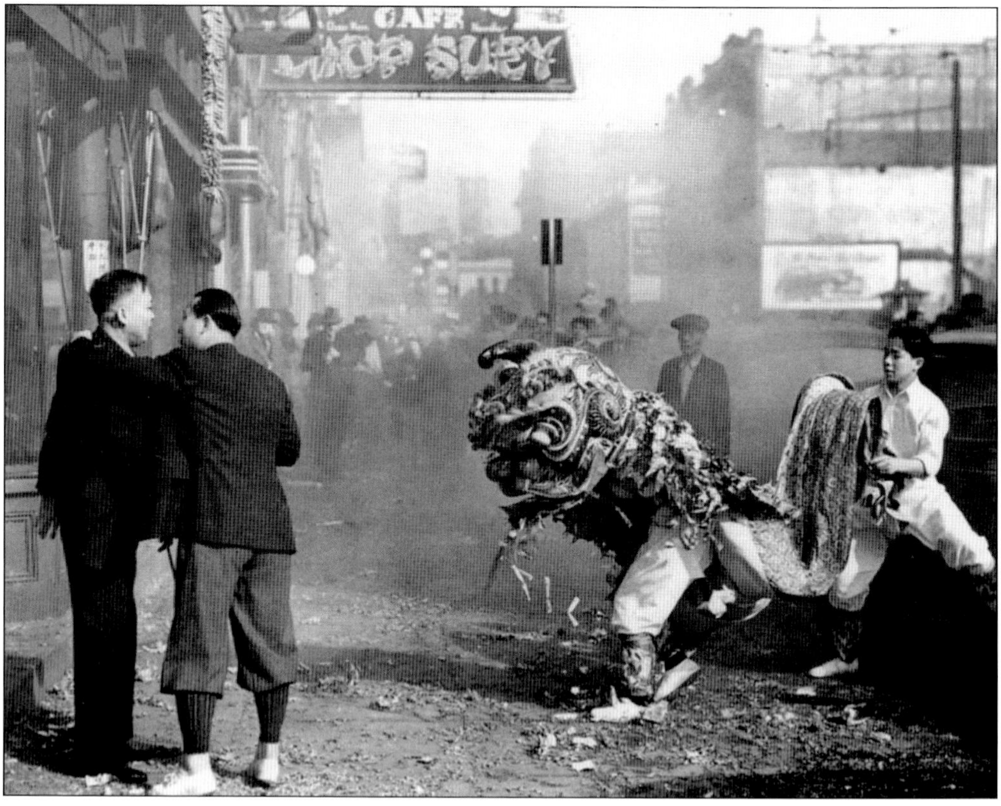

Betty Chin is pictured in 1939 burning incense for the Chinese New Year, a practice symbolizing respect for ancestors and deities. She wears a cheongsam, a traditional Chinese dress known for its elegant design. In front of her, incense burners and three cups of tea or wine are arranged as offerings, believed to appease spirits and deities, reinforcing cultural traditions that honor family and heritage. (Oregon Historical Society, bb013875.)

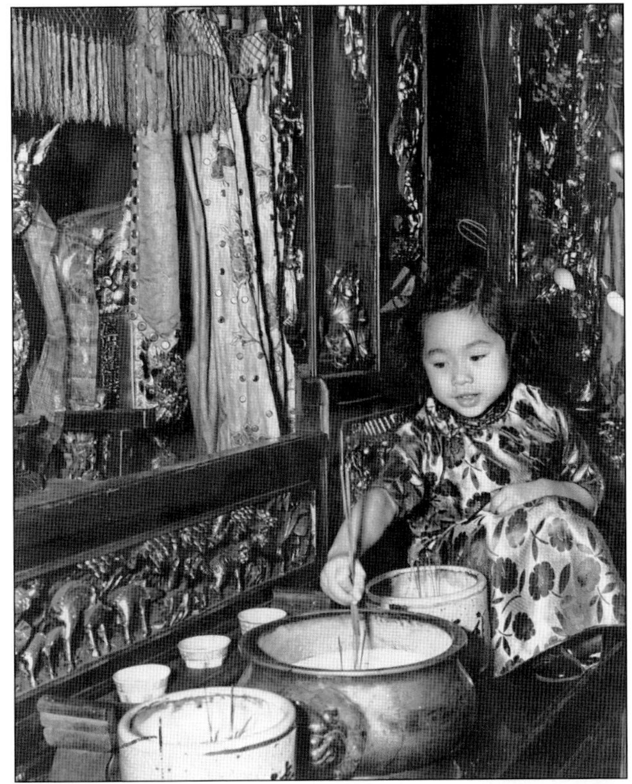

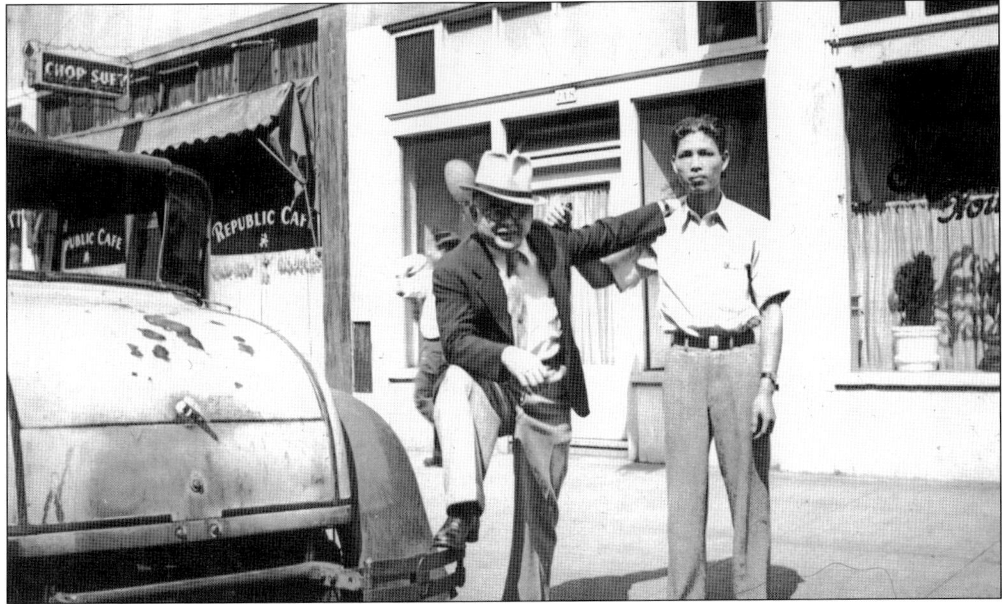

The Republic Café, established in 1922, specializes in Chinese American cuisine. It was surrounded by Japanese eateries like Tokyo Sukiyaki House and Yodogawa restaurant. In this photograph, principal owner and head chef "Sunny" Sam Soo Hoo stands on the right with a friend, capturing a moment in the late 1930s. This establishment is the longest-operating Chinese-owned restaurant in Portland. (Portland Chinatown Museum.)

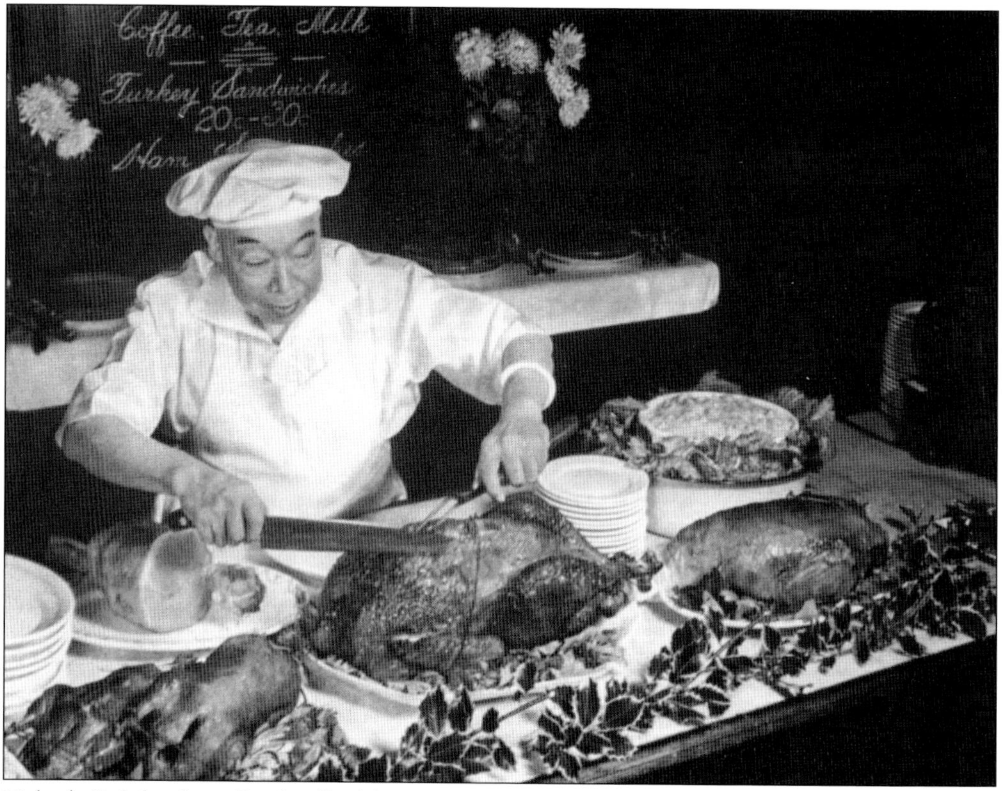

Huber's Café has been Portland's oldest operating restaurant since 1879. Huber's has been owned by the Louie family since 1940. Wei "Jim" Fung Louie immigrated to Portland in 1881 and started working at Huber's in 1891. After Augusta Huber's death, her son John partnered with Louie and sold his half of the business to him for a dollar. Louie became the chef manager, then owner, and the restaurant is still family-owned. This image appeared in *Collier's* magazine on December 23, 1939.

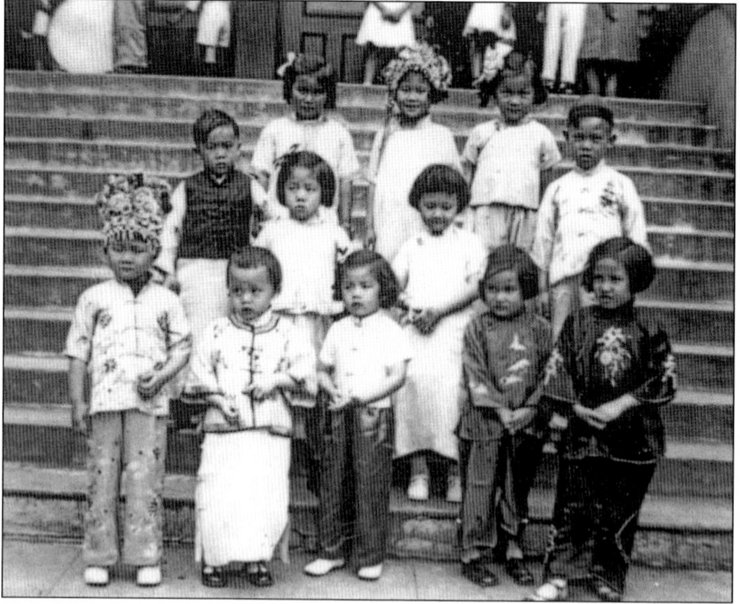

Children stand on the auditorium steps following a Chinese New Year performance in 1940 at Southwest Third and Clay Streets. Shown are, from left to right, (first row) Gloria Chang, Verna Lee, Sherrie Moe, Patricia Lee, and Carol Lee; (second row) Fred M. Wong, Virginia Koe, Eva Seid, and Richard Lee; (third row) Sally Seto, Janet Yut Locke, and Muriel Lee Wah. (Carol Lee.)

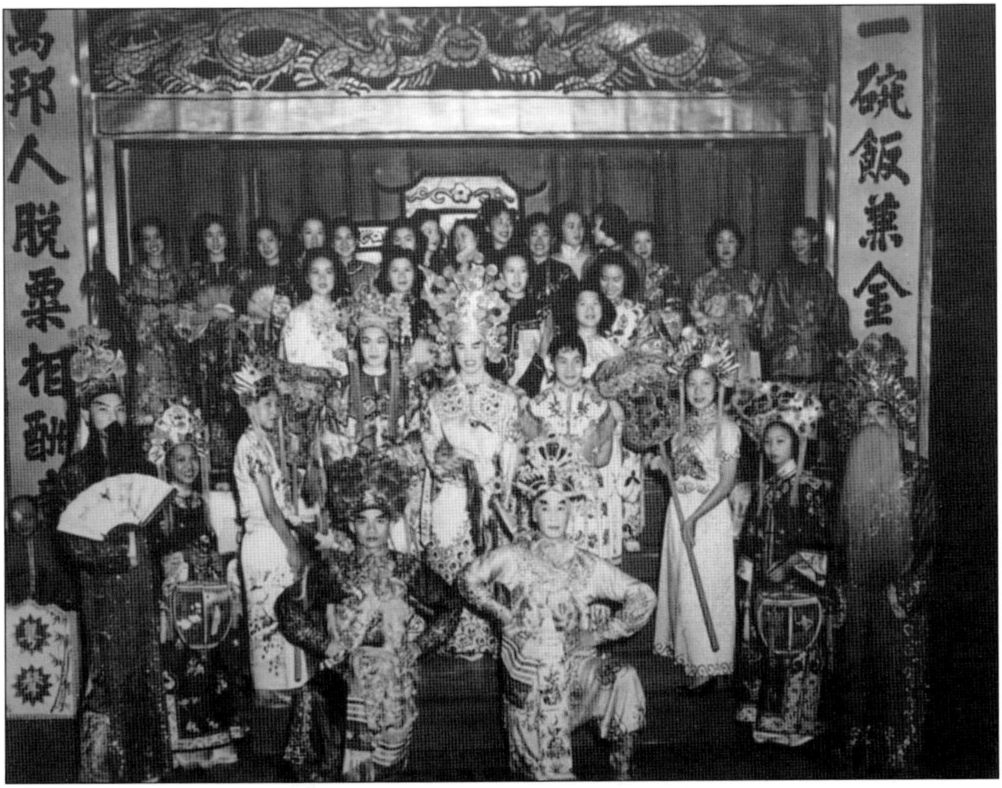

The "One Rice Bowl" China war relief fundraiser in Portland was organized by Chinese Americans during the Second Sino-Japanese War. Events were held in major Chinatowns across the country and included parades, concerts, and theatrical performances. This photograph was taken at the CCBA auditorium. Mary N. Leong is behind the girl holding the pole on the right. (George W. and Mary N. Leong family.)

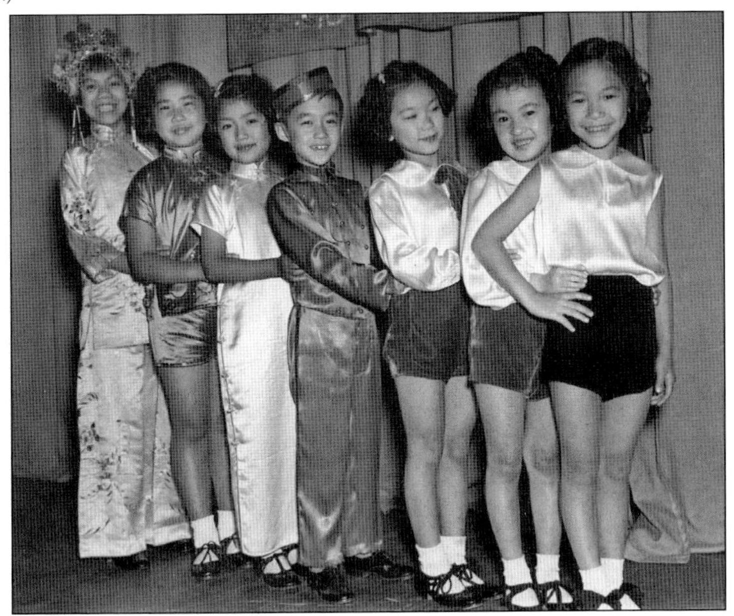

These tap-dancing children were part of numerous performances organized by the community to support China war relief in the early 1940s. These events raised funds and awareness, showcasing the talents of local performers and bringing the community together for a common cause. In the photograph on the far right is Ellen ?, and standing next to her is Audrey Leo. (Gordon Wong Collection.)

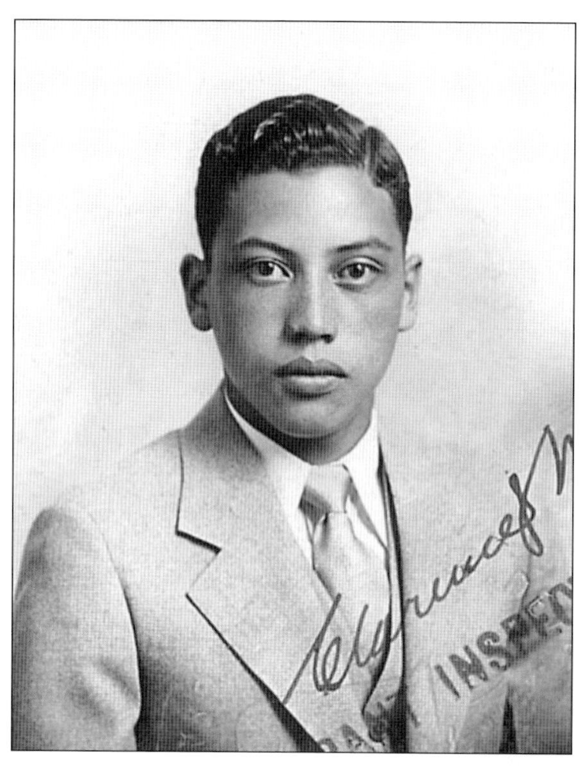

Arthur Chin, born in 1913 in Portland, graduated from the Al Greenwood Flying School in 1931. He volunteered with the Chinese Air Force during the Sino-Japanese War, which resulted in the loss of his US citizenship. While there, Chin met and married Eva Wu. During combat, his fuel tank caught fire from Japanese bombardment, and he suffered severe burns. While recovering at Liuzhou Airbase, Japanese bombers attacked, and his wife died while shielding him. Repatriated in 1945, Chin became the first American volunteer combat aviator and flying ace in World War II, earning the Distinguished Flying Cross and Air Medal. He became a postal worker, and a post office in Aloha, Oregon, honors him. In 1997, Chin was inducted into the Hall of Fame of the American Airpower Heritage Museum. (Left, US National Archives; below, Oregon Historical Society, OrHi_84171.)

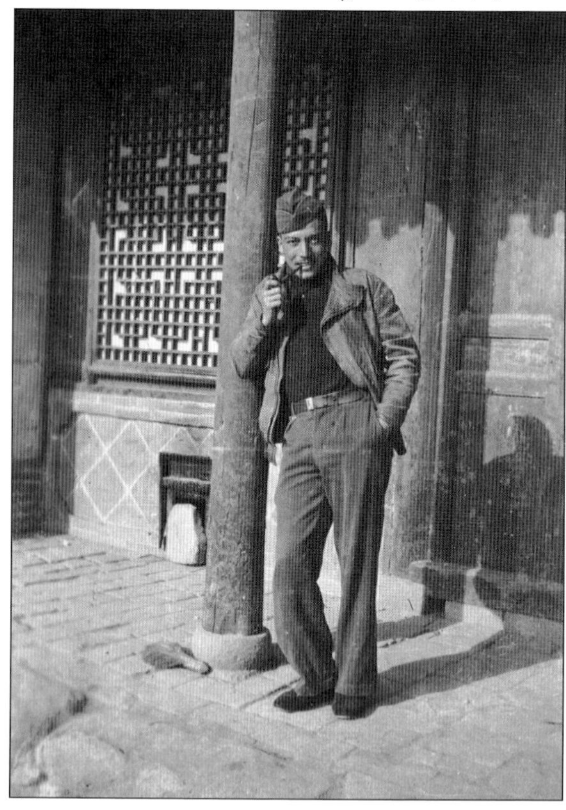

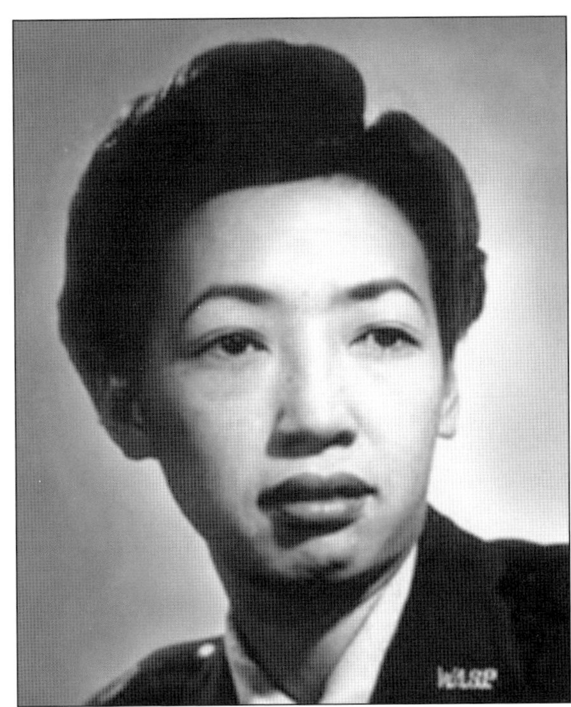

Hazel Ying Lee earned her pilot's license in 1932 from the Adcox School of Aviation. Excluded from the Chinese Air Force because she was a woman, she became a commercial pilot in China until the Sino-Japanese War. Returning to the United States, she joined the Women's Air Force Service Pilots (WASP), becoming the first Chinese American woman to fly for the US military. In 2010, she received the Congressional Gold Medal. (Portland Chinatown Museum.)

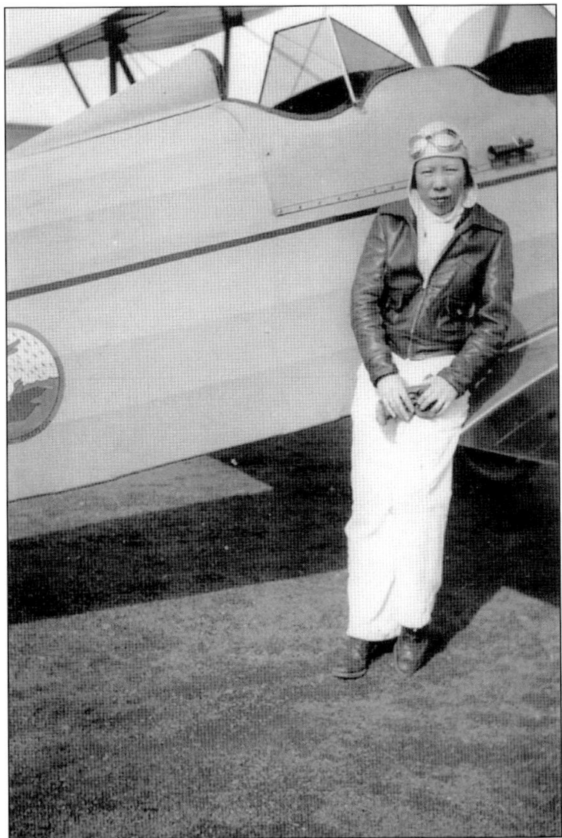

Leah Hing, born in Portland in 1907, earned a pilot's license from the Rankin Flying School in 1934. During World War II, she volunteered with the West Coast Civil Air Patrol, conducting ground training and repairing navigational equipment at the Portland Army Air Base. Her father forbade her from being a pilot in China, so she remained active in aviation organizations in the Portland community. (Portland Chinatown Museum.)

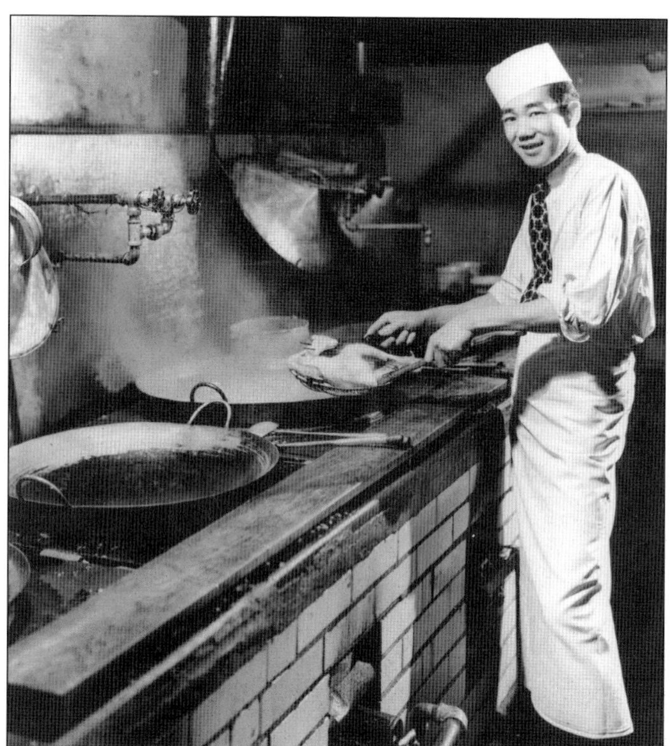

Leonard Yee, or Lee Sung, led the CCBA and opened a soup kitchen in 1937 to sponsor Chinese aviators at the Adcox Aviation School. In traditional Chinese society, men often had different names for life stages, including a given name, courtesy name, and professional name. Some also had an English name to ease assimilation. (Portland Chinatown Museum.)

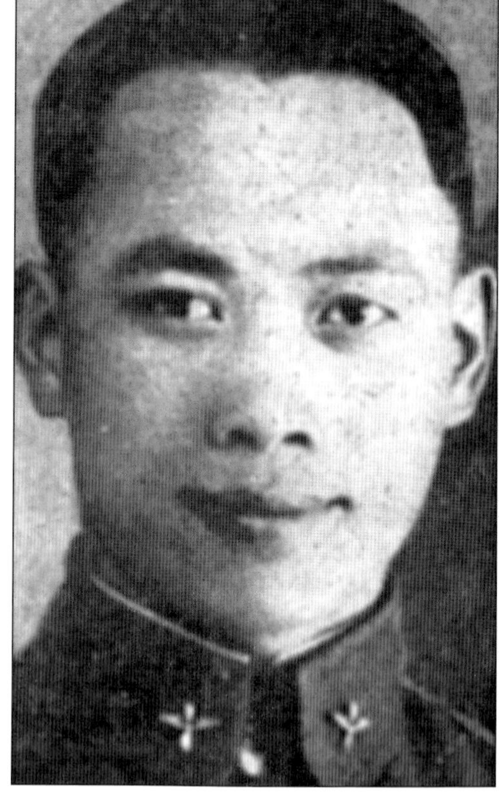

Mai Eoun Lam was a graduate of Lincoln High School and North Pacific Pharmacy College. At the age of 24, he made the ultimate sacrifice when he was shot down by Japanese forces in Nanchong, China, in 1938. Part of a group of 35 Portland Chinese pilots, he trained at the Al Greenwood Flying School to assist China during the Sino-Japanese War. (Portland Chinatown Museum.)

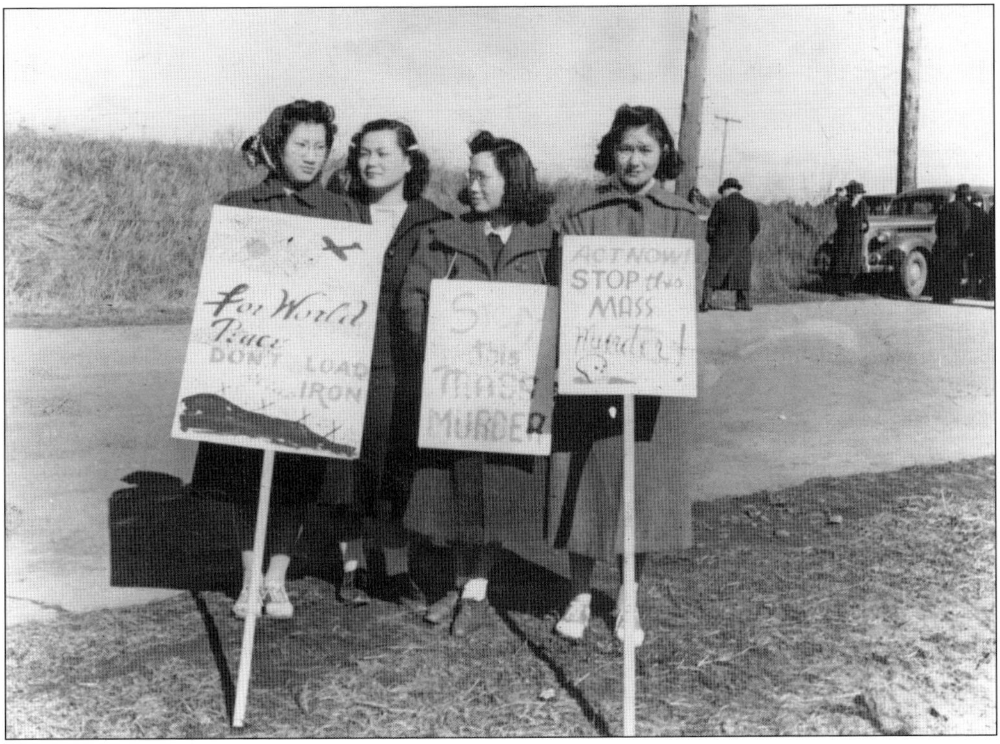

During the Sino-Japanese War, Chinese Americans in Portland protested US scrap metal exports to Japan, highlighting how these materials bolstered Japan's military operations in China. Though the United States was not at war with Japan, the exports directly fueled Japan's aggression, amplifying the devastation in Chinese territories. This activism demonstrated the Chinese American community's solidarity with their homeland and their awareness of the economic ties shaping global conflicts, foreshadowing similar dynamics in World War II. Pictured above, from left to right, are Mary N. Leong, J.C. Yee, Phyllis Klong Lee, and Elaine Young. In the image to the right, from left to right are Lily Chu Gum Lee, Lee Sing Sew, and Violet Chinn Wong. (Above, Portland Chinatown Museum; right, George and Verna Lee family.)

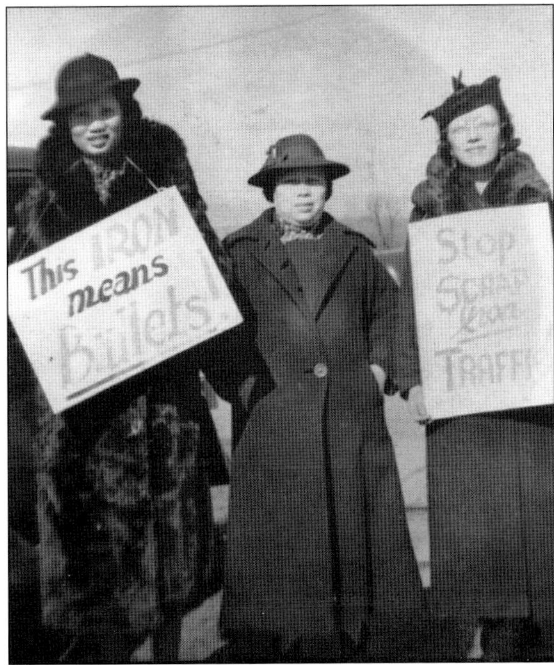

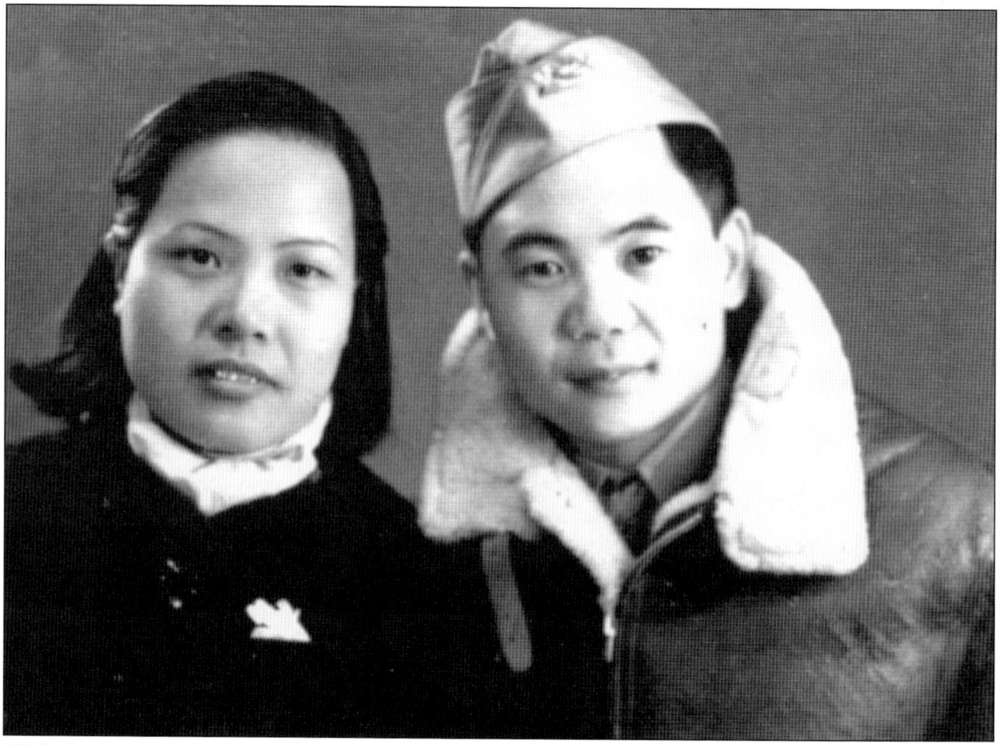

With the impending aggression of the Japanese in the early 1930s and the growth of the Communist movement under Mao Tse-tung, Pak On Lee left his wife, Sun Ying Lee, in China in 1935 to seek better opportunities in the United States. In 1941, he answered an advertisement in Portland's *Chinese Times* newspaper offering training and jobs in aircraft maintenance. This group of men became the original American Volunteer Group (AVG), or "the Flying Tigers." After graduation, they were assigned to China, and Lee saw this as an opportunity to return to his wife. After serving, Lee brought his wife and family back to the United States from China to pursue the American Dream. Lee worked for Majhor's Auto Electric, becoming a top electrical and carburetion technician and eventually becoming a partner in the business. (Both, Keith Lee.)

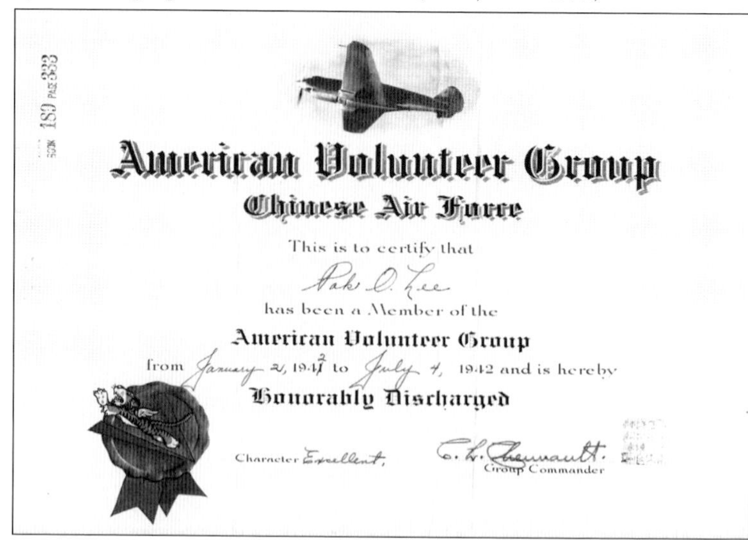

American Volunteer Group

Chinese Air Force

This is to certify that

Pak O. Lee

has been a Member of the

American Volunteer Group

from January 21, 1942 to July 4, 1942 and is hereby

Honorably Discharged

Character Excellent,

C. L. Chennault.
Group Commander

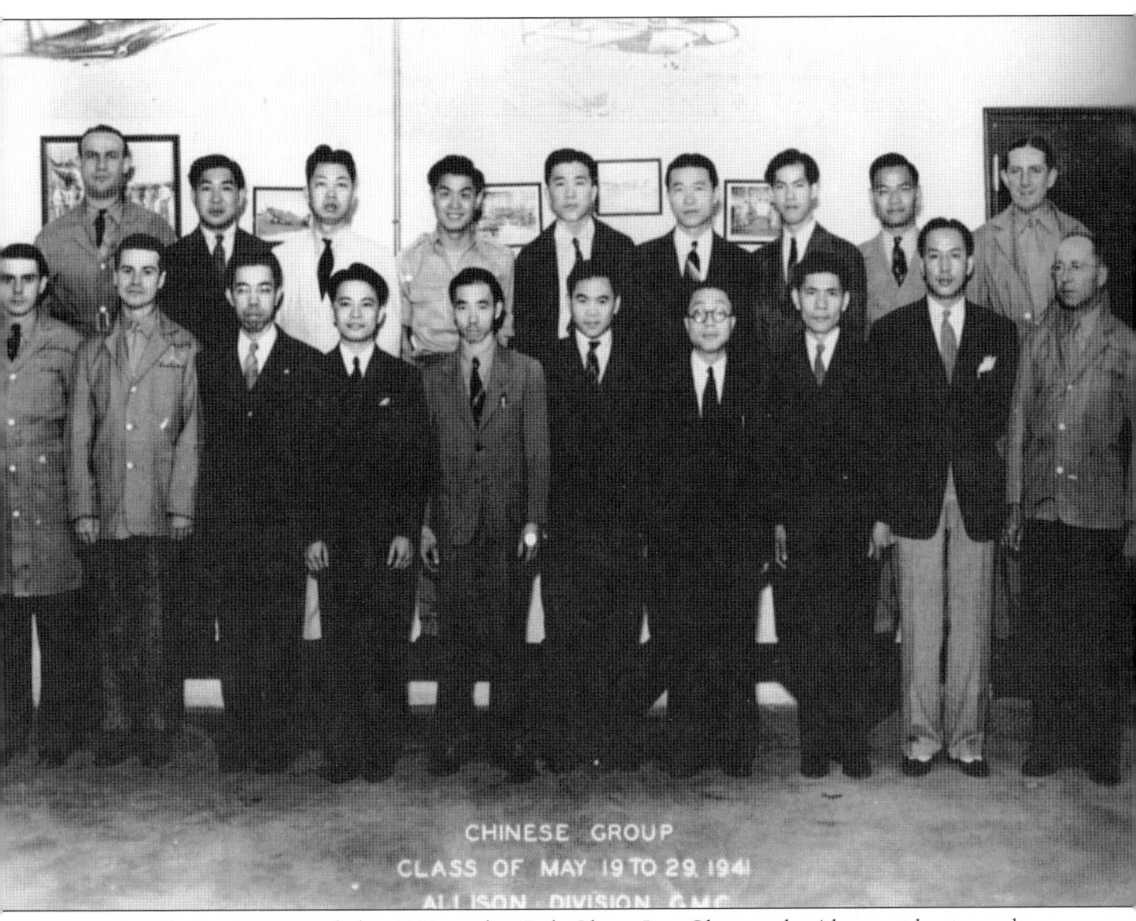

In 1941, Pak On Lee joined the AVG under Col. Claire Lee Chennault. Along with nine other Chinese men, they formed the Chinese American Volunteer Group (CAVG) and were trained as engine mechanics. They gained notoriety for their mission to defend the Burma Road during the Sino-Japanese War. World War II then started, and in 1942, the AVG disbanded, and it became the China Air Task Force. In 1943, the US Army Air Force absorbed the unit. These men showed patriotism to the United States along with giving back to China. This CAVG class photograph shows, from left to right, (first row) Leeds Lemex (instructor), R.H. Piper (instructor), Jack Eng, Lawrence Chow, Chun Gee, Pak On Lee, Leo Bow, Albert Gam, Nai-Chien Liu (counsel representative to China), and Fred Jainle (instructor); (second row) G.C. Pearce (instructor), Fred J. Wong, K.H.T. Ye Hon, Lem Git, Benny Fong, Lem Wu, Philip Pon, George Leo, and Harry Hartz (instructor). (Keith Lee.)

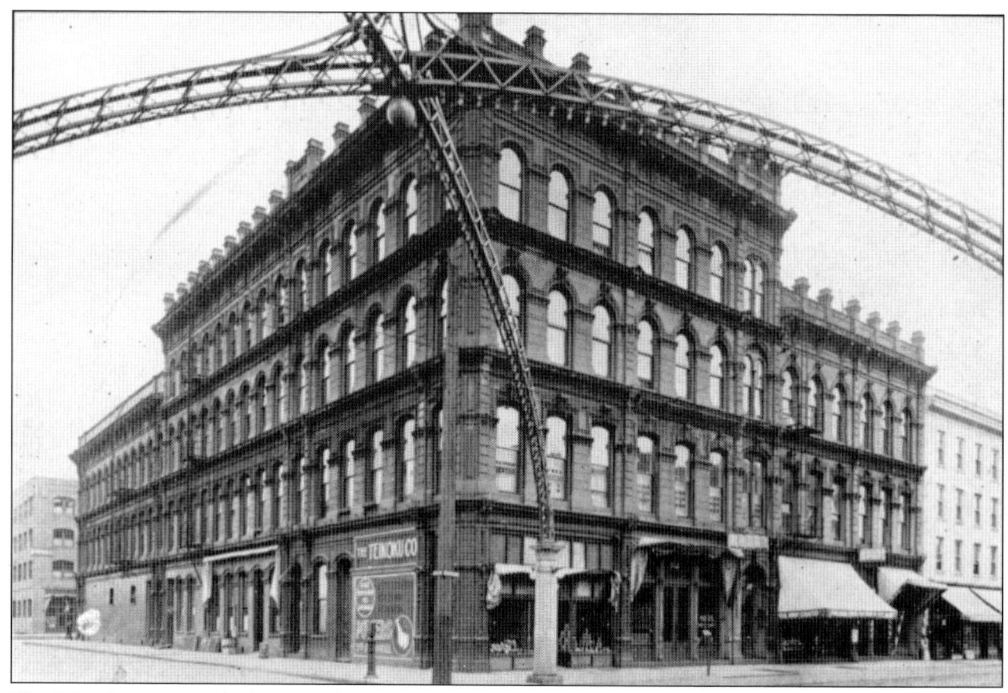

The Merchant, or Teikoku, Hotel was built in 1884 and was located at Northwest Third Avenue and Davis Street. It was an anchor in Japantown (Nihonmachi), which covered 20 blocks. Businesses in the Merchant Hotel building included the newspaper *Oshu Nippo*, Matsubu Bath and Laundry, dentist Dr. Kei Koyama, and mercantile Teikoku Company. Hotels like this offered a place for new arrivals working on railroads, timber mills, and canneries. (Japanese American Museum of Oregon.)

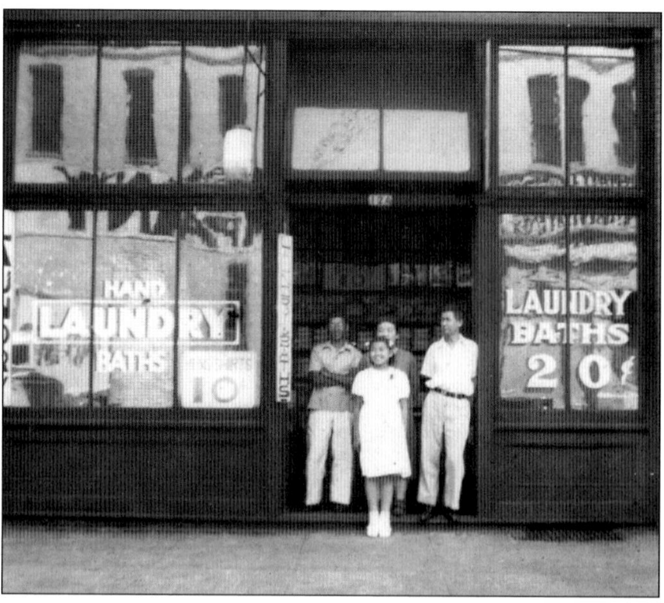

The Yabuki Laundry was located near Northwest Second Avenue and Couch Street. Starting in the 1890s, Japanese men sought economic opportunities in the United States, and many operated businesses like this laundry. Japanese immigrants also encountered job discrimination and exclusionary laws like the Chinese community. In the photograph are, from left to right, (first row) Mary Yabuki; (second row) Shizuta Yabuki, Ayako Yabuki, and Kazumasa "Jim" Yabuki. (Japanese American Museum of Oregon.)

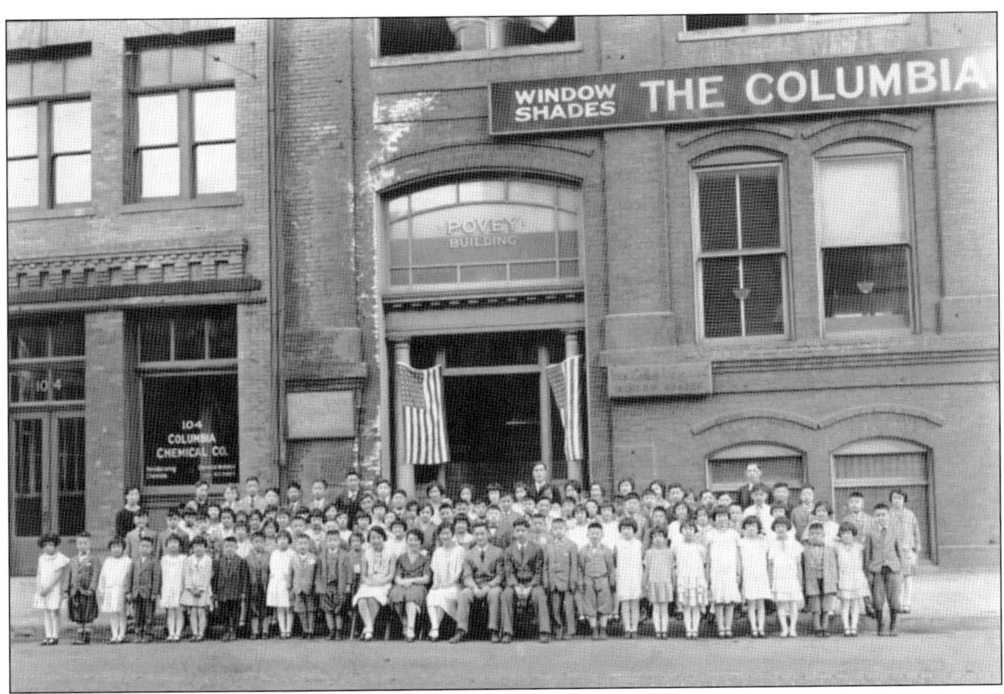

After attending public school during the week, Japanese children from kindergarten to 12th grade attended the Japanese language school Katei Gakuen in the afternoon to learn about the culture as well as speaking, reading, and writing. Kanji calligraphy was taught on Saturdays. It was located on the second floor of the Povey Building on Northwest Fifth Avenue and Flanders Street, which was a stained-glass window manufacturer. (Japanese American Museum of Oregon.)

Mosaburo Matsushima opened Teikoku Company in 1905 and offered Japanese goods, a post office, and money transfers. Following the Pearl Harbor attack in 1941, all Japanese, regardless of US citizenship, were sent to the Minidoka Relocation Center in Hunt, Idaho, in 1942, and Japantown disappeared within weeks. As a result, many Chinese businesses expanded into abandoned spaces. After the war, Matsushima returned and opened the store Anzen. (Japanese American Museum of Oregon.)

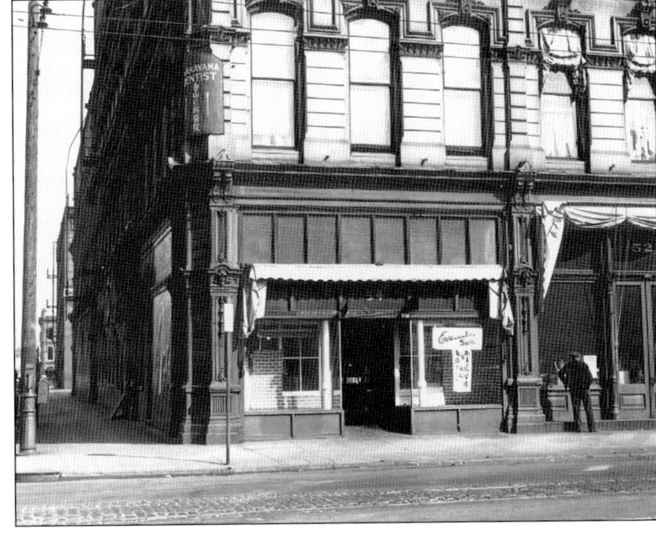

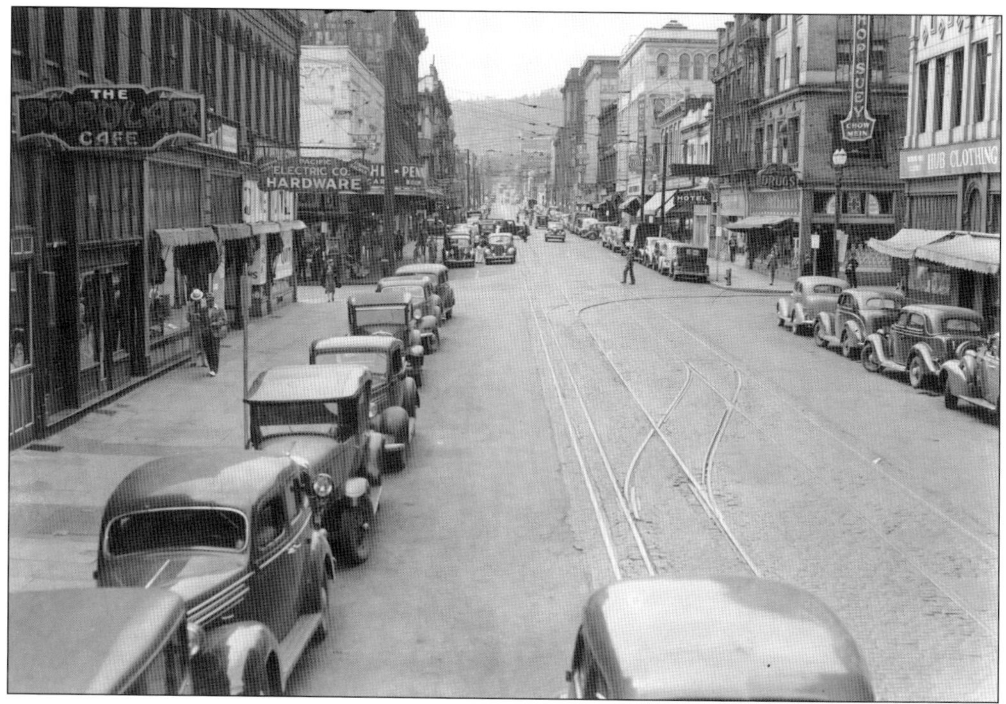

Looking toward Alder Street on Southwest Second Avenue, this was just outside of the immediate Chinatown area. By 1939, there were Chinese businesses interspersed among Japanese, Greek, and Jewish-owned stores and restaurants. During this time, many non-Chinese patrons shopped and ate at the Chinese restaurants, creating a diverse neighborhood. (City of Portland Archives, AP/6039.)

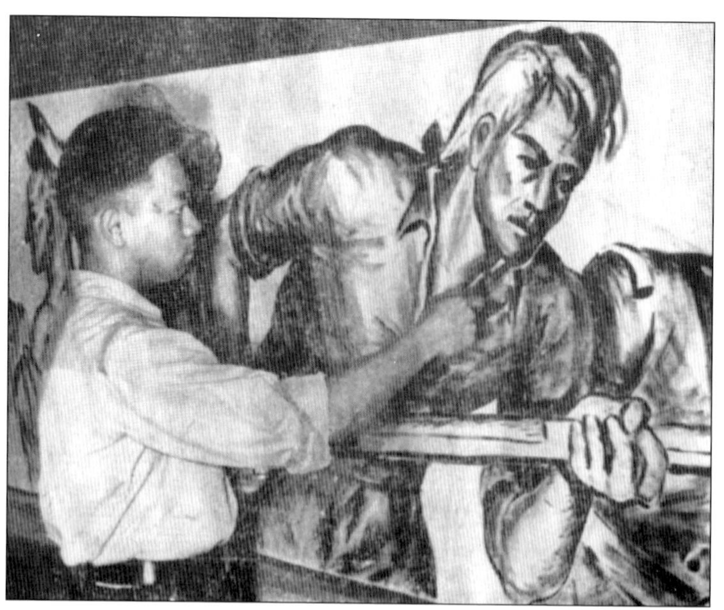

Fred Gong graduated from Lincoln High School in 1941. He was awarded the $1,000 first prize in *American Magazine*'s "Youth Forum Contest." Gong's winning entry, titled *What My Community Contributes to the Nation*, was selected out of 600,000 entries. His work was displayed at the Pioneer Post Office and the Portland Public Library. He went on to major in art at the University of Oregon. (Gholston Collection.)

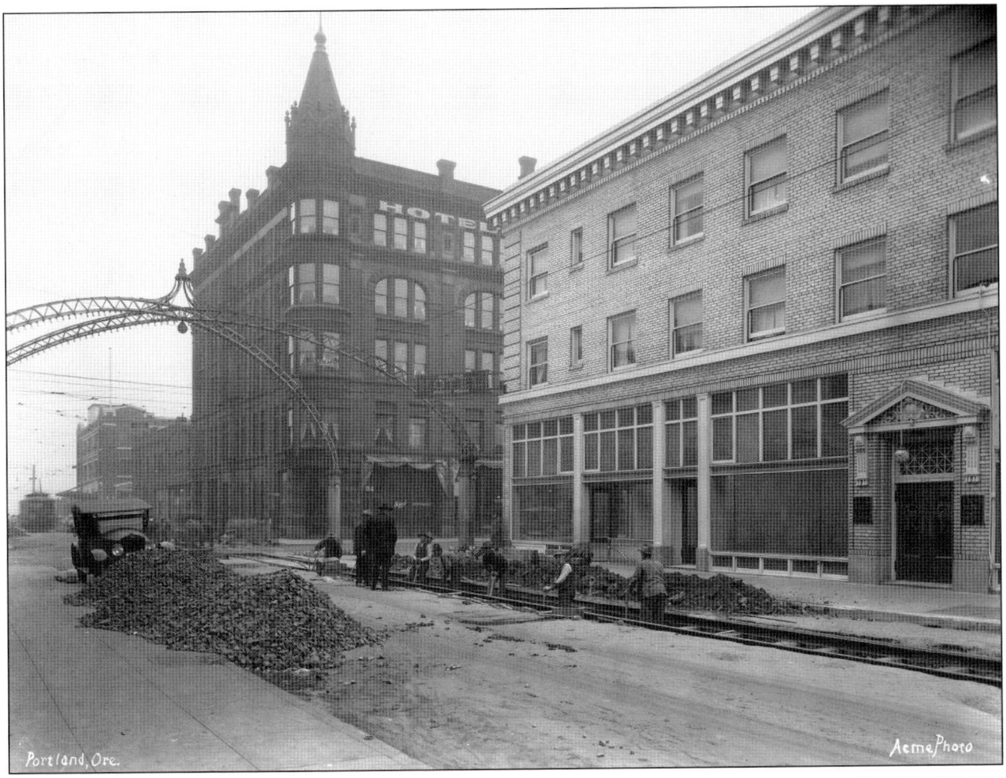

Built in 1913, the Royal Palm Hotel occupied the upper floors and was operated by the Japanese Kitayama family until their relocation to the Minidoka Relocation Center in 1942. The lower level housed businesses and Chinese families, including those of Fred M. Wong and George Lee. During a time of segregation, it welcomed African American workers, offering lodging during a time of restricted housing options. (Oregon Historical Society, OrHi_10493-a.)

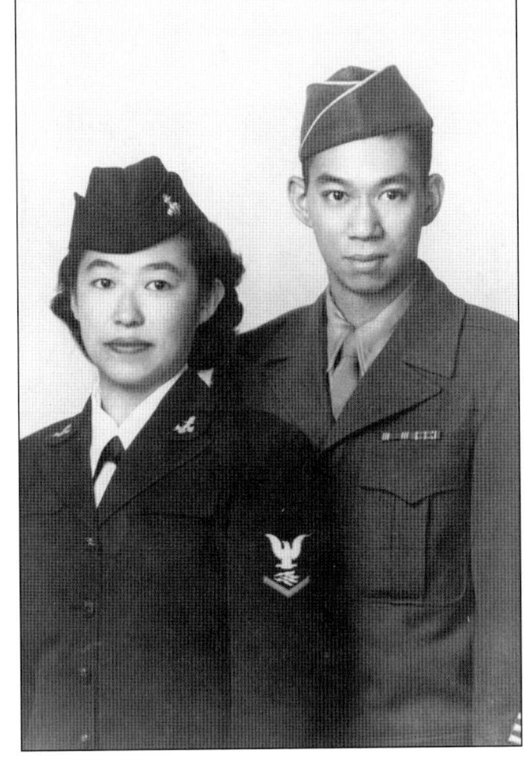

Nymphia Lam-Yok Taliaferro served as a radioman third class in the US Navy during World War II, specifically as the first Pacific Northwest Chinese WAVES (Women Accepted for Volunteer Emergency Service). Her role involved crucial communication duties, supporting naval operations in the Pacific theater. Next to her is Frank Lam, who served in the Army. Their contributions, like those of many others, were vital to the US war effort. (Portland Chinatown Museum.)

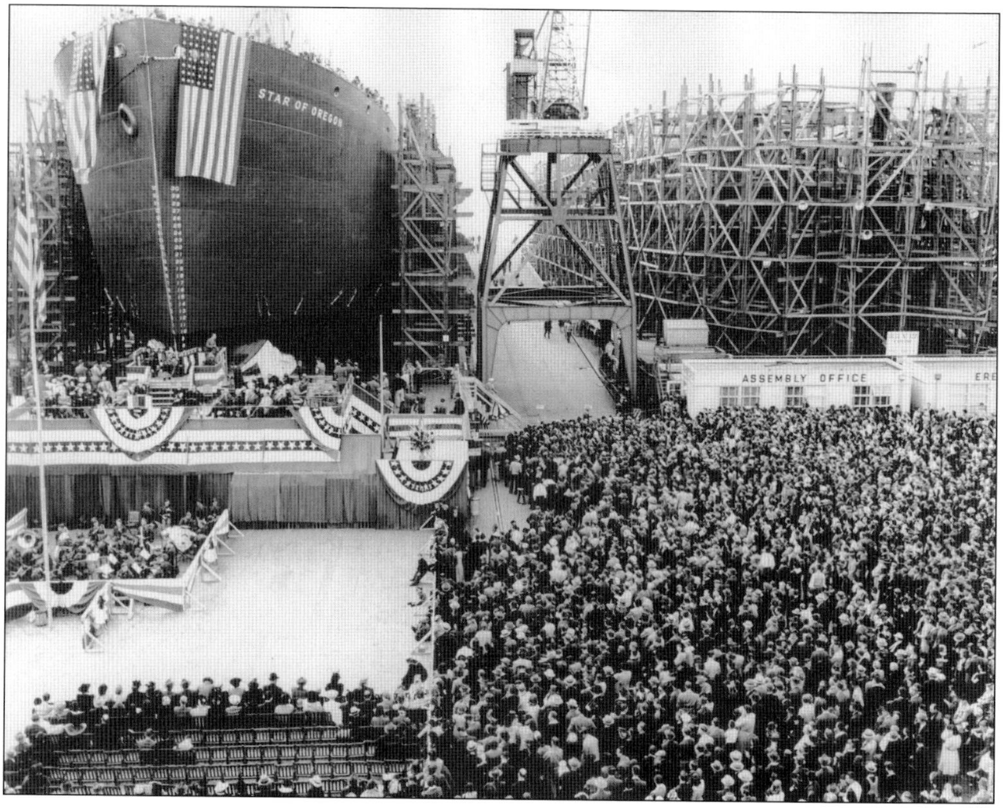

Henry J. Kaiser led the World War II shipbuilding effort with the Oregon Shipbuilding Corporation, Swan Island Shipyard, and the Vancouver Shipyard. Women of all nationalities, including many Chinese women, helped with the war effort. With 97,000 employees in the Pacific Northwest and 90,000 in Richmond, California, Kaiser, along with Dr. Sidney Garfield, created the first prepaid health plan, laying the foundation of what is now Kaiser Permanente. (Photo12/Alamy stock photo.)

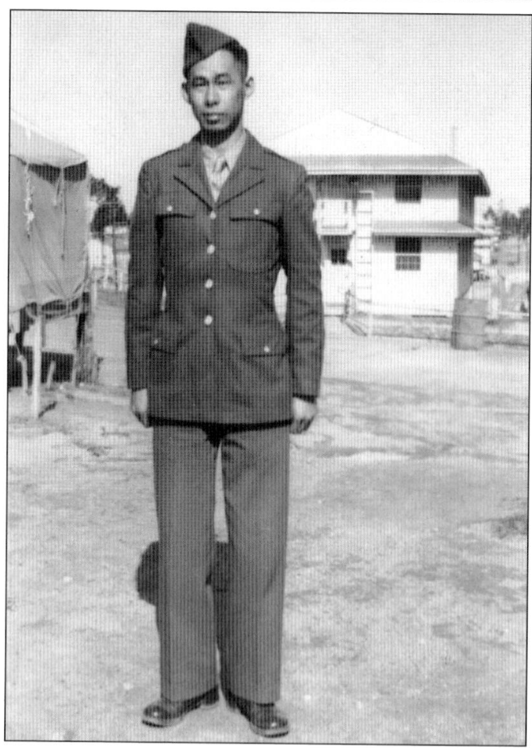

Ed Locke, born in Portland's Chinatown, attended Benson Polytechnic School with Arthur Chin, who became a fighter pilot. Locke went on to serve in the Army during World War II. With the highest IQ in his battalion, Locke was sent to Yale University to study Asian languages but was later deployed to Europe during the war. After serving his country, he worked in his family-owned lottery business in Chinatown. (Norman Locke.)

Brothers Billie and Fred Chin both served in World War II. As part of the Army Air Corps, Billie trained as an airplane and engine mechanic and also trained on Boeing aircraft in Seattle. He was the crew chief in charge of the maintenance of B-17 and C-47 aircraft. After the war, he was offered a job by the son of the founder of Boeing but turned it down, as he felt an obligation to return to Portland to run the family business, the Tea Garden Café. Fred, shown with the rifle, served in the Army and administered vision tests. He became an optometrist after the war, retiring from Columbian Bifocal. Both were honored as Chinese Americans who served in World War II, receiving the Congressional Gold Medal. (Right, Billie Chin family; below, Fred Chin family.)

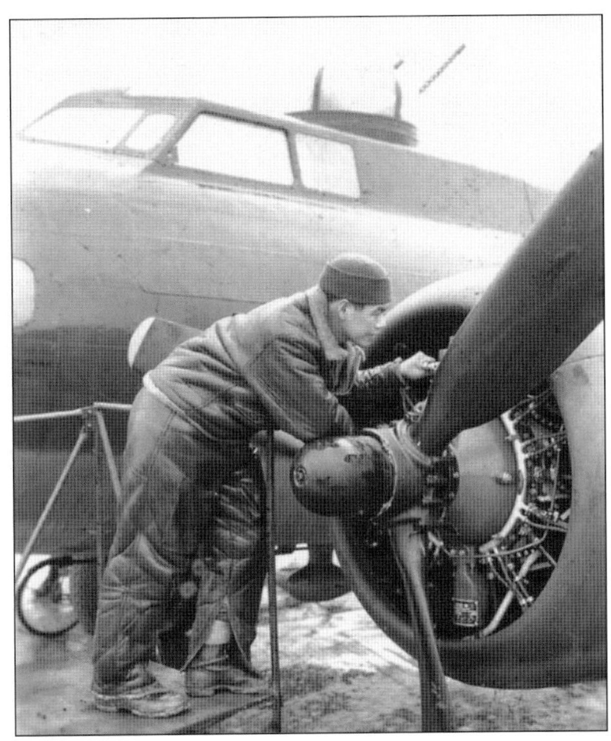

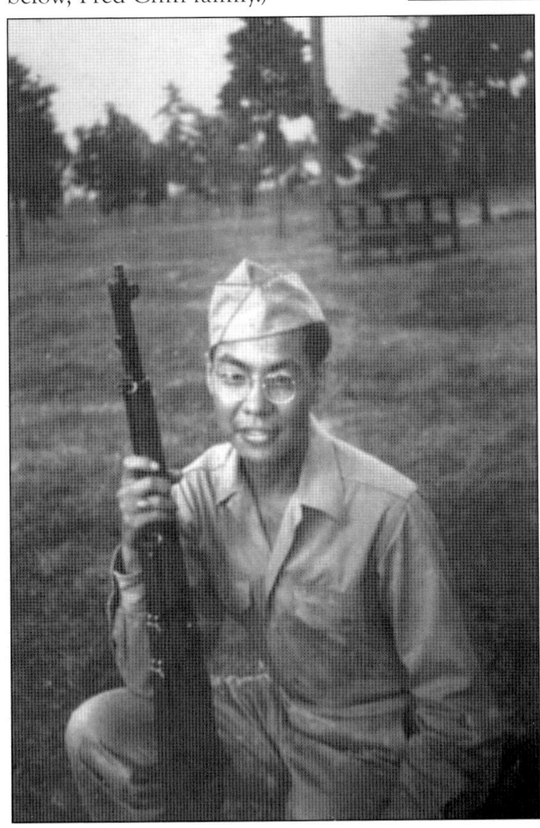

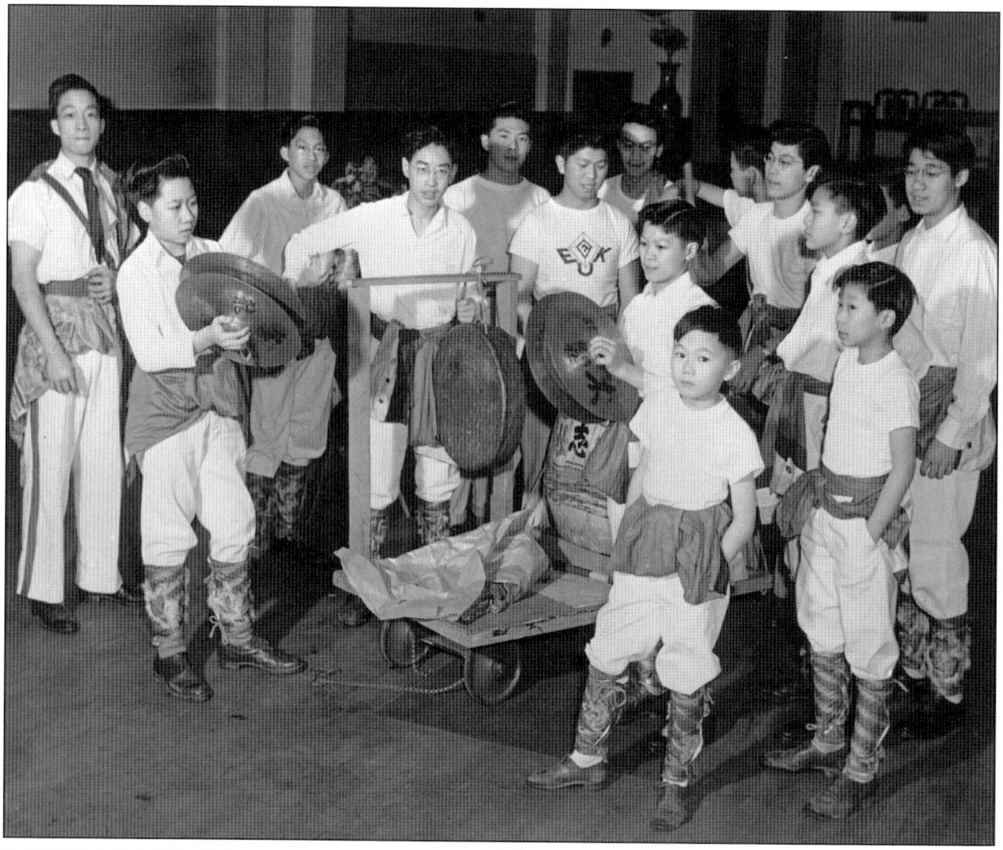

The CCBA Lion Dance Team from 1944 is preparing to perform in a cultural event. From left to right are (first row) Eddie Dong (with cymbals), Lawrence Chan (with gong), Ed Low, Jackie Lee (with cymbals), Fred M. Wong, Richard Chin (head turned), and Benny Lee; (second row) Paul Wong, Frank Wong, Kenny Lum, Bill Fong, unidentified (head turned), Gary Lee, and Lawrence Lee. (Oregon Historical Society, OrHi_79048.)

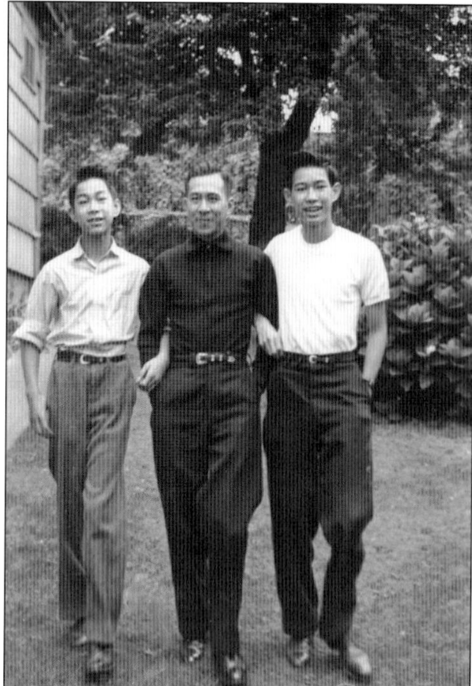

In 1944, Frank Locke's sons, Ron Locke (left) and Norman Locke (right), are pictured during a vacation in Seattle. In 1954, Norman opened Columbia Coin Company in downtown Portland. The family-owned and -operated business moved to Southeast Hawthorne Boulevard in 2006 and continues to specialize in US coins. This successful business is well known in the Portland community and beyond. (Norman Locke.)

Three

Post–World War II Chinatown 1946–1980

Portland's Chinatown underwent profound transformations after World War II, driven by changes in immigration policies and social, economic, and urban development factors. The Magnuson Act of 1943 repealed the Chinese Exclusion Act of 1882, allowing Chinese immigrants to gain citizenship and property rights, though an annual quota of 105 immigrants remained. Property ownership enabled many to move beyond Chinatown into the broader Portland metropolitan area, seeking better housing and opportunities. During this migration, most businesses in Chinatown continued under Chinese management. However, rising property values and urban redevelopment slowly contributed to displacing residents and businesses. Emerging Chinese neighborhoods, such as those in Southeast Portland, provided more affordable housing and new business prospects, shifting the cultural and economic focus away from historic Chinatown. National immigration laws further shaped these dynamics. The Immigration and Nationality Act of 1965 abolished the quota system, prioritizing family reunification and skilled labor, and significantly changed the demographic composition of immigrants, allowing more individuals from Asia, Africa, and Latin America. These legislative changes empowered Chinese Americans, particularly women, to break racial and gender barriers in various occupations. Generational and social changes also influenced this transition. The younger generation of Chinese Americans, born and raised in the United States, often pursued education and careers outside of Chinatown that were barred to previous generations. Examples include Lani Lee Louie, who was Oregon's first Chinese woman stockbroker, and Preston Wong, who was the Portland Police Bureau's first Asian police officer. Postwar Japantown struggled to recover, as many interned Japanese Americans did not return to downtown Portland. Over the decades, all of these factors have led to the shift in Chinatown's population. During that time, efforts continued to preserve the cultural heritage of Chinatown, led by local Chinese leaders, the Chinese Consolidated Benevolent Association, the Chinese American Citizens Alliance, family and tong associations, and other organizations in the community.

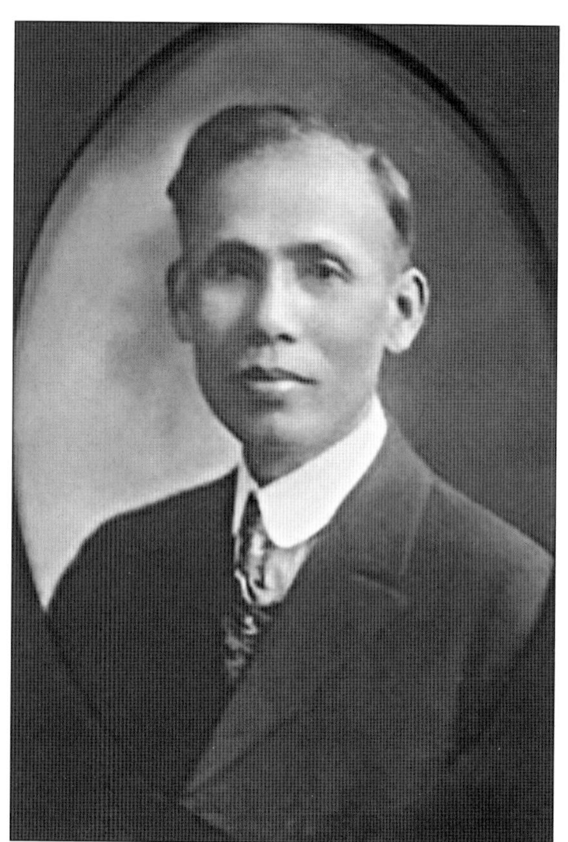

Mo Chung Way, also known as Mo Lee Tong, was a prominent businessman in the community. A CCBA board member and a founder of its new building at 315 Northwest Davis Street, he played a crucial role in Chinatown's development. As manager of John Wo and Company at 84 Second Street, he oversaw Chinese merchandise, wholesale and retail operations, and labor contracting, strengthening local commerce. (CCBA Museum.)

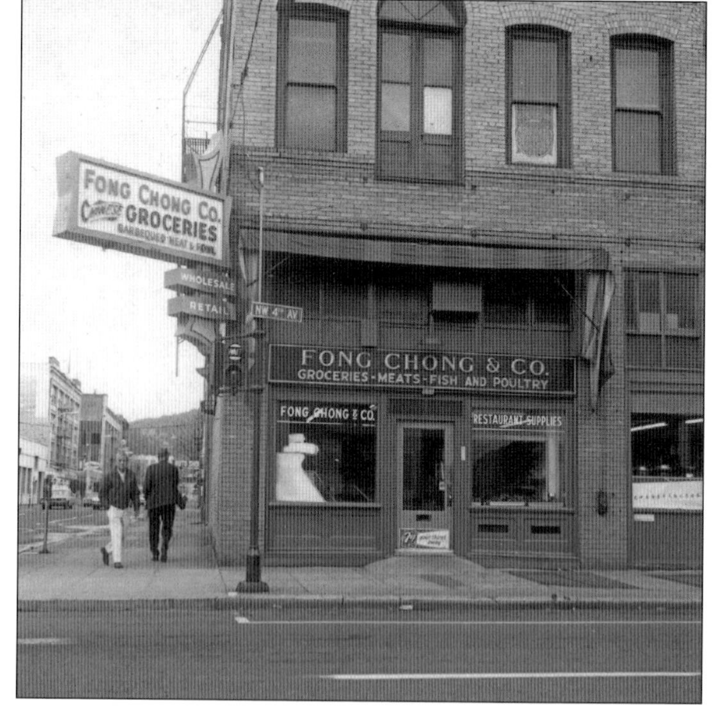

The three-story building on Fourth Avenue, between Everett and Flanders Streets, was built in 1905. Seid Gain owned the property from 1927 to 1934, defying restrictive property laws. In 1932, the Fong Chong grocery and restaurant opened at 301 Fourth Avenue. Over the years, it was operated in partnership by Bob Louie, Gregory Louie, Henry Louie, and Steven Louie. A fire in 1979 reduced the structure to one story. (Gholston Collection.)

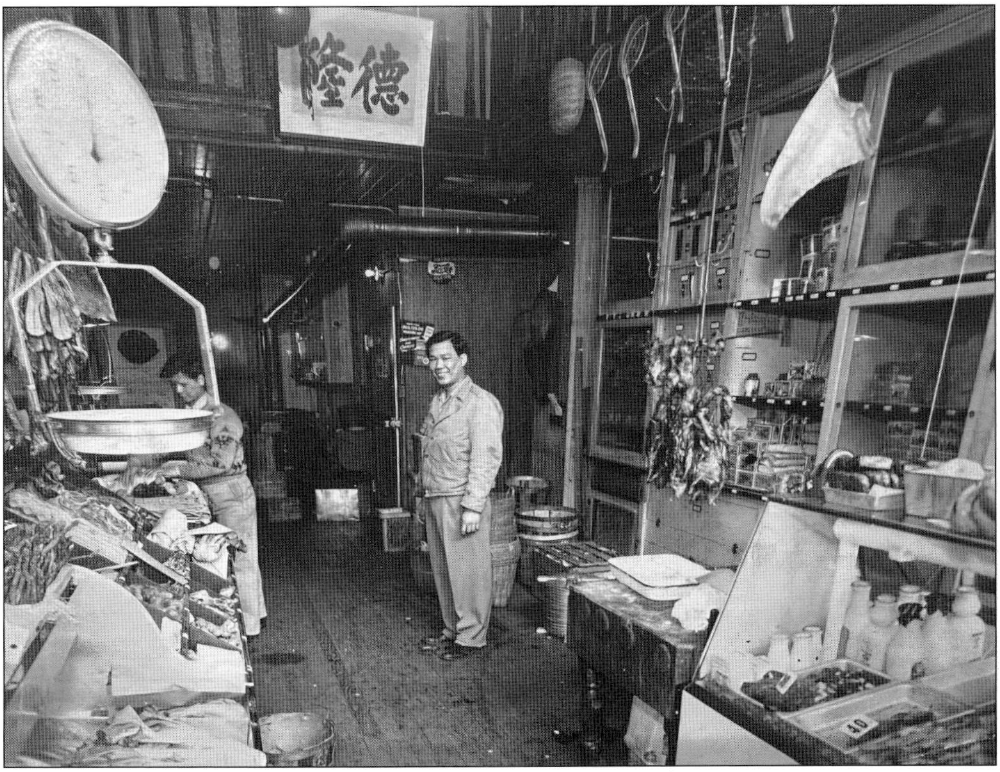

Wong Soon Yook arrived in Portland in 1920 as a merchant and became the owner of Tuck Lung by 1930. His sons, William and Francis, attended Atkinson Grade School and helped deliver groceries for the store. During World War II, Francis served in Europe. After the war, William opened a restaurant in North Dakota, while Francis (shown in the image) returned to help run Tuck Lung. (Francis Gang Wong family.)

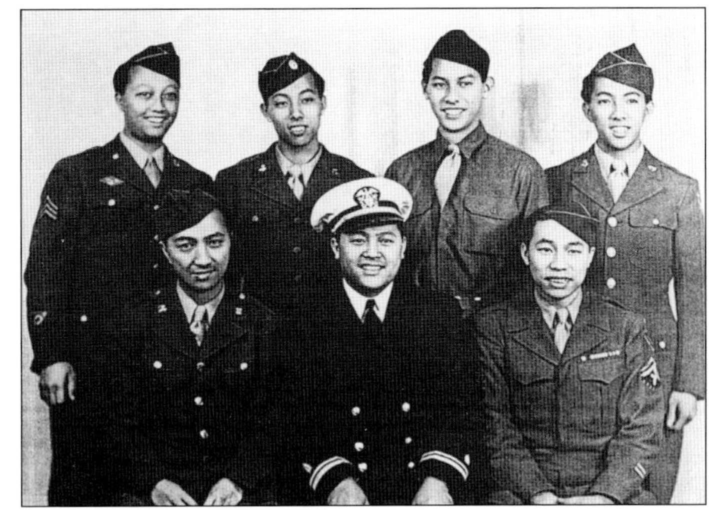

After World War II, many continued serving in the military. In 1946, the seven Lee brothers were granted emergency furloughs to be at their ailing mother's bedside. From left to right are (first row) Pvt. Jensen Lee, Lt. (j.g.) Sam Lee, and Cpl. William Lee; (second row) Sgt. George Lee, Cpl. Howard Lee, Pfc. Harry Lee, and Pvt. Fred Lee. This image was published in the *Oregonian* on January 27, 1946. (The *Oregonian*.)

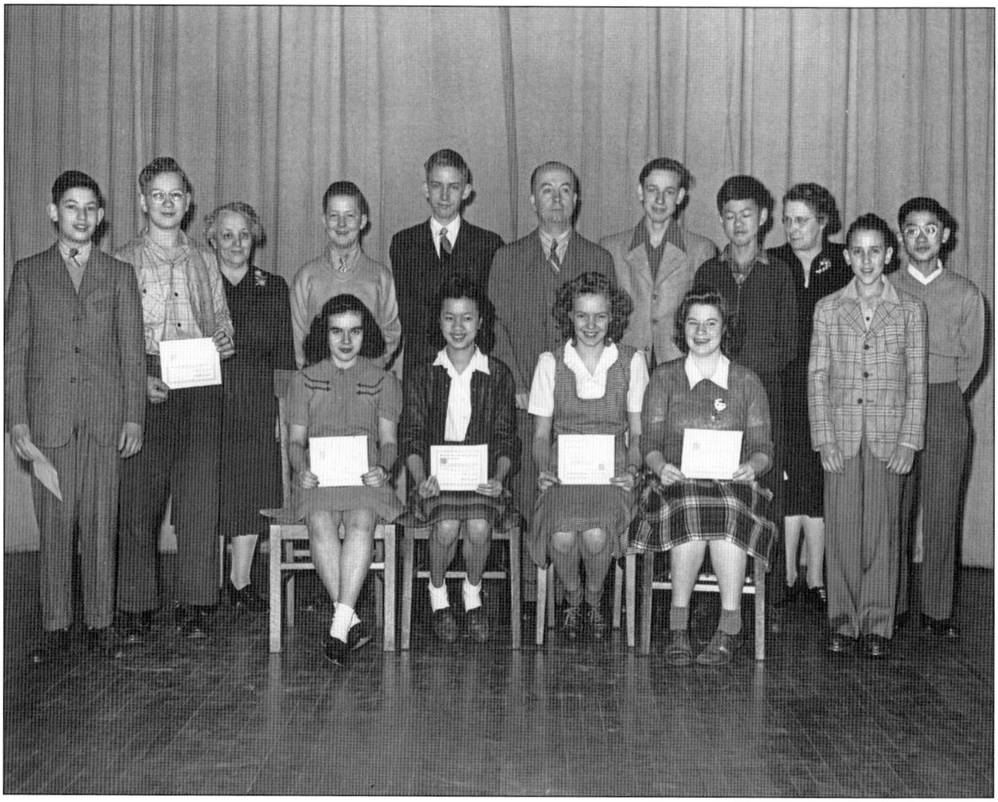

Many children from Portland's Chinatown, alongside other local students, attended Couch Elementary School, which was located at 2033 Northwest Glisan Street. It provided a diverse environment where students from various backgrounds could learn together. Despite facing societal challenges such as racial segregation and discrimination, the school helped shape a more inclusive experience for minority students. (Portland Chinatown Museum.)

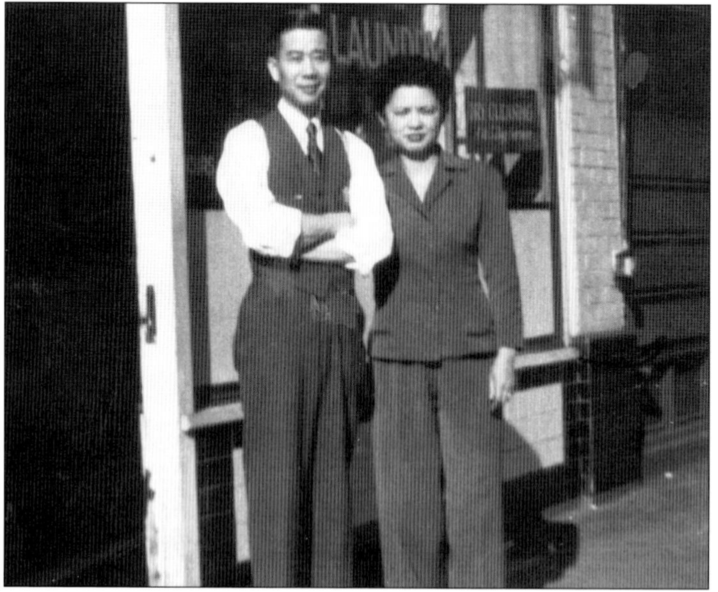

In 1942, Norman and Mabel Wong established New China Laundry and Dry Cleaners on Northwest Couch Street. For decades, they provided trusted service, earning a strong reputation within the community. In 1979, they expanded and relocated to Northeast Portland, continuing their commitment to quality care and reliability, ensuring their business remained a vital resource for their customers. (Gordon Wong Collection.)

Established in 1922, Republic Café, at 222 Northwest Fourth Avenue, remains a Chinatown cultural landmark, attracting a diverse clientele. The restaurant offers classic Chinese American cuisine like chow mein, chop suey, and egg foo young, alongside an extensive menu. On Sundays, it became a favorite among the Jewish community, and it has long been a Mother's Day tradition. The restaurant has also hosted celebrities such as Louis Armstrong, Shaquille O'Neal, and Harry Belafonte, along with city officials. The Ming Lounge, one of Portland's oldest bars, still draws a late-night crowd. With its historic neon sign and nostalgic ambiance, Republic Café continues to preserve the rich heritage of Portland's Chinatown. (Both, Gholston Collection.)

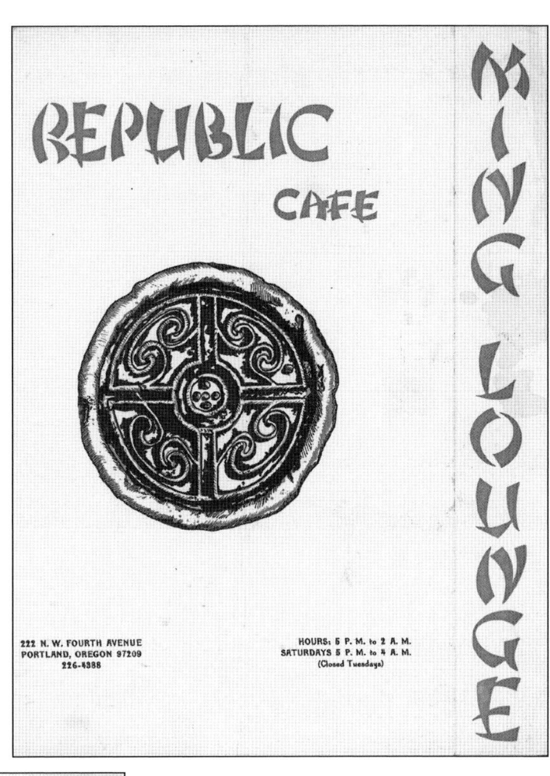

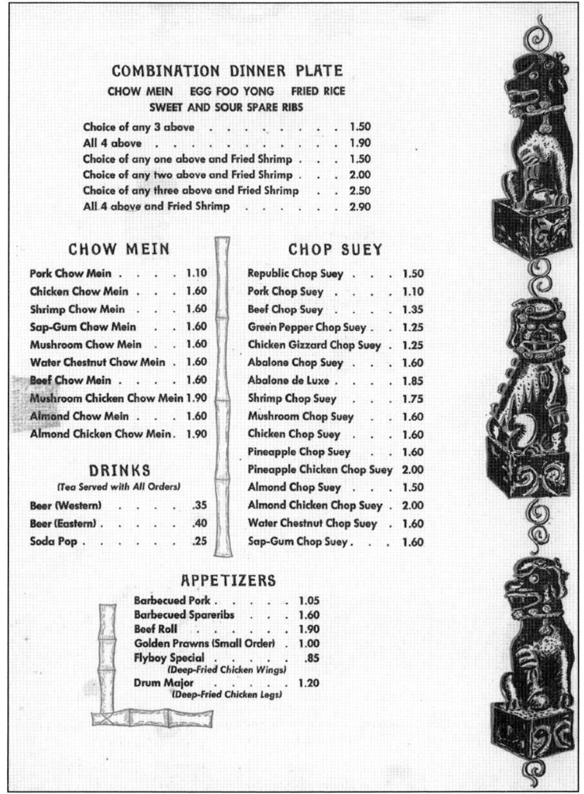

COMBINATION DINNER PLATE

CHOW MEIN EGG FOO YONG FRIED RICE
SWEET AND SOUR SPARE RIBS

Choice of any 3 above	1.50
All 4 above	1.90
Choice of any one above and Fried Shrimp	1.50
Choice of any two above and Fried Shrimp	2.00
Choice of any three above and Fried Shrimp	2.50
All 4 above and Fried Shrimp	2.90

CHOW MEIN

Pork Chow Mein	1.10
Chicken Chow Mein	1.60
Shrimp Chow Mein	1.60
Sap-Gum Chow Mein	1.60
Mushroom Chow Mein	1.60
Water Chestnut Chow Mein	1.60
Beef Chow Mein	1.60
Mushroom Chicken Chow Mein	1.90
Almond Chow Mein	1.60
Almond Chicken Chow Mein	1.90

DRINKS

(Tea Served with All Orders)

Beer (Western)	.35
Beer (Eastern)	.40
Soda Pop	.25

CHOP SUEY

Republic Chop Suey	1.50
Pork Chop Suey	1.10
Beef Chop Suey	1.35
Green Pepper Chop Suey	1.25
Chicken Gizzard Chop Suey	1.25
Abalone Chop Suey	1.60
Abalone de Luxe	1.85
Shrimp Chop Suey	1.75
Mushroom Chop Suey	1.60
Chicken Chop Suey	1.60
Pineapple Chop Suey	1.60
Pineapple Chicken Chop Suey	2.00
Almond Chop Suey	1.50
Almond Chicken Chop Suey	2.00
Water Chestnut Chop Suey	1.60
Sap-Gum Chop Suey	1.60

APPETIZERS

Barbecued Pork	1.05
Barbecued Spareribs	1.60
Beef Roll	1.90
Golden Prawns (Small Order)	1.00
Flyboy Special *(Deep-Fried Chicken Wings)*	.85
Drum Major *(Deep-Fried Chicken Legs)*	1.20

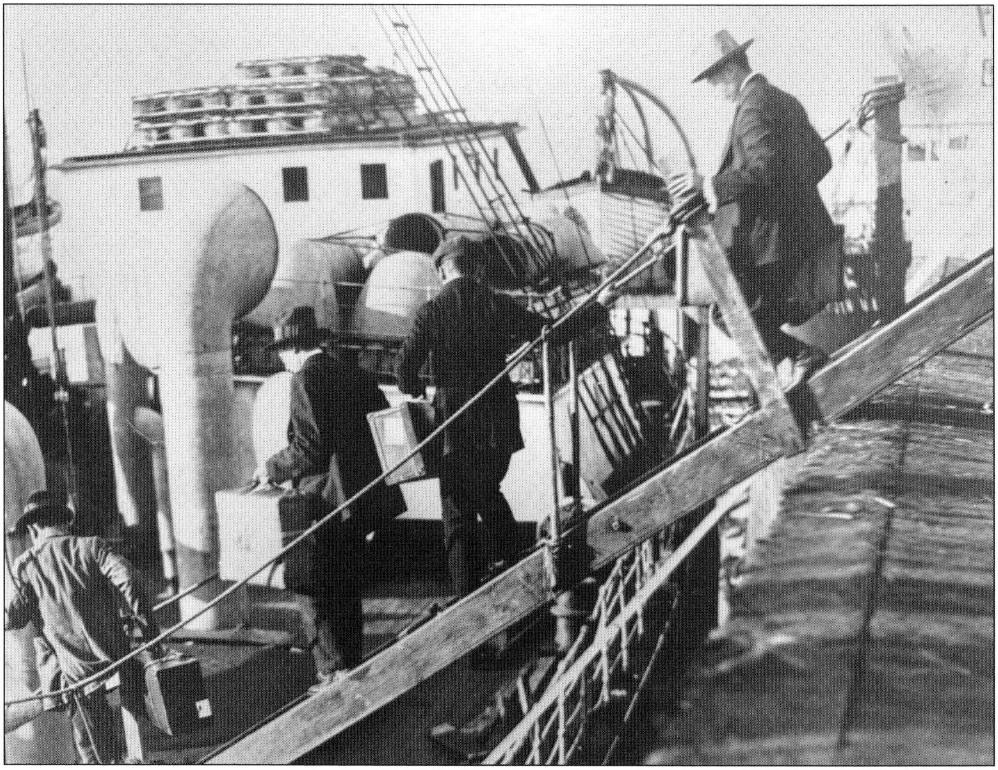

Even after the Chinese Exclusion Act was repealed in 1943, a cap of 105 Chinese immigrants per year remained. The 1965 Immigration and Nationality Act abolished the National Origins Formula, allowing for more equitable immigration policies. This 1946 photograph shows individuals who were denied entry, reflecting the restrictive immigration policies still in place at that time. (CCBA Museum.)

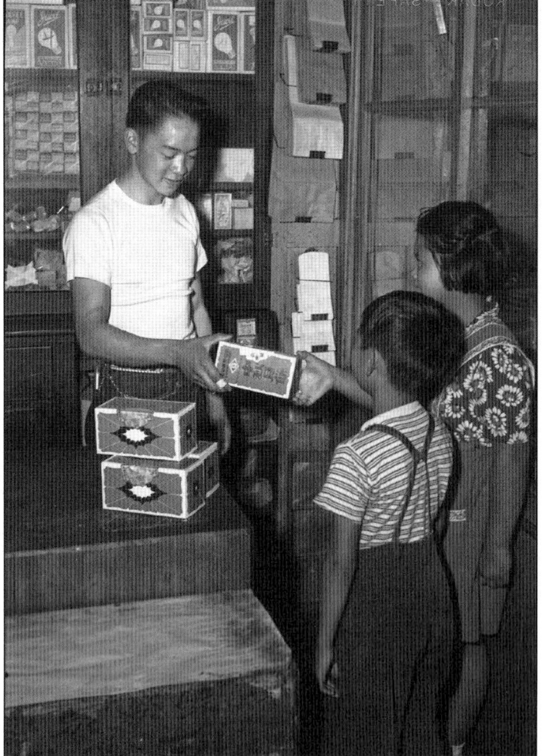

Fong Chong grocery and restaurant was known for its traditional Cantonese cuisine and dim sum. The grocery store stocked a wide array of traditional Chinese foods for the community. In this 1945 photograph, Willy Fong (left) is seen handing moon cakes to Michael Gong (middle) and Kathleen Law (right). Moon cakes, available during the Mid-Autumn Festival, symbolize the harvest season and family unity. This image appeared in the *Oregonian* on September 16, 1945. (The *Oregonian*.)

Ruth Fong, a student at Commerce High School, made history in 1946 as the first nonwhite Rose Festival Princess. This significant milestone marked a step toward greater inclusivity and diversity in the history of the Rose Festival. Fong is shown shaking hands with Bill Berry, the president of the Urban League, symbolizing the recognition of her achievement and the progress toward diversity. (Oregon Historical Society, 0313P316.)

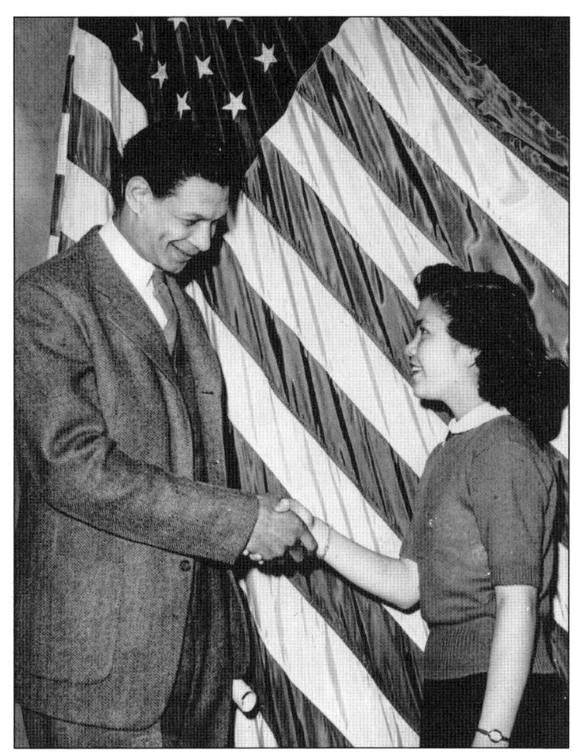

Following World War II, Caryle and Helen Lee established Cottage Weavers, a business specializing in invisible reweaving. Before the war, they operated a grocery store in Portland's Chinatown, near what is now Keller Auditorium. This photograph from 1946 captures them inside their Northeast Hassalo Street storefront, marking a new chapter in their entrepreneurial journey. (Gordon Wong Collection.)

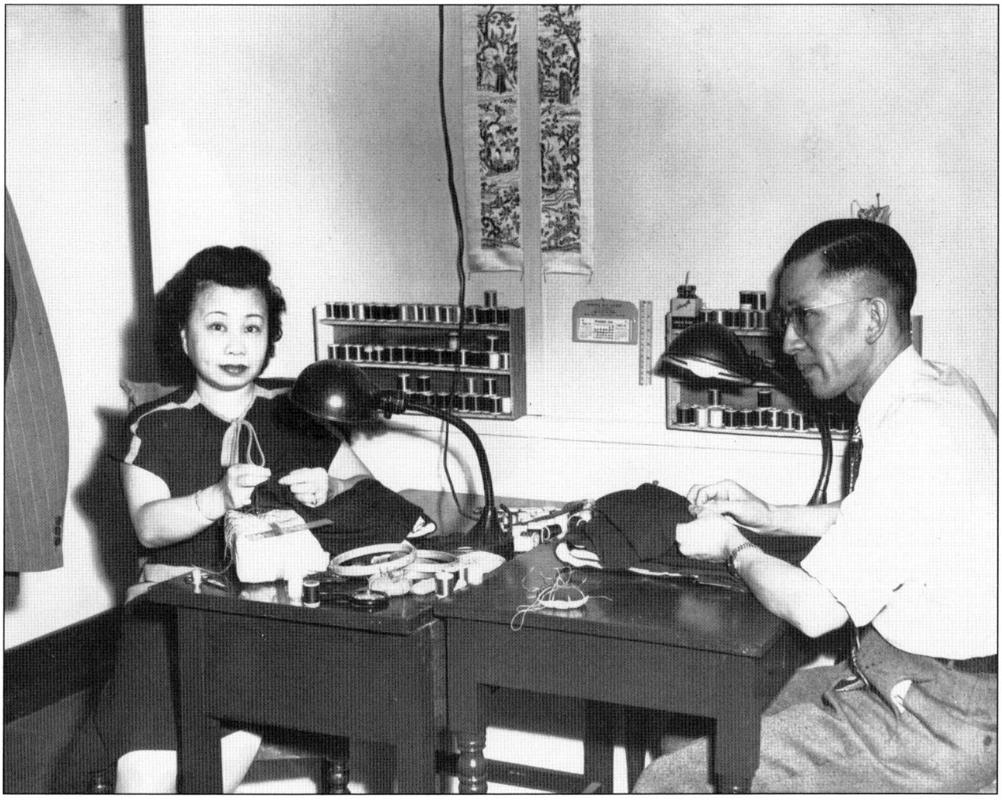

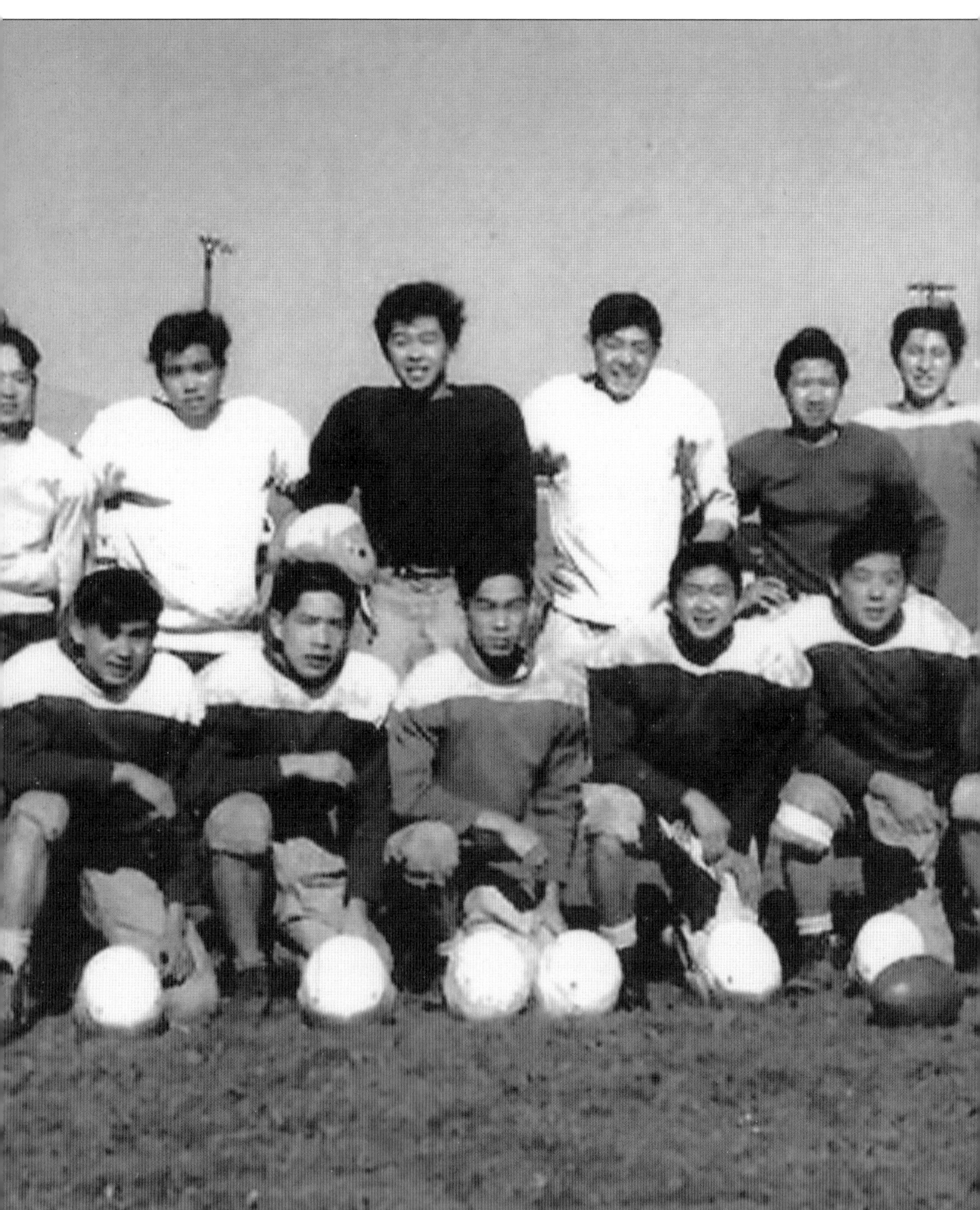

From 1946 to 1948, Chinese football teams from Portland and Seattle Chinatowns were formed, consisting of high school and college-aged players. Pre-game social events fostered friendships between the cities. Coach Herman DeVault owned DeVault's Wishing Well Lounge in Portland, which eventually became a Chinese restaurant in the 1960s. Portland teammates included, from left to right, (first row) Gordon Wong, Eugene Chin, Ronald Locke, Harlan Luck, Kenneth Lum,

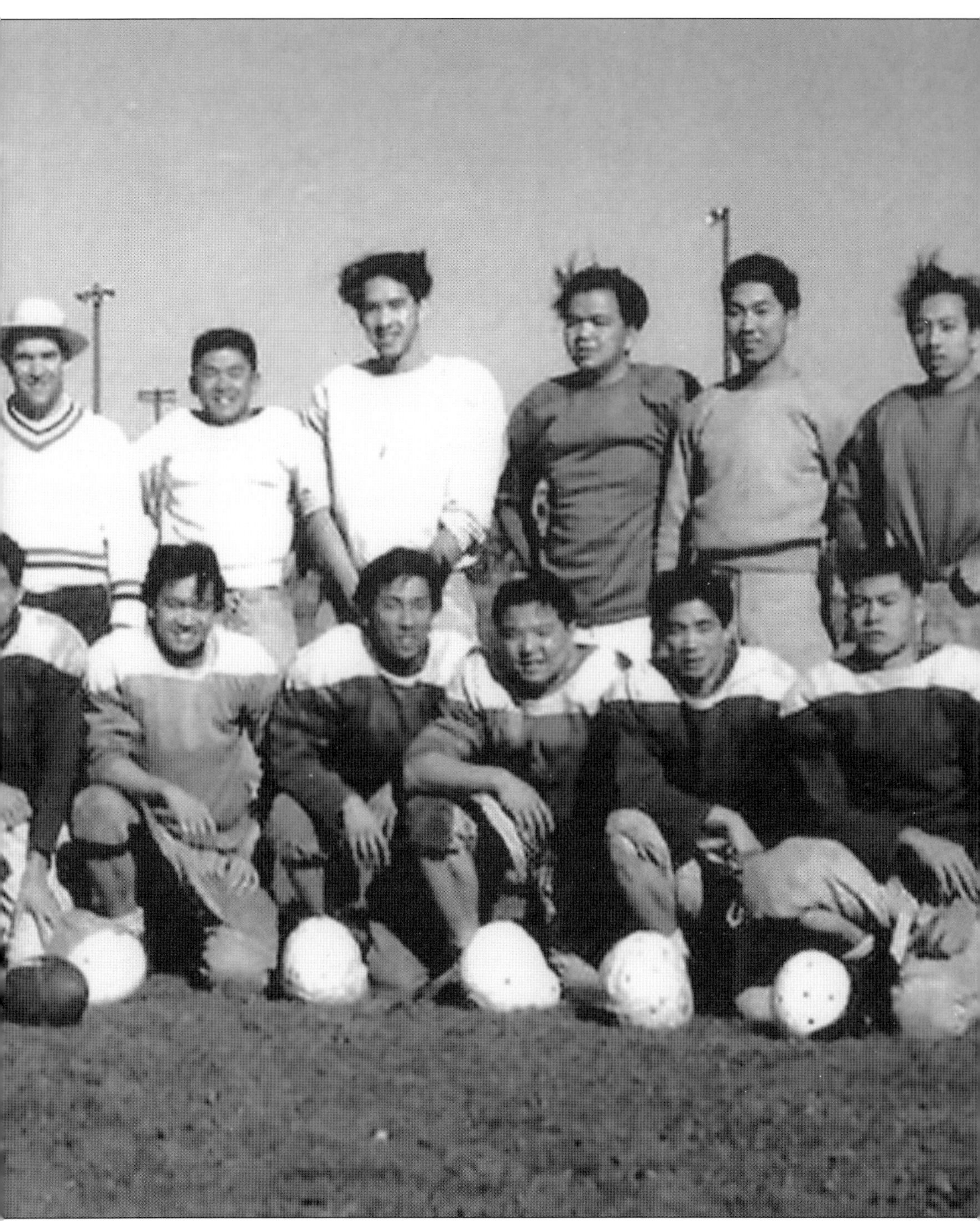

Robert Luck, William Fong, Fred Lee, Tot Earl Lee, Sidney Leo, and Clifford Wong; (second row) Willie Wong, Herert Leo, Edwin Chen, Bruce Wong, Edward Dong, Richard Low, coach Herman DeVault, Phillip Wing, Gay Chin, Ralph Moe, Richard Moy, and Howard Lee. (Gordon Wong Collection.)

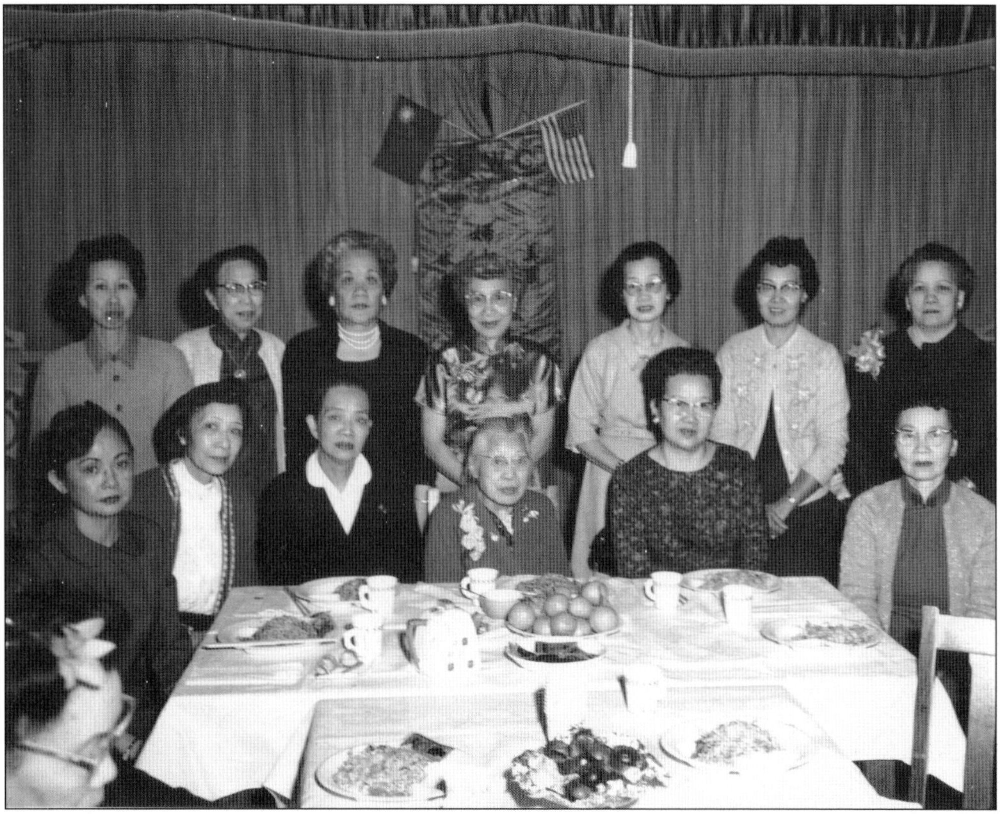

The Chinese Consolidated Benevolent Association initially addressed the needs of early bachelor immigrants. Around the 1930s, the Chinese Women's Club was established, focusing on community welfare and the preservation of cultural traditions. Mabel Wong, facing the camera, is sitting on the far left during this gathering. (Carey Wong.)

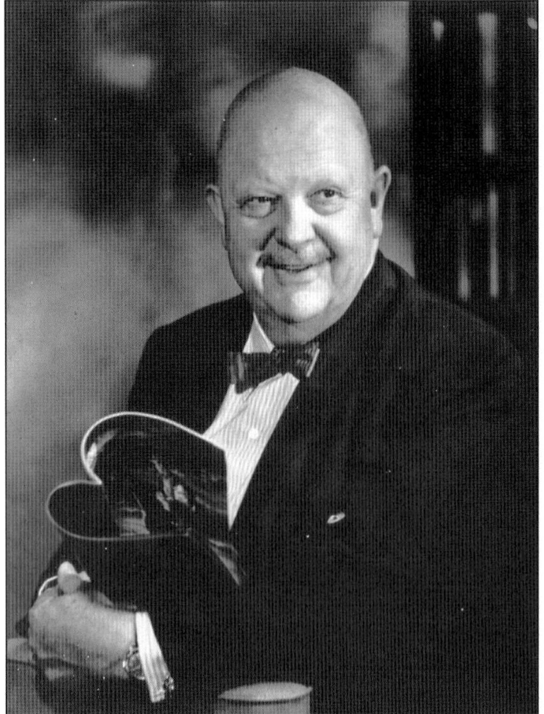

The mother of renowned American chef James Beard, Elizabeth Beard, hired Jue-Let as the family cook. Growing up in Portland, Beard grew fond of the Jue-Let's dishes, including oyster vol-au-vent, braised lamb curry, and terrapin stew. One of Beard's earliest memories was being bedridden with malaria and only craving Jue-Let's chicken jelly. Beard frequently expressed his admiration for Jue-Let, acknowledging his influence in shaping his culinary philosophy. (Everett Collection Historical/Alamy Stock Photo.)

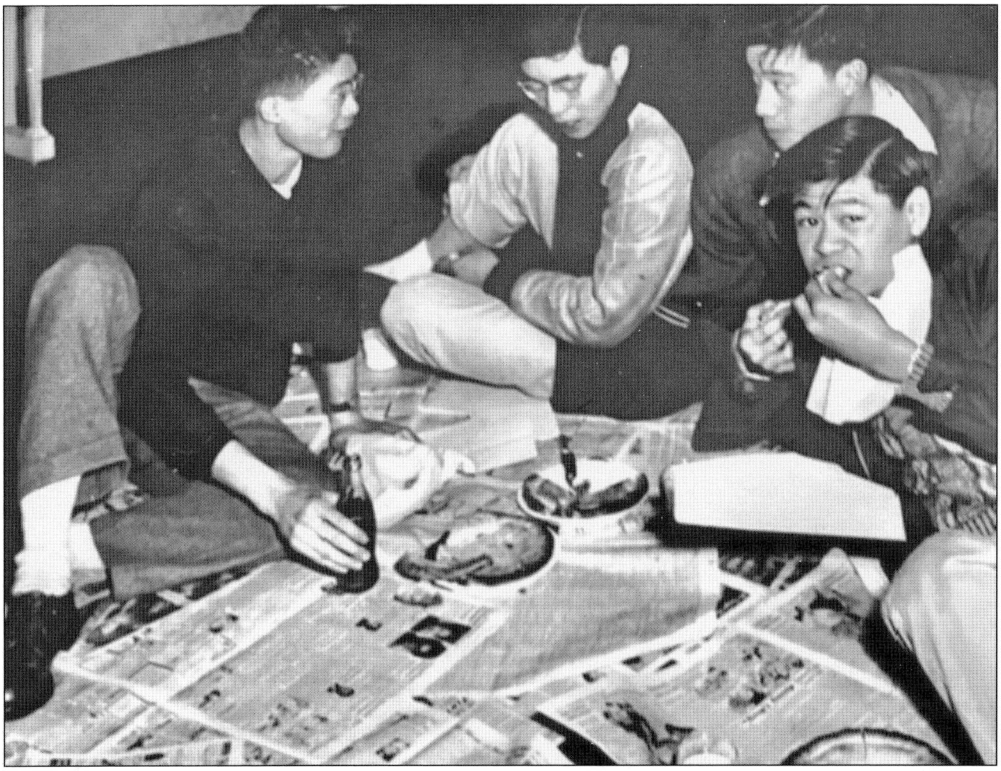

Portland Chinese football teammates Robert Luck (far left) and Clifford Wong (far right) are shown sharing a pizza after a game, along with two football players from Seattle's Chinatown team. These social activities played a key role in fostering camaraderie and friendship between Portland and Seattle's Chinese communities. This sense of unity and shared experiences helped form new friendships between the two cities. (Robert Luck.)

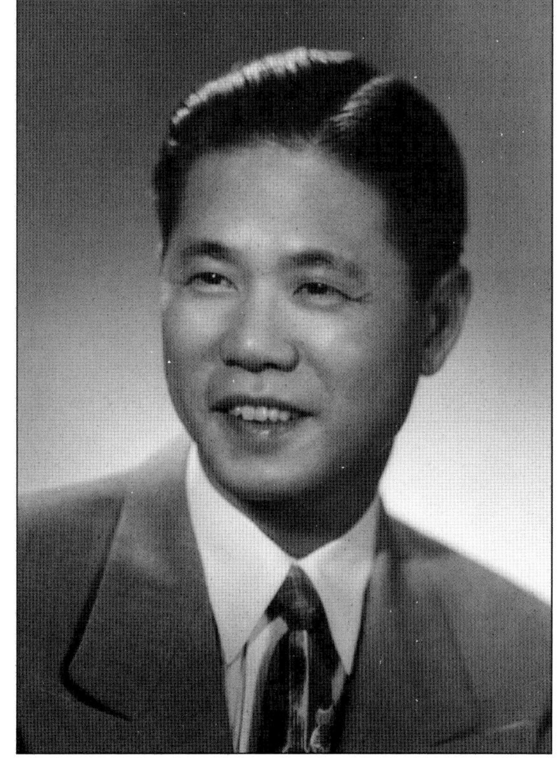

Leland Chin founded Pagoda Restaurant and later Chin's Kitchen in Portland's Hollywood neighborhood. Starting in the 1940s, Chin's white vans were the first in Portland to offer Chinese food delivery service. He expanded his business to include Chin's Import Export, which still supplies Asian food products and restaurant supplies and remains family-owned. (Oregon Historical Society, 002P194.)

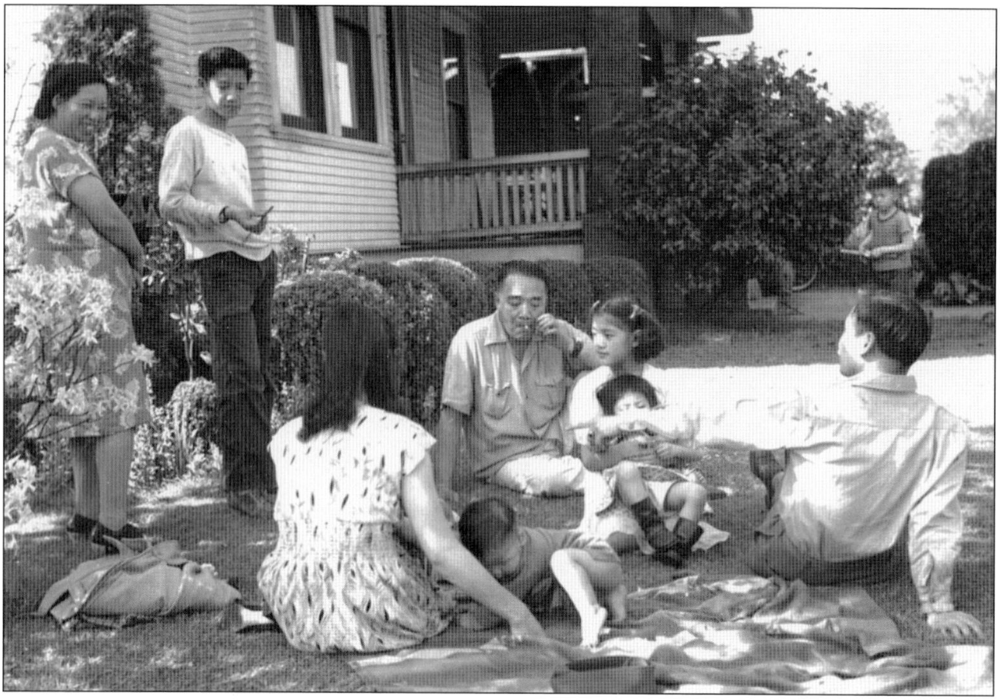

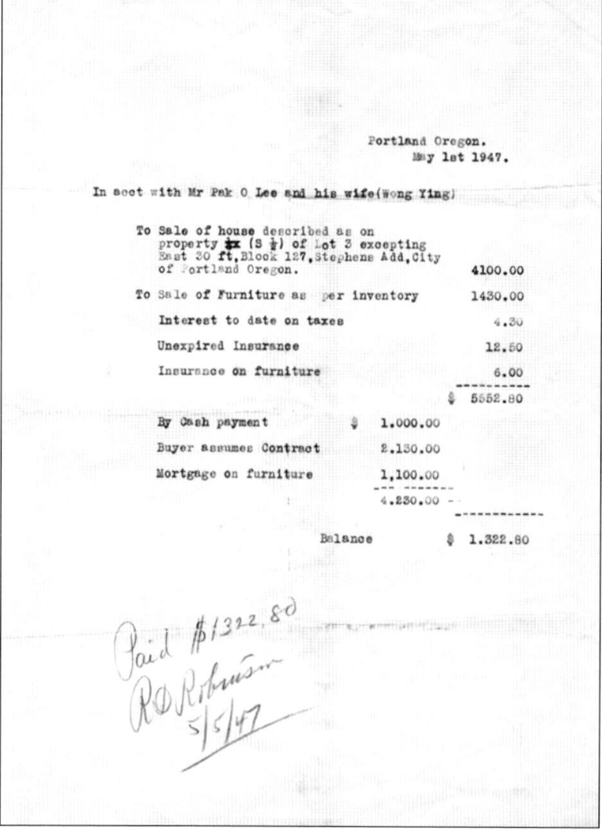

Portland Oregon.
May 1st 1947.

In acct with Mr Pak O Lee and his wife(Wong Ying)

To Sale of house described as on property ~~xx~~ (S ½) of Lot 3 excepting East 30 ft, Block 127, Stephens Add, City of Portland Oregon.		4100.00
To Sale of Furniture as per inventory		1430.00
Interest to date on taxes		4.30
Unexpired Insurance		12.50
Insurance on furniture		6.00
		$ 5552.80
By Cash payment	$ 1.000.00	
Buyer assumes Contract	2.130.00	
Mortgage on furniture	1,100.00	
	4.230.00	
Balance		$ 1.322.80

Paid $1322.80
R D Robinson
5/5/47

Before World War II, Ladd's Addition was one neighborhood where Chinese and other Asian families could buy homes. Due to racial discrimination, buyers often had to use Caucasian intermediaries to purchase properties, later transferring the title. In 1947, Pak On Lee bought a two-story, three-bedroom, one-bath home for $5,552.80. This house represented a pathway to the American Dream for the Lee family. This photograph above captures a moment while visiting the Sue family, who also lived in Ladd's Addition. From left to right are Bessie Sue, Frank Sue, Sun Ying Lee with Keith Lee (baby), Ah Soon Sue, Bonnie Sue with Ruth Sue (child), Pak On Lee, and Kenny Fong (standing). (Both, Keith Lee.)

Chungking Café, located by Union Station at Northwest Sixth Avenue and Glisan Street, was opened in the mid-1940s by four cousins. Later, it was sold to Wing K. Wong, known as "Giggles." He is shown on the right with his son Sun Wong. Situated on the ground floor of the Ranier Hotel, the restaurant catered to travelers from both the hotel and the train station, serving classic American Chinese cuisine. (Fred B. Wong.)

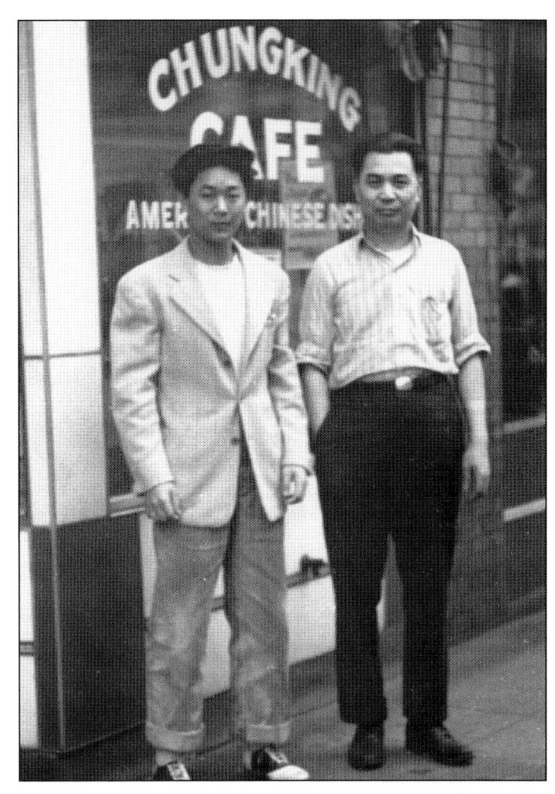

Chinese immigrants and American-born Chinese have long served in the US military, beginning with the Civil War in 1862. Unlike other enlisted minorities, the Chinese served in integrated units. Shown in the photograph is Bob Luck (center) along with two comrades in the US Air Force. They were in San Francisco in 1951 on their way up to Alaska during the Korean War. (Bob Luck.)

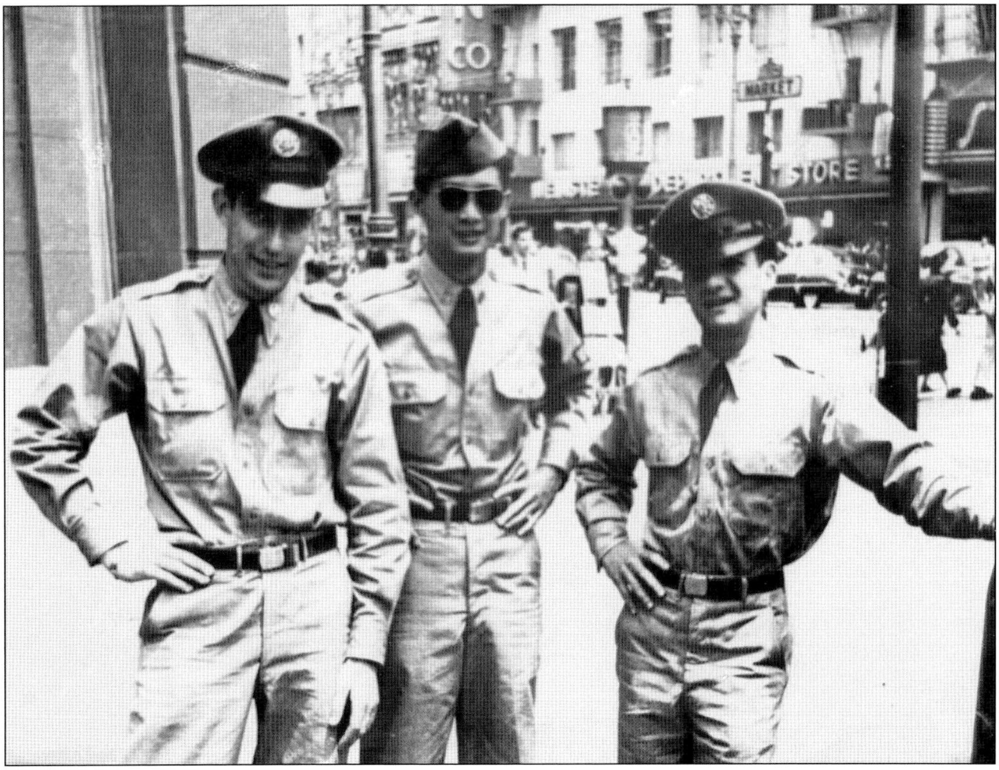

NON-NEGOTIABLE RECEIPT

PORTLAND TRUST AND SAVINGS BANK

PORTLAND, OREGON

DATE FEB 6TH 1951

RECEIVED FROM PAK Q LEE

2L28 SE 11TH AVENUE PORTLAND ORE

THREE HUNDRED FIFTY ONE & 50/100 U.S. DOLLARS $ 351.50

FOR TRANSFER OF

THREE HUNDRED FIFTY & 00/100* * * * (AMOUNT IN WORDS) 350.00 U S (AMOUNT IN FIGURES)

BY [ ] MAIL [X] AIR MAIL [ ] CABLE

TO HOO JUNG WONG C/O ON HING CHONG

NAME AND ADDRESS OF BENEFICIARY TO BE TYPED OR PRINTED

273 DES VOEUX RD C HONGKONG

FOREIGN MONEY TRANSFER No. 192171

THIS TRANSACTION SUBJECT TO CONDITIONS ON REVERSE SIDE

BY ______ AUTHORIZED SIGNATURE

RATE	DOLLAR EQUIVALENT	HANDLING CHARGE	AIR MAIL CHARGES	CABLE CHARGES	TOTAL
	350.00	1.50			351.50

F. X. 1818

Overseas Chinese sent remittances to support their families in China, which helped build homes, start businesses, and provide education and healthcare. Contributions also helped with local community development projects like schools, roads, and hospitals. Remittances played a crucial role in stability and progress, improving the quality of life and fostering community development and economic stability in many areas in China. (Keith Lee.)

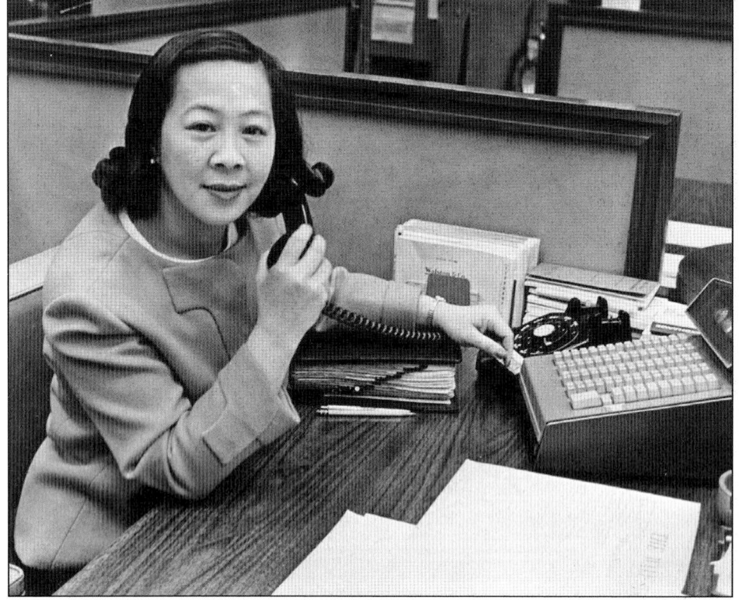

Lani Lee Louie made history in 1956 as the first Oregon woman to register as a broker with the New York Stock Exchange. She broke barriers at a time as a woman and an ethnic minority in a white, male-dominated field. In addition, in 1962, she and her husband, Bob Louie, opened Lani Louie's restaurant in Milwaukie, where she also worked in the evenings. (Oregon Historical Society, CN_021743.)

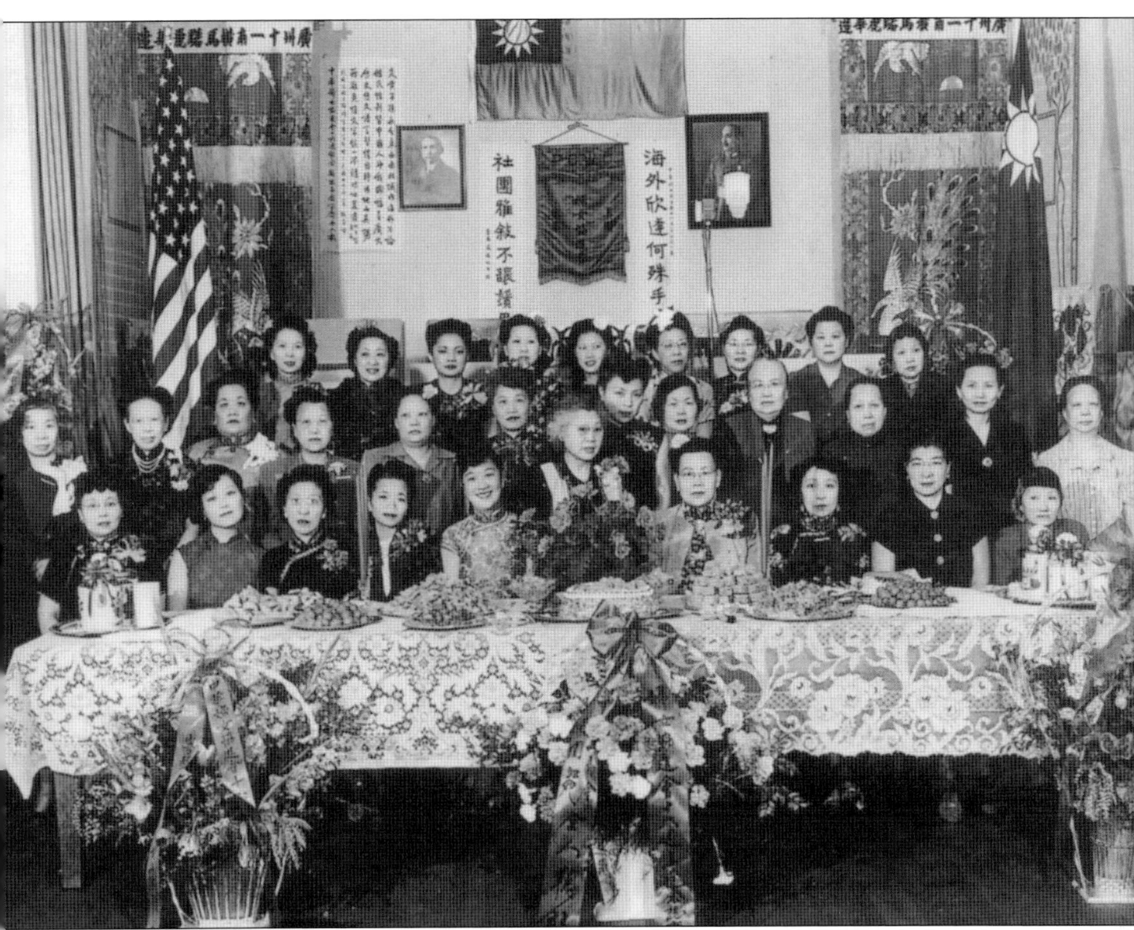

In the 1940s, the CCBA's Chinese Women's Club marked its anniversary, celebrating 16 years of dedicated activism and leadership within the local Chinese community. The event honored the organization's ongoing contributions to social welfare, cultural preservation, and civic engagement, reflecting its role in empowering Chinese women and strengthening community ties in Portland's Chinatown. Those identified at the event include, from left to right, (first row) Low Moy Fong (first), Mrs. Lee Fong (second), Rose Loy (third), Lillian Chin (eighth), and Violet Chinn Wong (ninth); (second row) Ching Wan (first), Mrs. Ngan Locke (second), cofounder Ho Sui Jower (seventh), cofounder Mrs. Winge Lee (eighth), and Wong See Lee (twelfth); (third row) Mabel Wong (third). (George W. and Mary N. Leong family.)

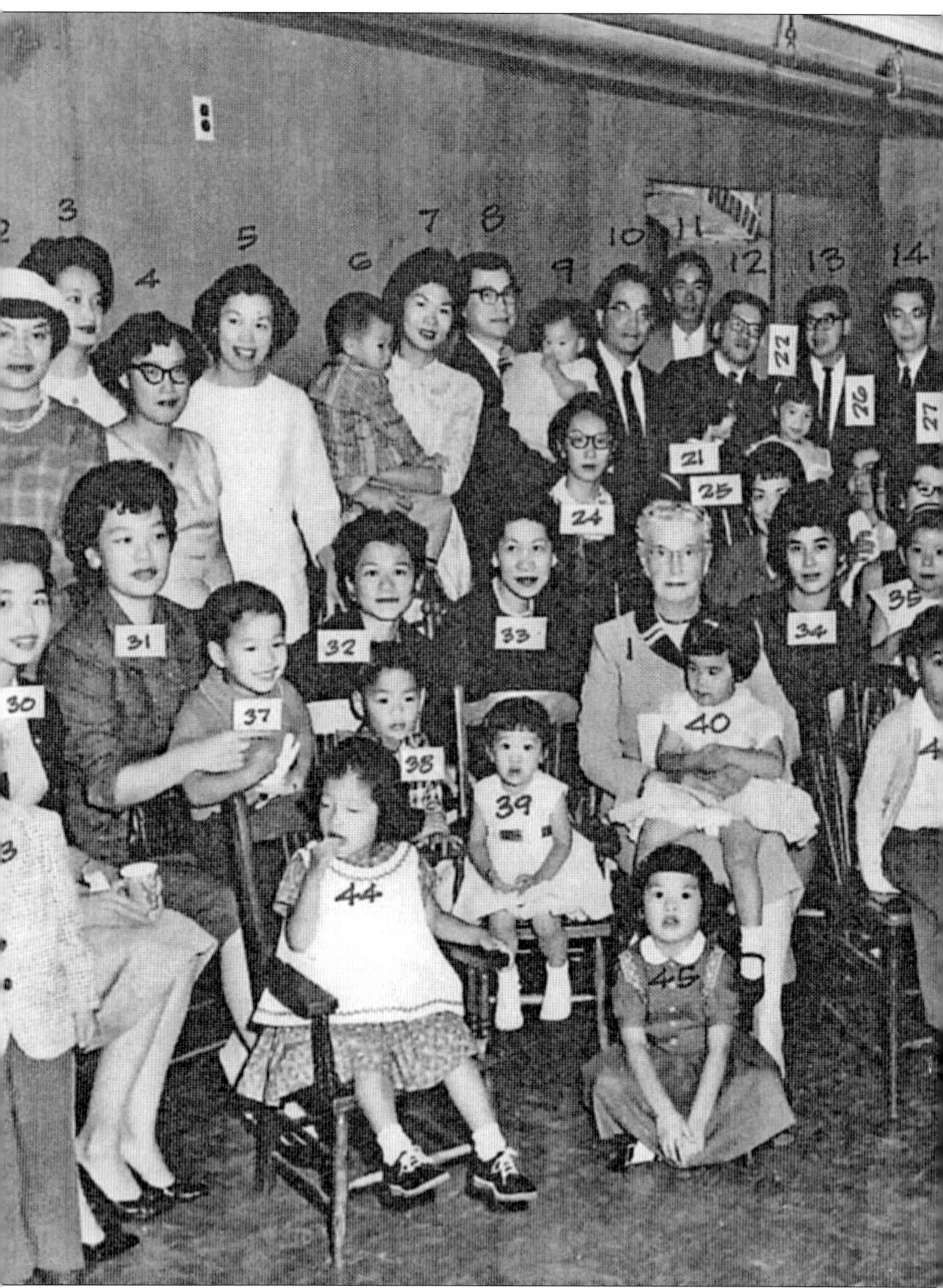
2 3 4 5 6 7 8 9 10 11 12 13 14
22 26 27
21 25 24
31 32 33 1 34 35
30 37 38 39 40
44 45

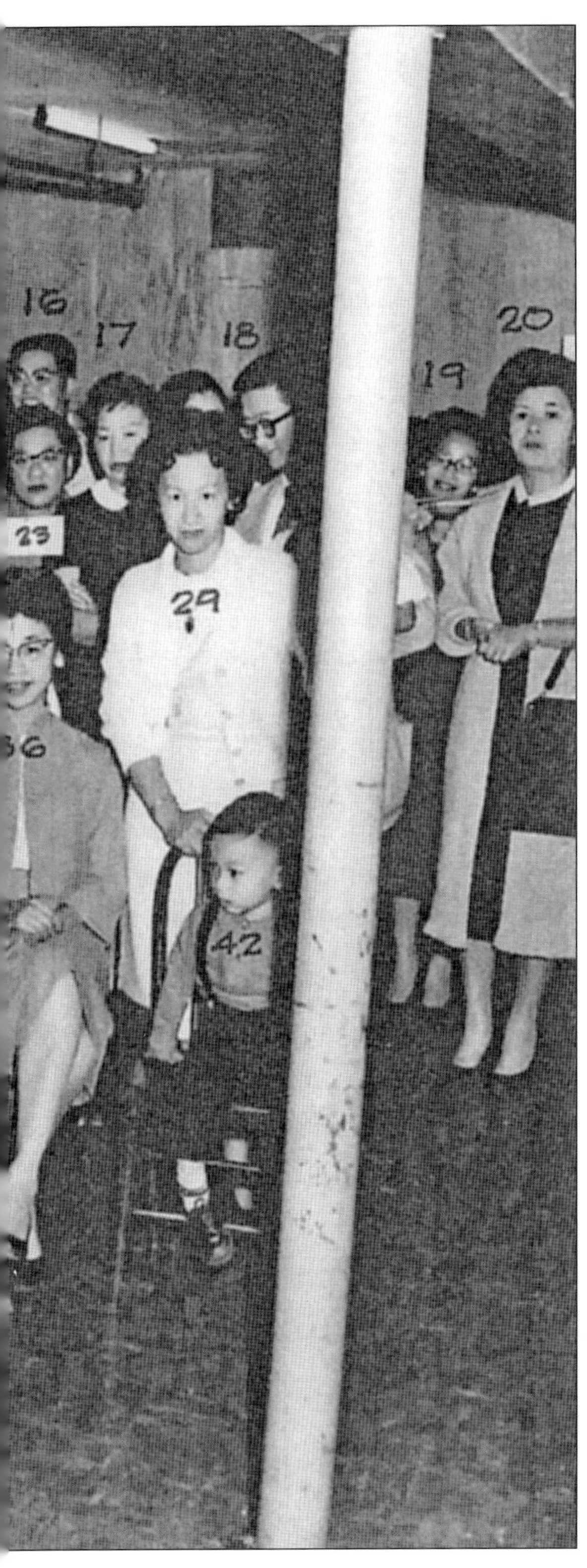

In 1960, Holt Presbyterian celebrated teacher Sarah Phillips's birthday, including (1) Sarah Phillips, (2) Vivian Wong, (3) Patricia Lee, (4) Joan Lee, (5) Irene Loy, (6) Jon Locke, (7) Janet Locke, (8) Norman Locke, (9) Nancy Locke, (10) Way Lee, (11) Gordon Wong, (12) Richard Chin, (13) Franklin Quan, (14) Gary Lee, (15) Debbie Leo, (16) Herbert Leo, (17) Lillian Okazaki, (18) Harlan Luck, (19) Juanita Lee, (20) Isabelle Low, (21) unidentified, (22) unidentified, (23) Doris Louie, (24) Dorothy Lee, (25) Mary Wong, (26) unidentified, (27) Lily Lee, (28) unidentified, (29) Lily Quan, (30) Lolita Tsujimura, (31) Anita Leo, (32) Johanne Chan, (33) Rheitha Wah, (34) Flora Wong, (35) Marci Dove, (36) Patsy Lee, (37) Steve Leo, (38) Martin Wong, (40) Allison Wong Toso, (41) Stuart Lee, (42) unidentified, (43) Michael Wong, (44) Delissa Wong, and (45) Debra Wong. (Franklin Quan.)

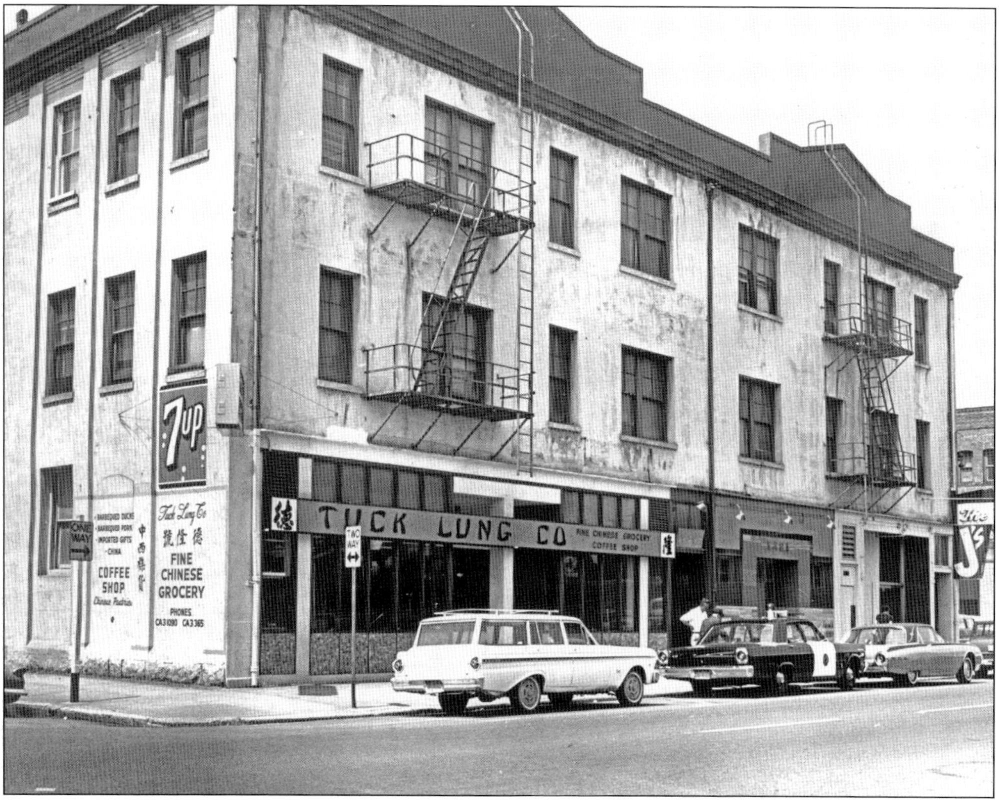

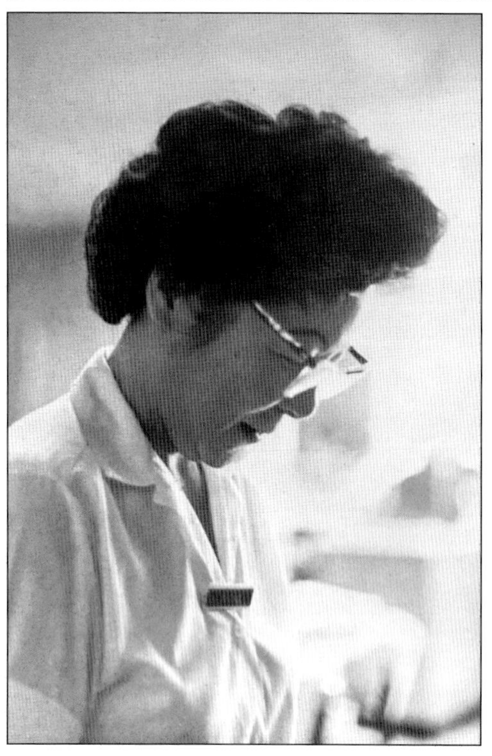

In 1962, Francis Wong partnered with his son Albert to expand and relocate their family business, Tuck Lung, to 205 Northwest Fourth Avenue. Albert managed the grocery retail and wholesale operations, while Francis and his wife, Helen, oversaw the newly added coffee shop. Francis applied skills he had learned during his earlier years at Hung Far Low restaurant. The coffee shop quickly became a favorite spot for locals to exchange news and socialize within Chinatown. Eva Wong Woo, featured to the left, was the first waitress at Tuck Lung's coffee shop. Her sister Dorothy Mah joined as a waitress later on, and they worked together. (Above, Portland Chinatown Museum; left, Harry and Eva Wong Woo family.)

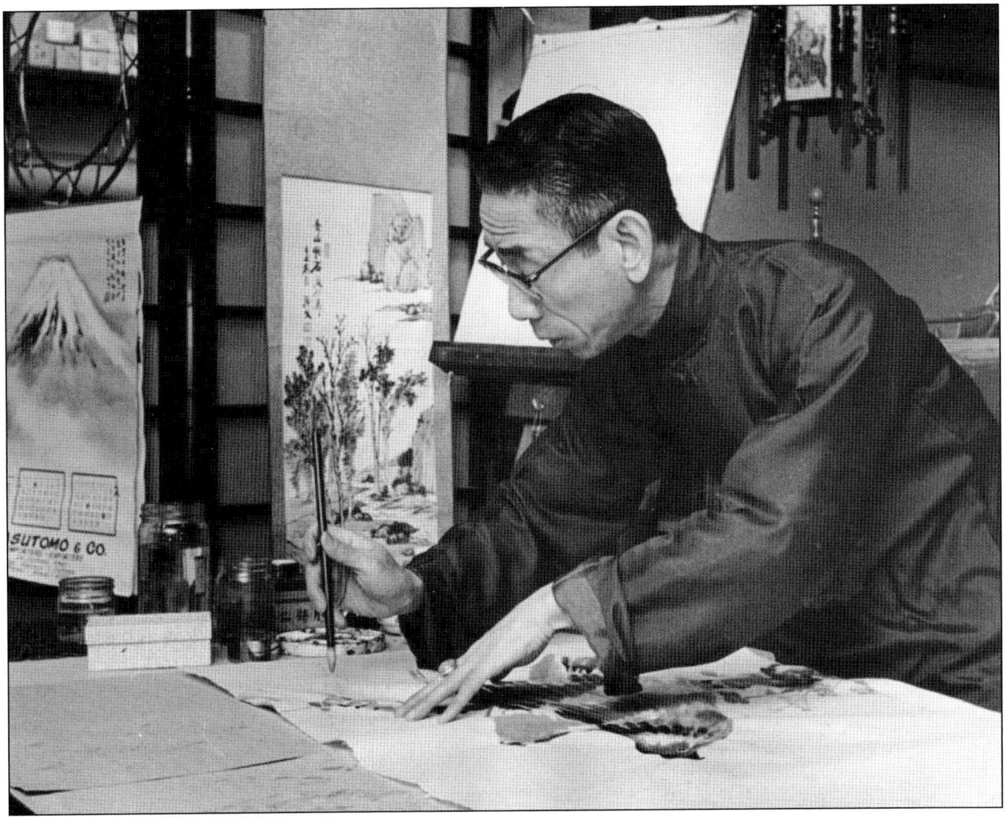

Bong Wai Chen, an acclaimed artist and educator, was trained in traditional Chinese art in China before immigrating to the United States in 1936. He became a leading authority in Chinese painting and calligraphy, dedicating his career to teaching, exhibiting, and lecturing. In 1960, he established the Chinese Art Studio, where his artistry inspired generations of students. He also served as the first principal of the CCBA Chinese Language School. (Oregon Historical Society, 0022P132.)

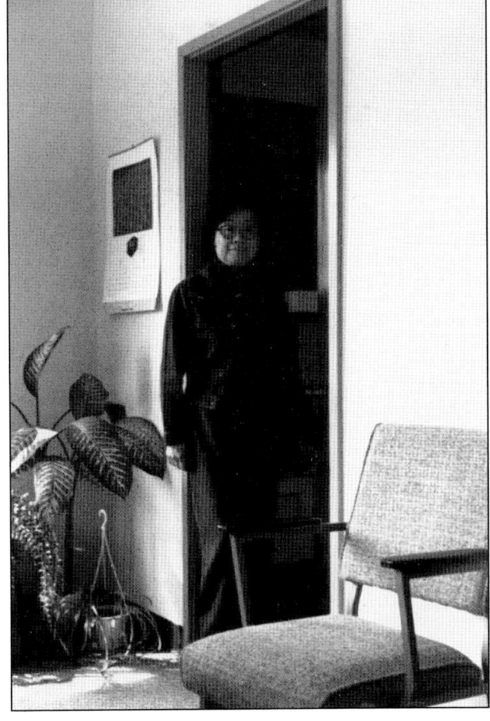

In 1954, Edith Yang became the first minority woman to earn her architect's license in Oregon. She worked on various commercial and residential projects, including on the Oregon State University campus and the Kaiser Vancouver Shipyard during World War II. Despite facing discrimination as a Chinese woman, she helped break barriers and inspired others to pursue architecture. (Edith Yang Papers [MSS Yang], OSU Special Collections and Archives Research Center, Corvallis, Oregon.)

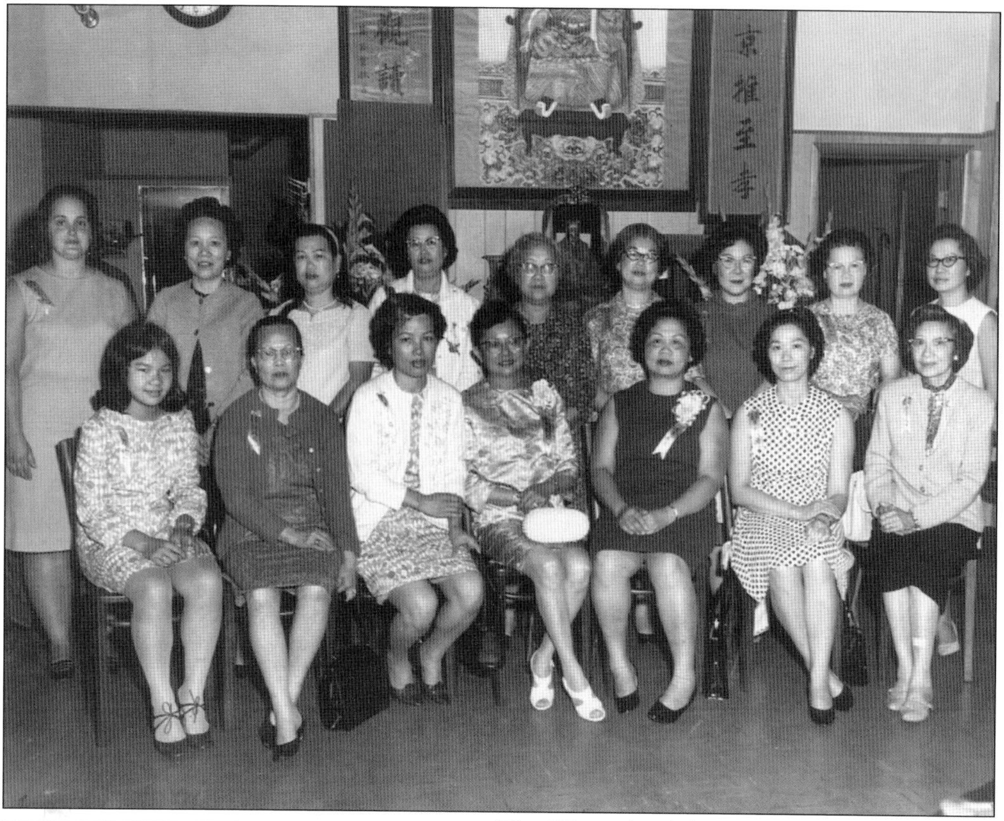

The Women's Club was photographed inside a Chinese family association hall. Mabel Wong, a dedicated member and president, helped shape the club's activities and outreach. Her leadership reflected the growing influence of Chinese American women in civic and cultural organizations during the mid-20th century. Known from left to right are (first row) Mabel Wong (fourth), Tiana ? (sixth), and Mrs. John Wong (seventh); (second row) Elizabeth Wong (sixth). (Carey Wong.)

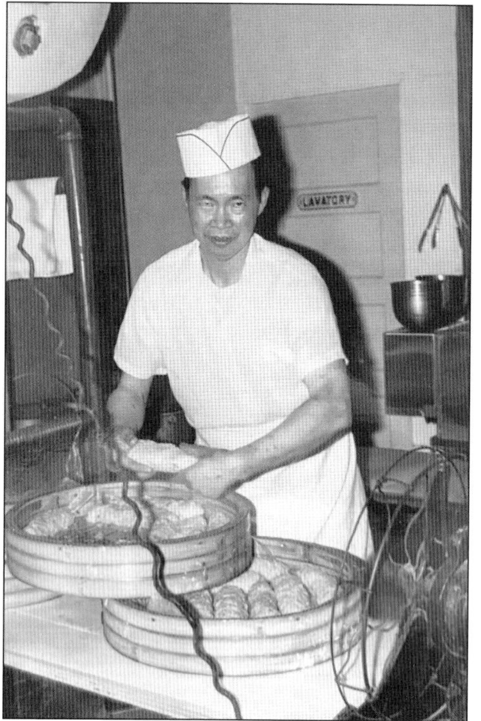

Harry Wong Woo began working at the Republic Café before the 1960s and worked for over a decade there, becoming the beloved chef. His leadership in the kitchen contributed to Republic Café's reputation as a community staple, attracting both locals and visitors. When not at work, he enjoyed fishing for bass and was an active member of Suey Sing Tong. (Harry and Eva Wong Woo family.)

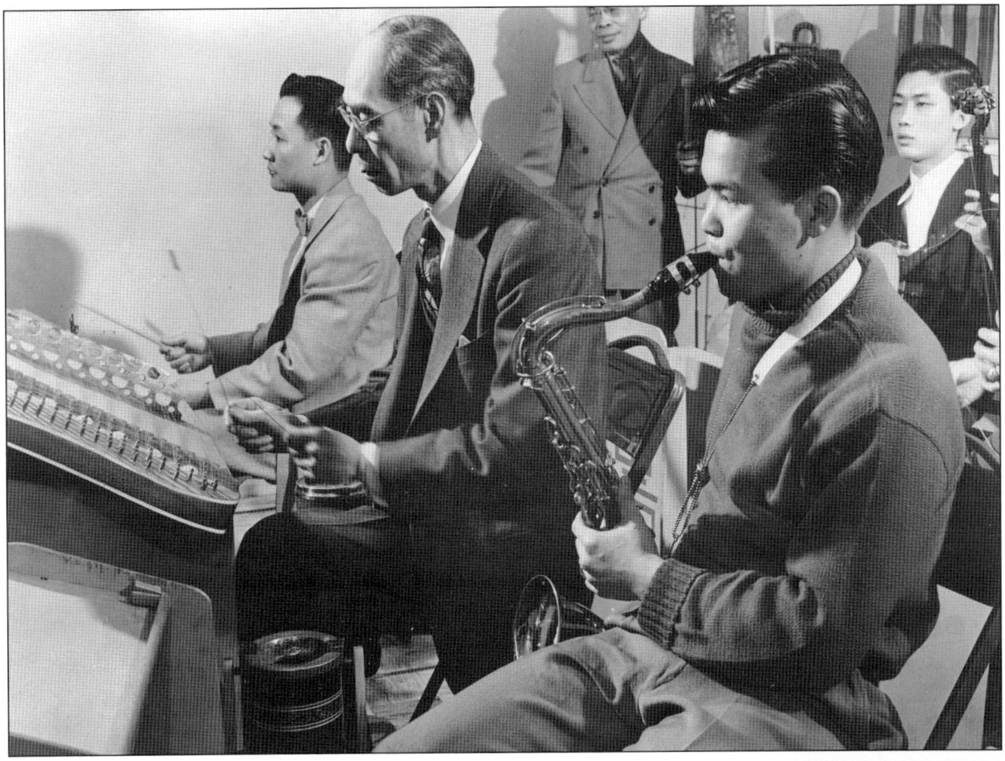

Founded in 1941 by Chinese immigrants to raise funds for China's defense against Japan, the Yat Sing Music Club has remained vital to the Chinese community since World War II. It continues to preserve Chinese opera and performs at numerous events in Portland. Known in the photograph are Carl Jew Yet Ngan (far left) and John G. Lee on the saxophone. (Oregon Historical Society, OrHi_60617.)

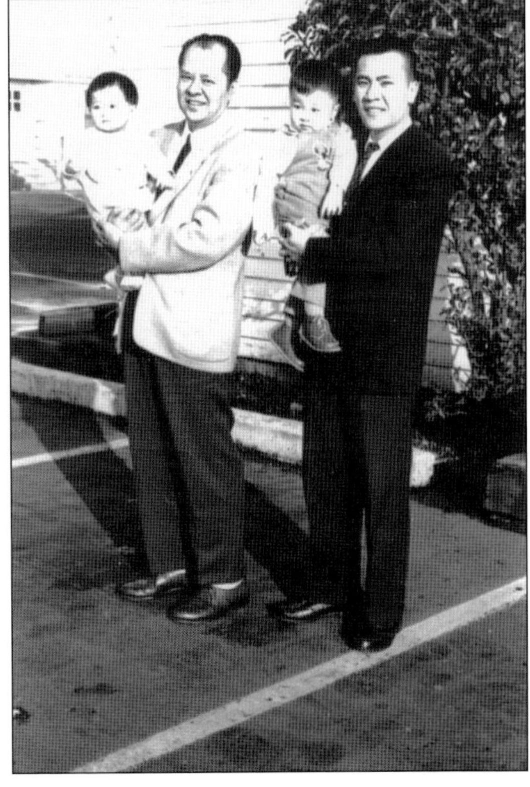

Yin K. Leong, a Kaiser Shipyard welder and Army medic in World War II, gained US citizenship through the 1943 Magnuson Act, which enabled family reunification. After 27 years apart, this 1962 image captures Leong meeting his son Wing K. Leong for the first time. From left to right are Lisa Leong Tsang, Yin K. Leong, Joseph Leong, and Wing K. Leong. (Wing K. Leong family.)

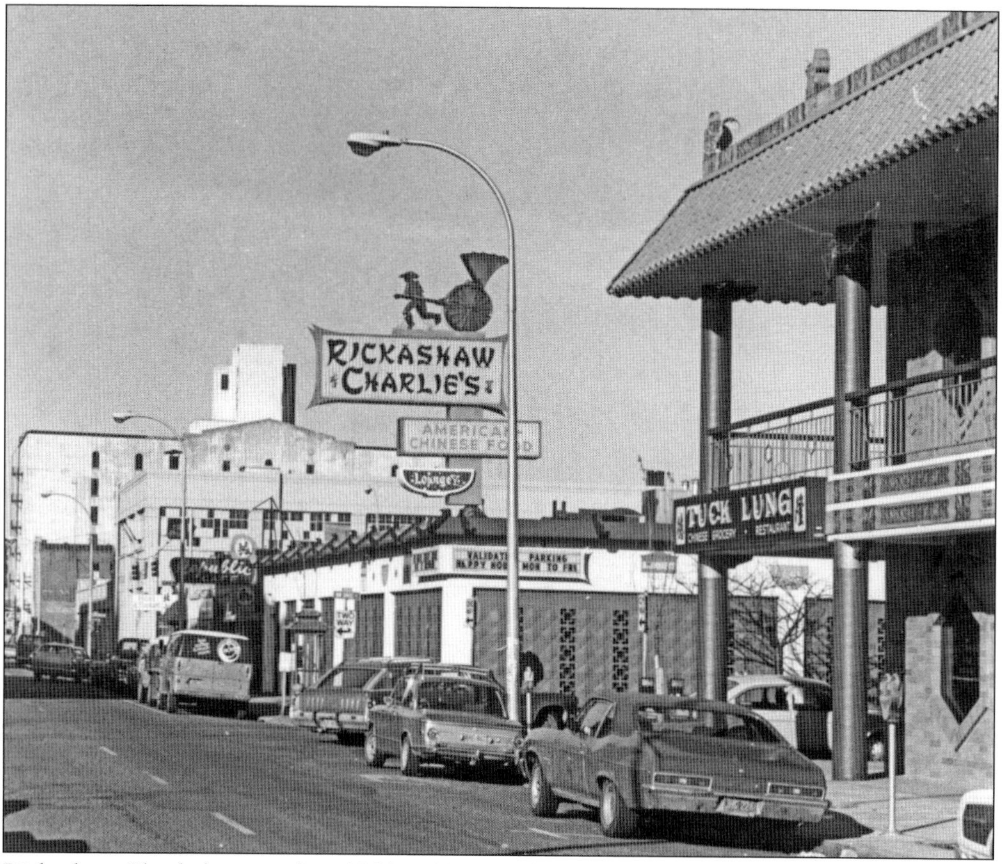

Rickashaw Charlie's opened in 1966 at 331 Northwest Davis Street, serving Cantonese and American cuisine. The restaurant featured a lively lounge with live piano music, creating a vibrant atmosphere, and was known for its animated neon sign that lit up at night. Its distinctive decor and popular menu items made it a beloved spot in Portland's Chinatown for diners. (Portland Chinatown Museum.)

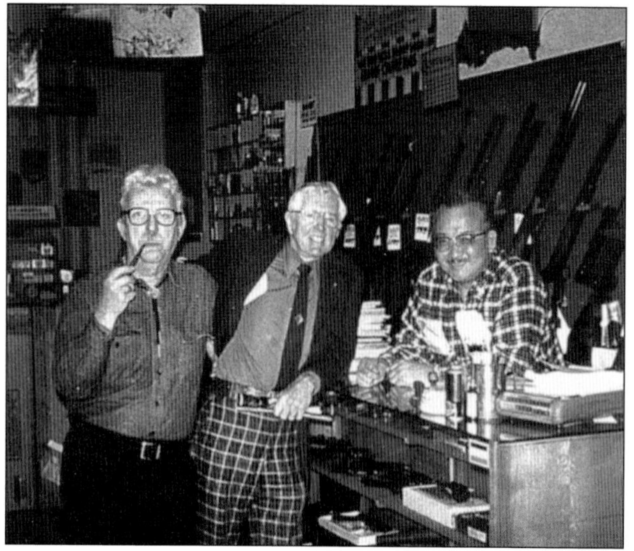

B'wana Junction Sporting Goods was opened in 1966 by Joe Lae (or Lee) on Southwest Third Avenue between Stark and Oak Streets. He is shown on the far right with Fred Goetz (far left), an outdoor writer for various publications, and Tom McAllister (middle), an outdoor columnist for the *Oregon Journal* and the *Oregonian*. The store was well loved by both the Chinatown community and the wider Portland area. (Marcus Lee.)

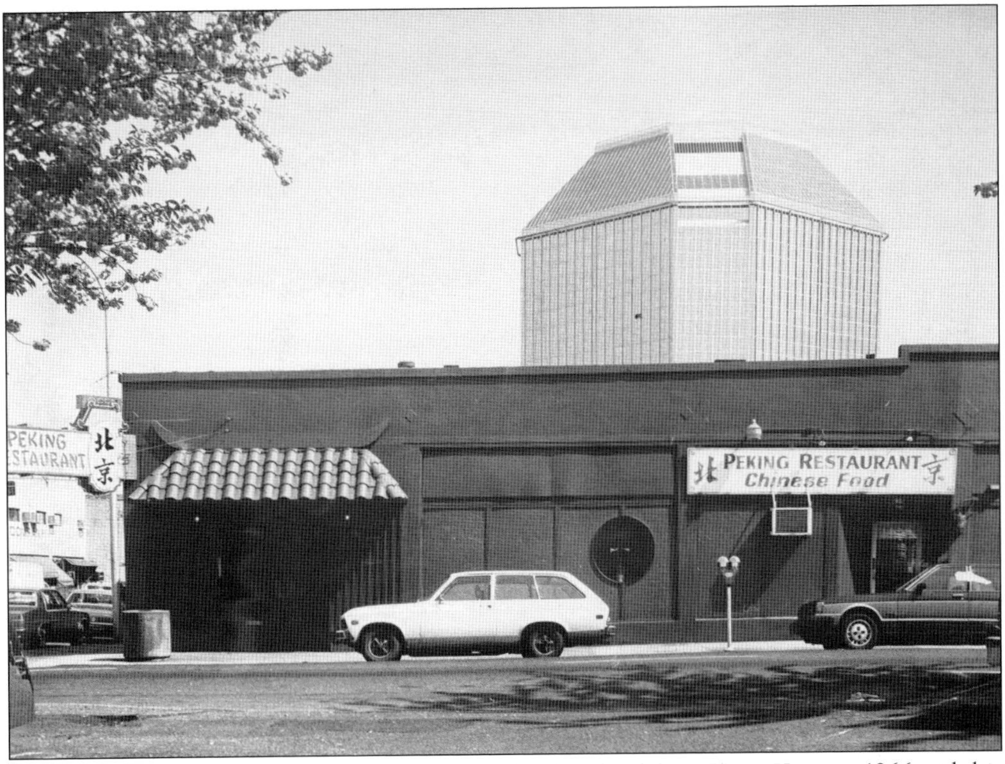

Henry Choi, born in Canton, China, immigrated to Portland from Hong Kong in 1966 with his wife, Diane Choi, and their five children. He worked as a chef at the Hi-Hat and Pagoda restaurants before establishing Peking Restaurant in Chinatown at 238 Northwest Fourth Avenue during the 1970s, and he successfully operated it for 16 years. Choi was very active in the Bing Kong Association and with the CCBA. (Henry and Diane Choi family.)

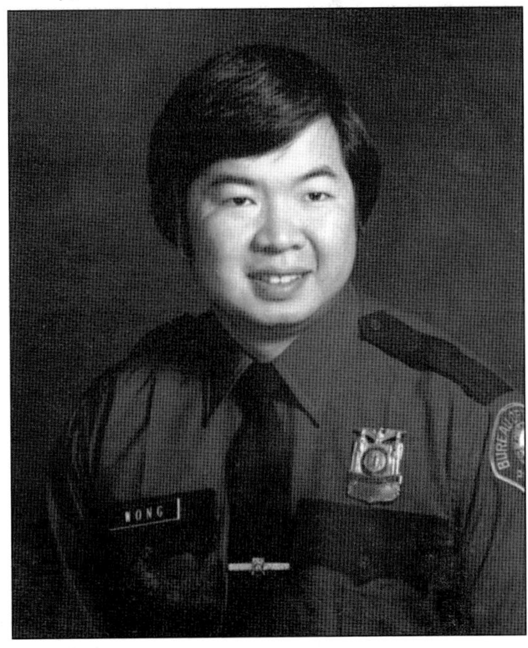

Preston Wong was the Portland Police Bureau's first Asian police officer when he was hired in 1973. He worked in the Southeast Precinct for the Drug and Vice Division and also on the Gang Enforcement Team. He helped mentor high school students as well as high-risk immigrant youth. His father, Henry Wong, was a chef at Rickashaw Charlie's restaurant in Chinatown. (Portland Chinatown Museum.)

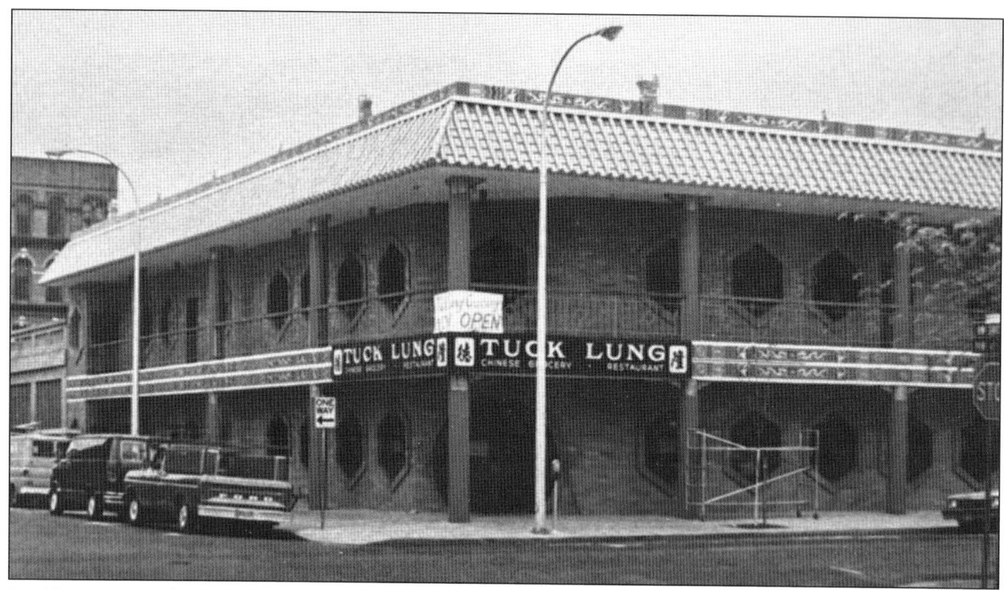

In 1977, ground was broken to relocate Tuck Lung to 140 Northwest Fourth Avenue by Albert Wong and his wife and business partner, Vivian Wong. Edwin Chen, the designer, incorporated elements of Chinese Tang Dynasty–inspired architecture into the facade. The restaurant became popular for dim sum and banquets, and the grocery store was popular for Chinese groceries. (Roberta May Wong.)

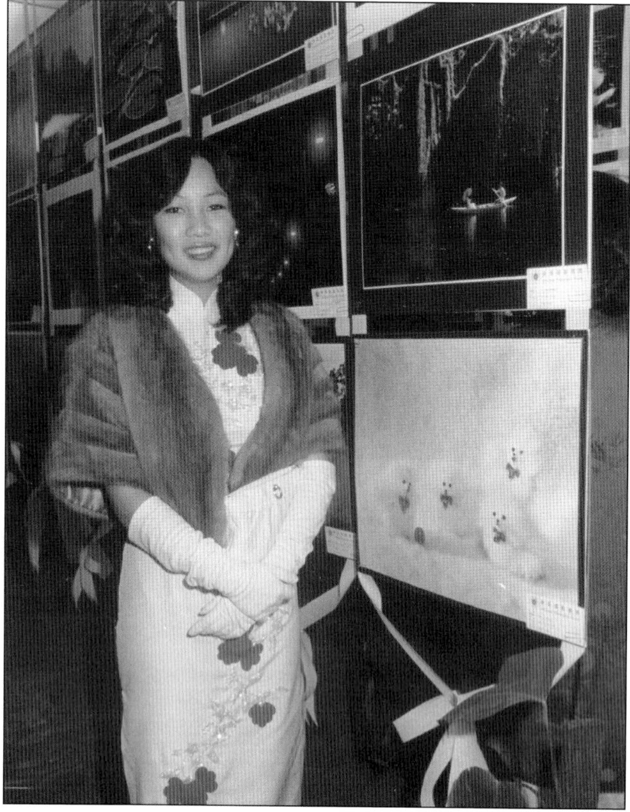

The first Miss Chinatown officially started in 1953 in San Francisco. It became so popular with locals and visitors that, in 1958, the Chinese Chamber of Commerce expanded it nationwide, and it became the Miss Chinatown, USA Pageant. In 1980, Allison Wong Toso was selected as First Princess of the Miss Portland Chinatown pageant. (Allison Wong Toso.)

Four

New Generations and the Future 1981–Present

Chinatowns in the US face significant challenges threatening their survival. Economic pressures, the lingering effects of COVID-19, gentrification, rising property values, and large-scale developments are displacing long-standing communities and businesses. Renovating aging infrastructure in historic neighborhoods is hindered by stricter building codes and rising construction costs. Chinatowns were safe havens for those from Southern China who faced discriminatory laws like the Chinese Exclusion Act, offering a sense of community. By the 1980s, many families relocated to the suburbs, yet Portland's Chinatown remained a hub for shopping, dining, and cultural education. Landmarks such as the Chinatown Gateway, built in 1986, and newer immigrant enclaves like the Jade District in Southeast Portland reflect this evolving history. Today, civic and cultural institutions such as the Portland Chinatown Museum and Lan Su Chinese Garden preserve traditions by hosting community events. Organizations like the Chinese Consolidated Benevolent Association, Bing Kung Tong, and the Lee Family Association have long provided resources, social networks, and legal aid, while continuing to play vital roles in fostering community pride and unity. For Chinatown to thrive, these organizations must appeal to the wide diaspora of newer Chinese immigrants from countries such as Taiwan and Vietnam as well as ethnic minority groups from China, acknowledging their unique traditions and languages, as they may not have direct ties to Chinatown like previous generations. Despite these challenges, projects such as the Society Hotel's revitalization of the Mariners' Building highlight how renewal efforts can preserve these cultural enclaves. In 1977, the western edges of the New Chinatown/Japantown Historic District, which overlap with the Skidmore/Old Town Historic District, were given a national historic landmark designation. Then, in 1989, the New Chinatown/Japantown Historic District was added to the National Register of Historic Places, recognizing its historical significance within the city. As Portland's Chinatown faces challenges from urban development, community and city leaders are working to preserve this historic neighborhood and ensure it remains a thriving part of the city's cultural landscape for generations to come. It is also important for residents to show their support to businesses and organizations by shopping, dining, and participating in local events.

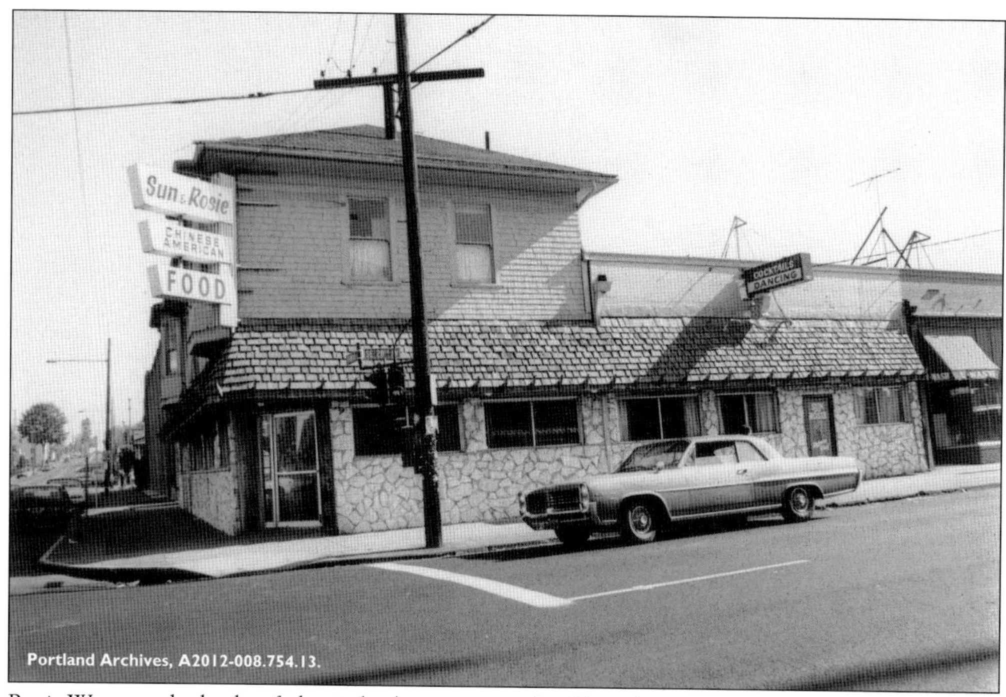

Rosie Wong worked at her father-in-law's restaurant, the Chungking Café, and then was a seamstress at Jantzen Woolen Mills before opening a restaurant with her husband, Sun Wong, in 1964. The Sun and Rosie restaurant was one of the first Chinese restaurants on the east side of Portland at Twenty-Eighth Avenue and East Burnside Street. On this block, the family also owned three other commercial spaces. This included son Fred B. Wong and wife Ivy Wong's F&I U-Wash. As part of the American Dream, Chinese were able to move outside of Chinatown into the surrounding communities when the city's property laws changed. Shown from left to right are Wong Shee Yup, Rosie Wong, and Sun Wong. (Above, City of Portland Archives, AP/78260; below, Fred B. Wong.)

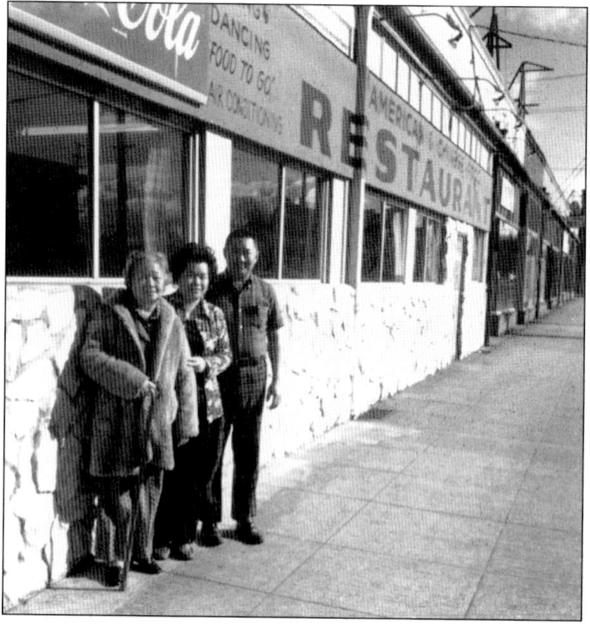

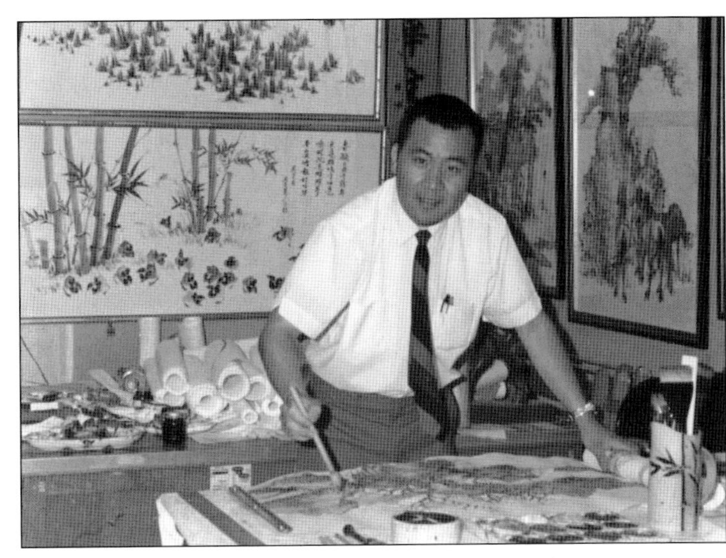

Wing K. Leong, a fine arts graduate from Hong Kong, brought his passion for Chinese art to Portland in 1962 when he immigrated. He founded the Chinese Art Studio, offering art supplies, picture framing, and classes in Chinese painting and calligraphy. Beyond his studio, Leong also taught at community colleges and art schools, sharing his expertise and inspiring others. (Wing K. Leong family.)

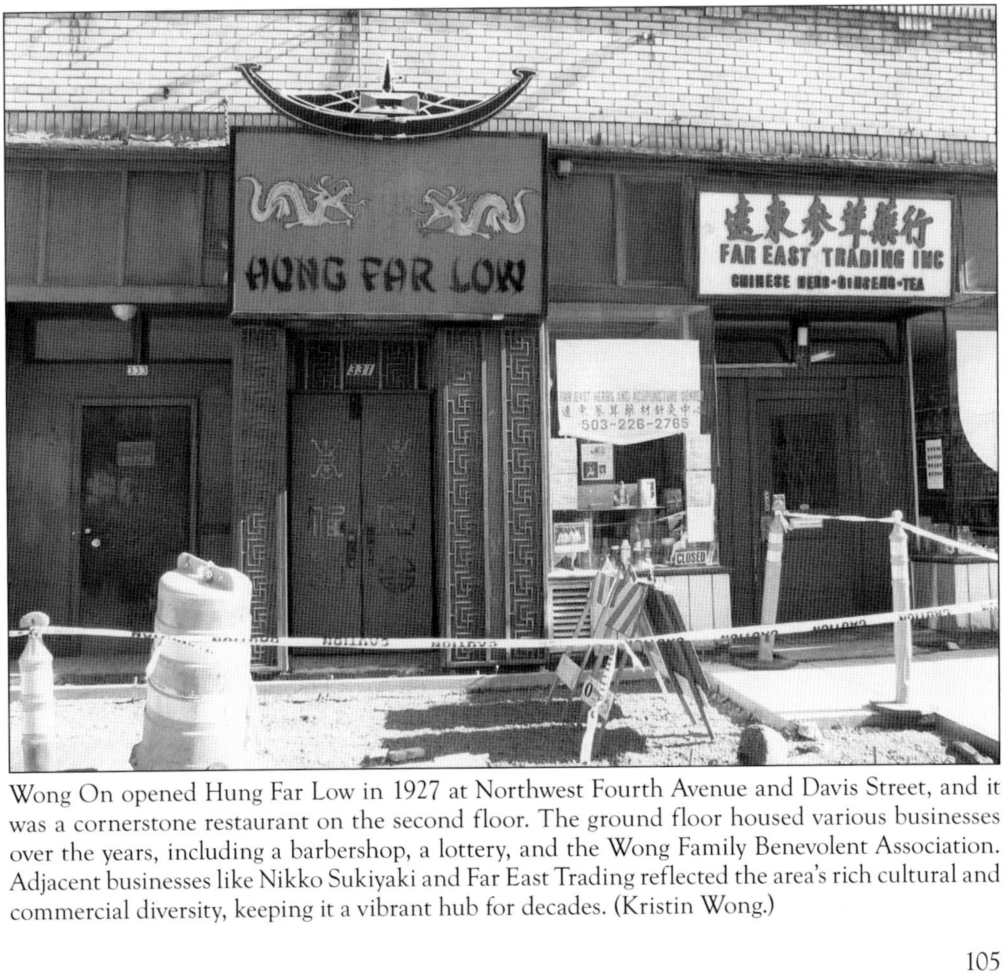

Wong On opened Hung Far Low in 1927 at Northwest Fourth Avenue and Davis Street, and it was a cornerstone restaurant on the second floor. The ground floor housed various businesses over the years, including a barbershop, a lottery, and the Wong Family Benevolent Association. Adjacent businesses like Nikko Sukiyaki and Far East Trading reflected the area's rich cultural and commercial diversity, keeping it a vibrant hub for decades. (Kristin Wong.)

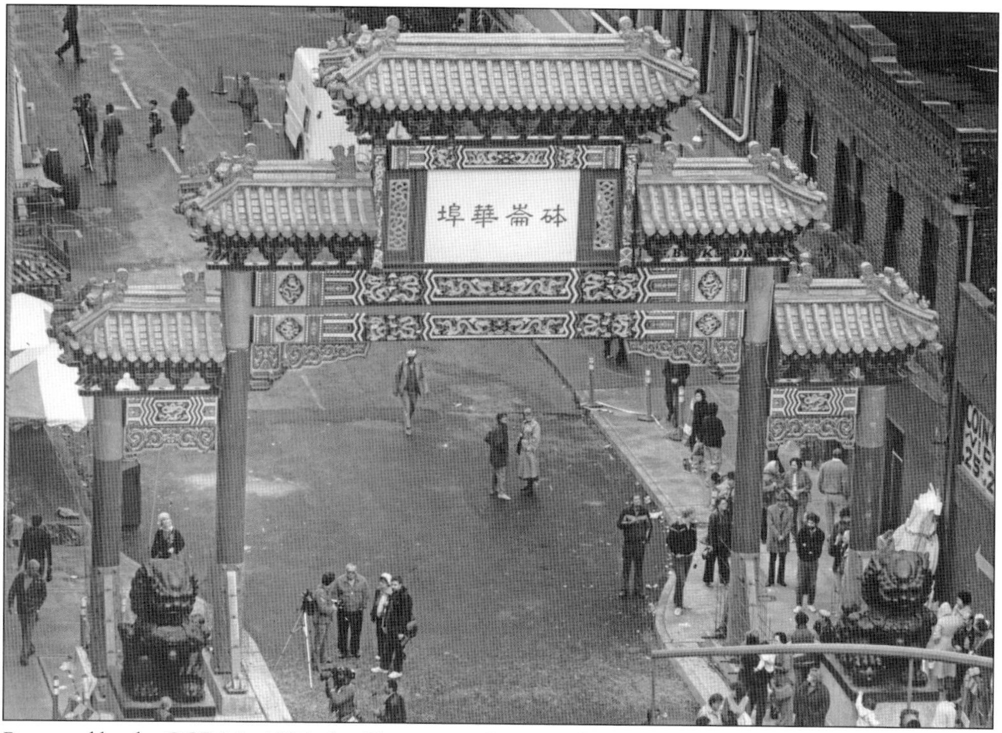

Proposed by the CCBA in 1984, the Chinatown Gate was designed and built by Ting Hwa Architects in Taiwan and dedicated in 1986. It was the largest structure of its kind in the US until the one in Washington, DC, was completed later that year. The gate at West Burnside Street and Northwest Fourth Avenue remains a landmark welcoming visitors to the historic Chinatown district. (Portland Chinatown Museum.)

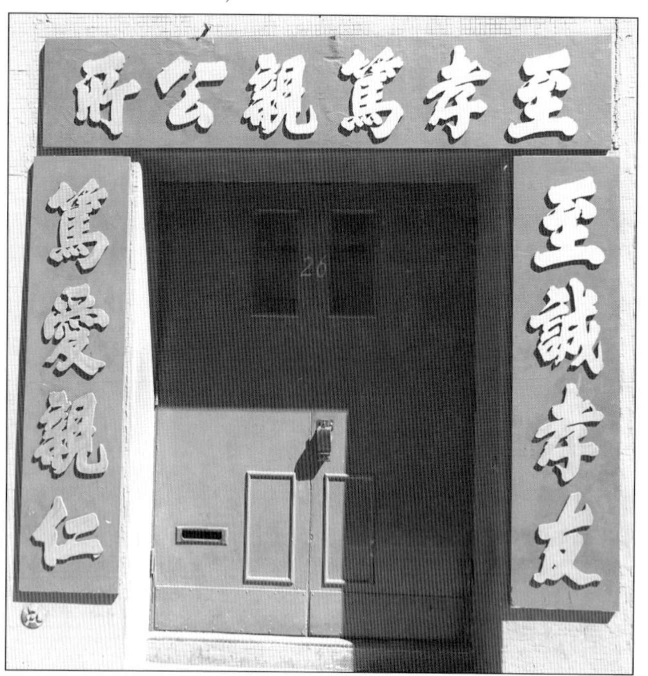

Built in 1905, the Gee How Oak Tin Association building on Northwest Fourth Avenue was acquired by Leland Chin and has housed the association on the top floor since 1963, with restaurant and retail businesses below. The association represents the surnames Chan, Woo, and Yuen. From 1934 to 1942, the Holt Chinese Presbyterian Mission occupied space in the building, reflecting its historical role in Chinatown's evolving community landscape. (Zoonar GmbH/Alamy Stock Photo.)

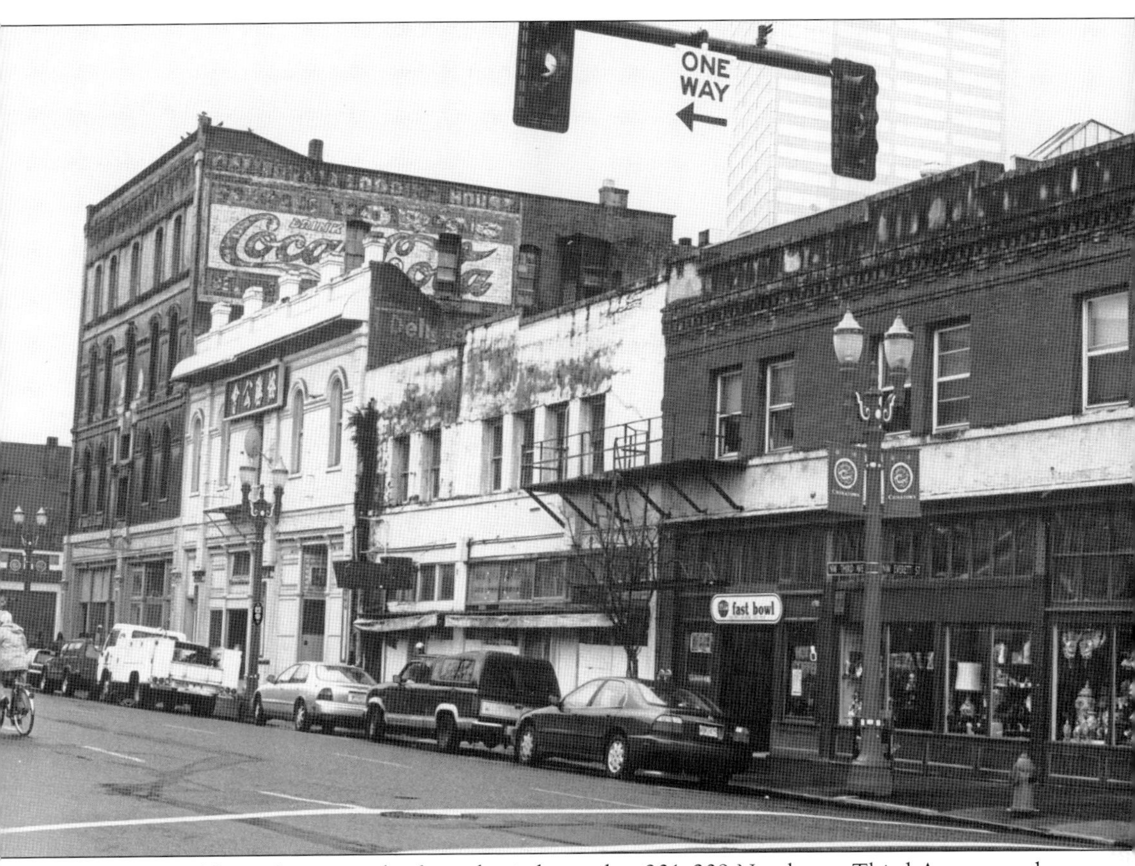

The Pallay Building, shown on the far right, is located at 231–239 Northwest Third Avenue and Everett Street. It was constructed in 1908 and played a significant role in the area's development. The second floor housed several Japanese-run hotels, including Mikado Hotel (1930–1936), New Palace Hotel (1936–1943), and the Glendale Hotel. The ground-level businesses included Hasagawa Company (1910–1932), Mikado Laundry (1930–1934), a Chinese lottery, Hip Sing Tong, and the Hoy Yin Association. In the basement were Mikado-yu Japanese bathhouse, a Filipino cannery workers' union, and the Yat Sing Music Club. Next door at 221–223 Northwest Third Avenue, built in conjunction with the Pallay Building, was Don Rosenberg's furniture and hardware store (1928–1934), Ben Shaman's secondhand store, and Wing Lee's tea room (1934). As World War II began, Wong's Laundry took over the vacant storefront, marking the continued evolution of the building. Most recently, Great Era Oriental Imports at 239 Third Avenue, shown as the storefront on the far right, operated from the 1980s to the 2010s. (Portland Chinatown Museum.)

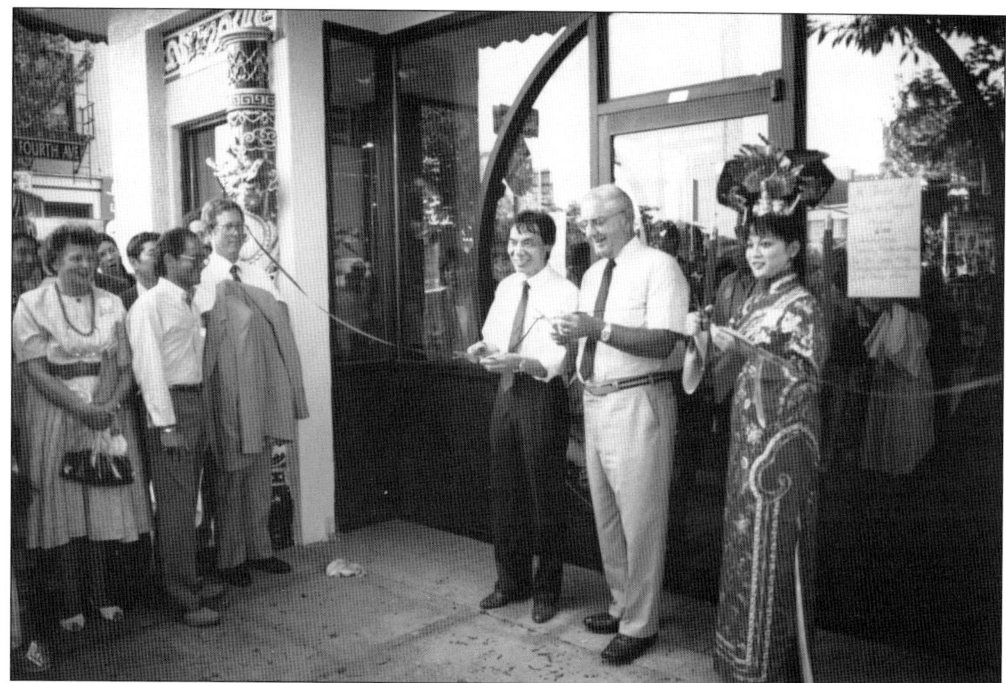

The House of Louie, located at 331 Northwest Davis Street, was renowned for its dim sum lunches and elaborate dinner banquets, becoming a cherished culinary institution in Portland's Chinatown. Its architecture prominently featured Chinese-inspired elements, including a circular "moon gate" entrance, symbolizing heaven. The exterior of the building included ornate decorations featuring depictions of a dragon and a phoenix. These symbols are deeply significant in Chinese culture, representing balance, harmony, and prosperity. Captured in these 1988 grand opening images, Steven Louie is seen with Gov. Vic Atiyeh. Below, the CCBA Lion Dance Team performs a traditional ceremony to bring prosperity and good fortune. (Both, Steven Louie and family.)

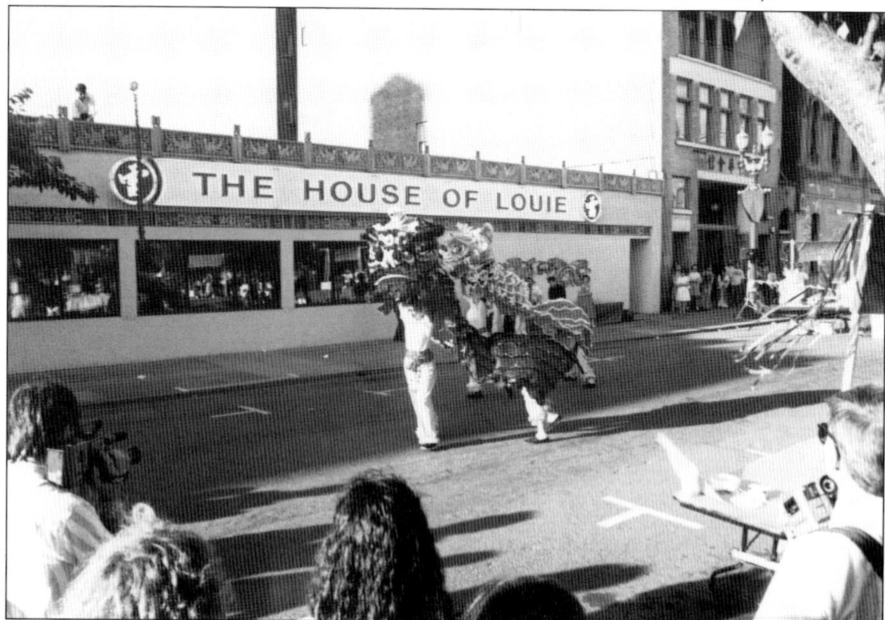

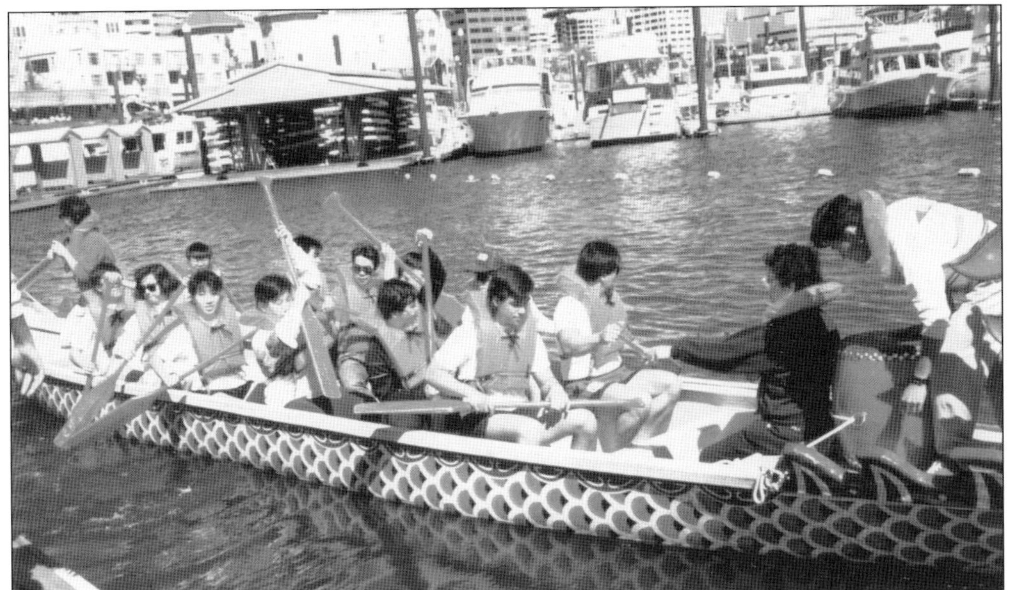

Since 1989, the Portland-Kaohsiung Sister City Association has organized the Portland Rose Festival's Dragon Boat Race, drawing teams from the Pacific Northwest and beyond. This event celebrates an ancient tradition while fostering camaraderie and teamwork. Pictured second from right is Mary N. Leong guiding the CCBA Dragon Boat Team during a practice in 1989. (George W. and Mary N. Leong family.)

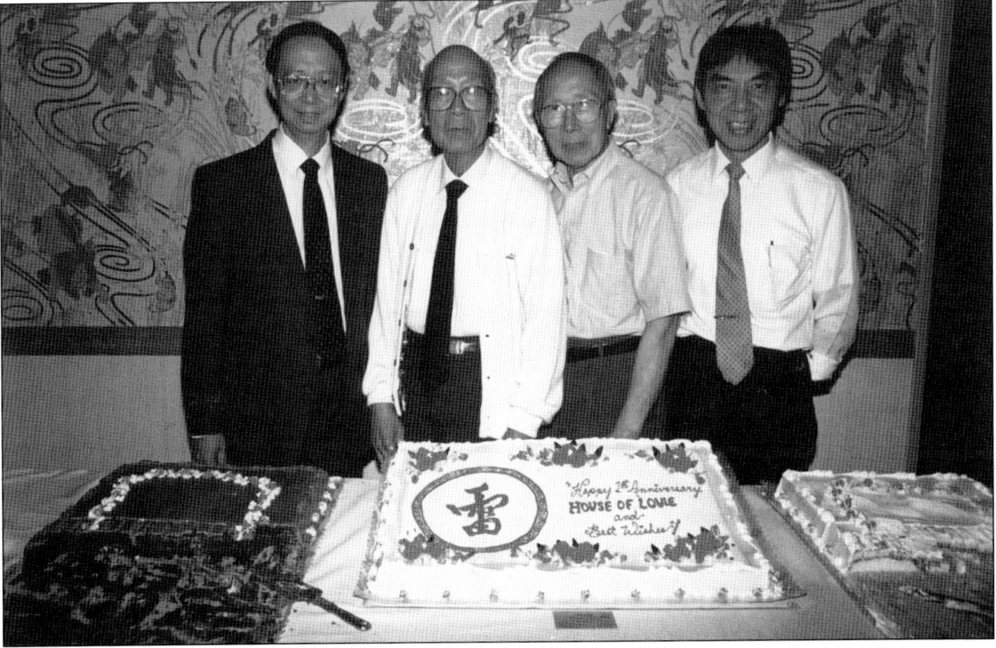

Members of the Louie family clan, including, from left to right, Gregory Louie, Henry Louie (father), Bob Louie, and Steven Louie (son), successfully started and partnered in several Chinese restaurants in the Portland area, including House of Louie, Hi-Hat, New Cathay, Lani Louie's, Bill's Gold Coin, Silk Hat, and Fong Chong grocery and restaurant. This photograph captures the first anniversary of House of Louie in Chinatown in 1989. (Steven Louie and family.)

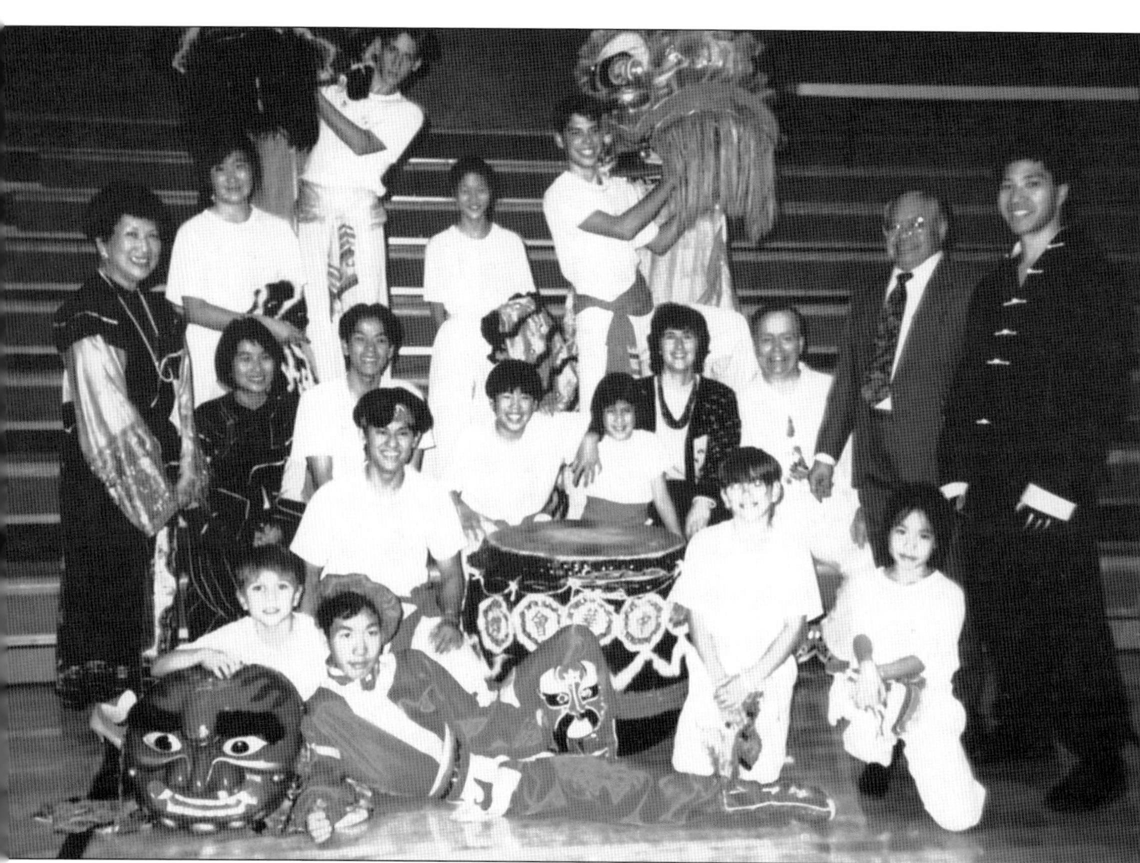

Coach Robert H. Leong played a significant role in the Chinese Consolidated Benevolent Association Lion Dance Team, contributing to its cultural presence in Portland's Chinatown. In this image from 1992, the team performed in Pendleton, showcasing the artistry and tradition of lion dance to the community. His parents, George W. and Mary N. Leong, were also active in the team performances, helping with various aspects such as costumes, props, and transportation. Shown from left to right are (first row) Scott Foster, Victor Tang, Tyler Foster, and Leslie Tang; (second row) D.D. Chen, Lance Watanabe, and Abbie Nim; (third row) Shan-Mei Leong, A-Mun ?, Mrs. Foster, Grandpa Foster, George W. Leong, and Robert H. Leong; (fourth row) Mary N. Leong, Marcia Watanabe, Brendan Foster, TaiLee Mathis, and Andy Rother. (George W. and Mary N. Leong family.)

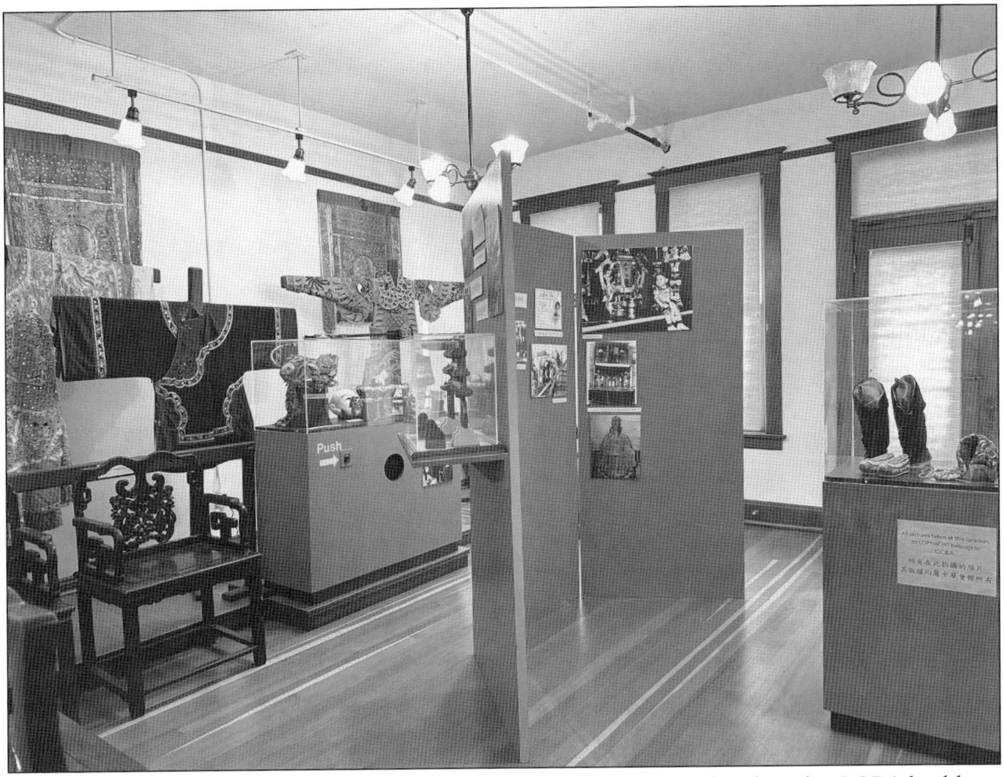

The Chinese Consolidated Benevolent Association Museum, located within the CCBA building, showcases the rich history of Portland's Chinese community, beginning in the 1850s with the first Chinatown and its current location in the New Chinatown/Japantown Historic District. The museum helps preserve the past for future generations. It is staffed by volunteers and is open by appointment. (CCBA Museum.)

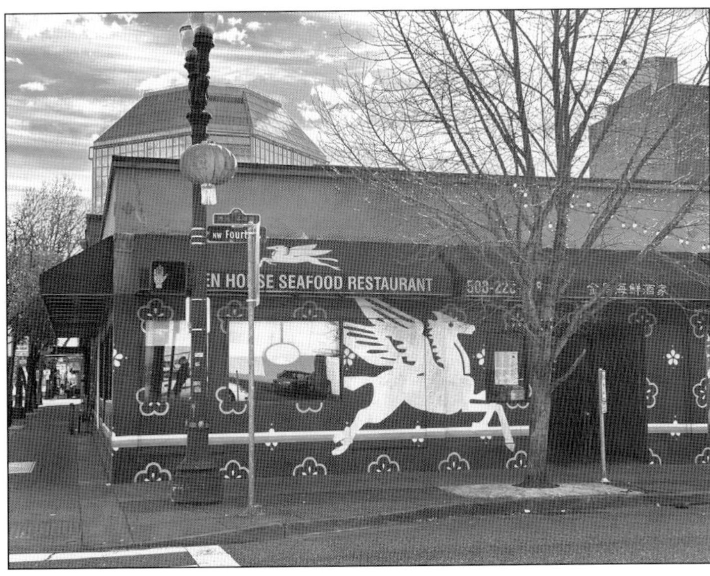

Golden Horse Seafood Restaurant, a cherished Chinatown establishment since 1989, is located at 238 Northwest Fourth Avenue. Sophy Li and her husband, Guang Cai, began their journey there as employees in the restaurant and kitchen before becoming its owners. Today, Golden Horse remains a beloved culinary landmark, serving an array of delicious Cantonese and Mandarin dishes. (Kristin Wong.)

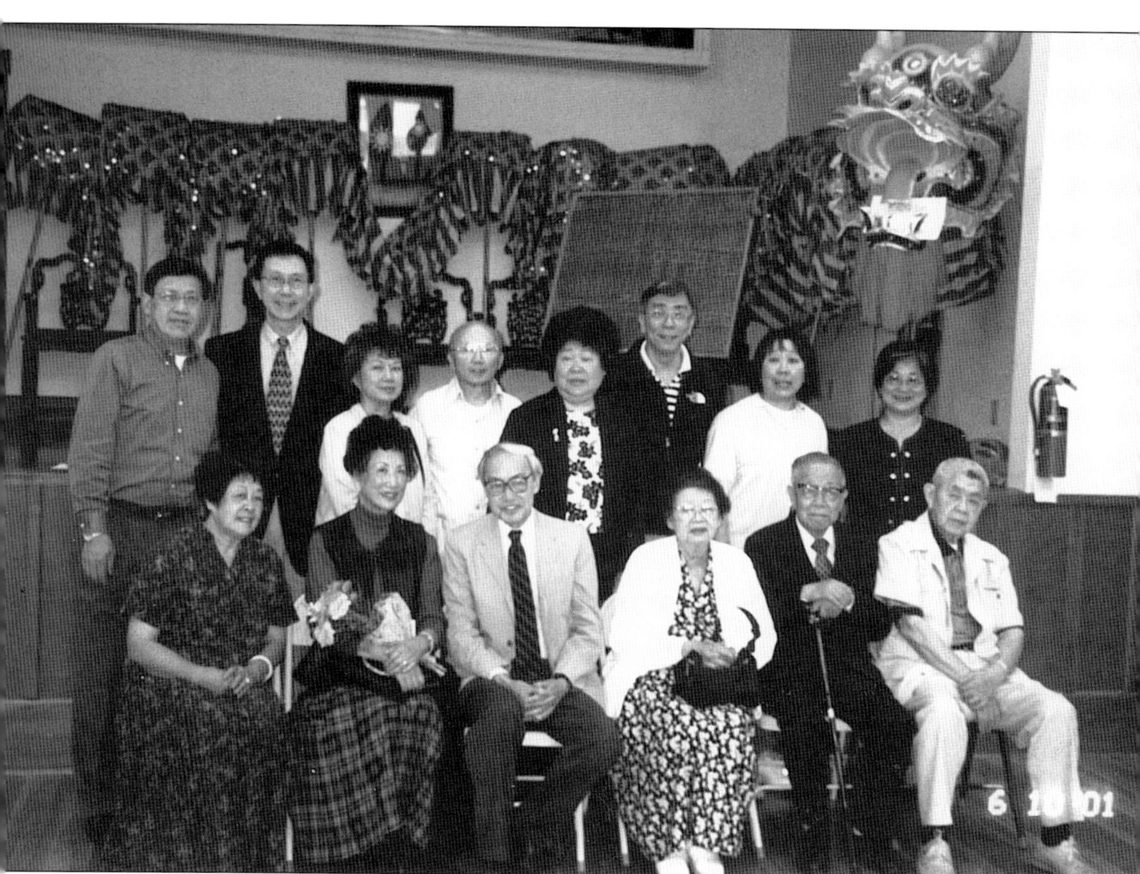

The Portland Chinese Scholarship Foundation (PCSF), originally established by the Chinese Consolidated Benevolent Association, now operates independently but in full cooperation with the CCBA to support Oregon high school graduates of Chinese ancestry through scholarships funded by community organizations and private individuals. Founded in 1965, the PCSF awards scholarships based on academics, leadership, service, financial need, and athletic achievement. Since 1963, the foundation has granted over $750,000, with 29 endowment scholarships, continuing its tradition of supporting future generations in their pursuit of higher education. This 2001 photograph shows the supporters and donors at the scholarship presentation event at the CCBA auditorium. From left to right are (first row) Gloria Wong, Mary N. Leong, Kelly Wong, Isabella Low, Yao Chun Lee, and Shelton Low; (second row) Patrick Chan, Philip Tang, Jane S. Wong, Fred M. Wong, Kim Luey, Tarcy Lee, Shirley Yee, and Rebecca Liu. (Jane S. Wong.)

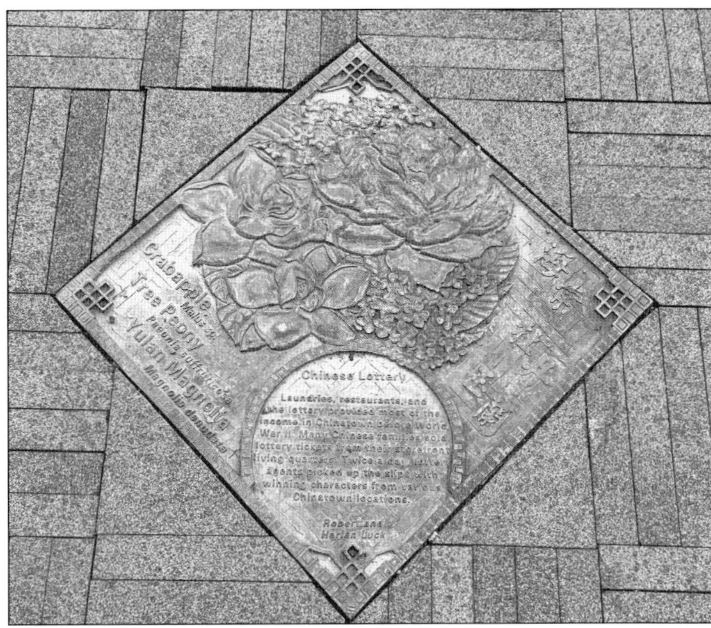

Since the 1850s, the New Chinatown/Japantown Historic District has been shaped by Chinese, Japanese, Italian, Jewish, Greek, Filipino, Romani, Scandinavian, and African American workers and their families. Urban designer Suenn Ho co-led the installation of 20 bronze plaques that highlight significant landmarks, businesses, and events, creating a walking history tour that celebrates the area's rich cultural heritage. (Kristin Wong.)

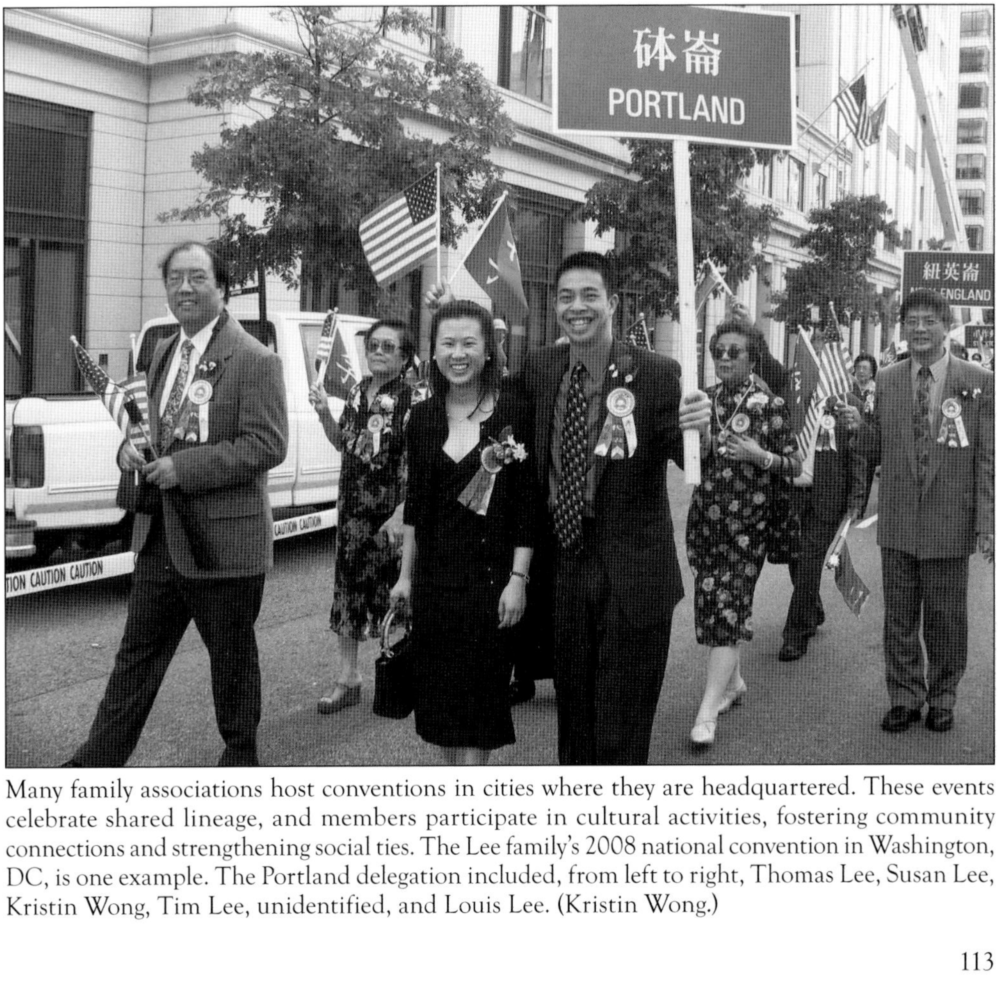

Many family associations host conventions in cities where they are headquartered. These events celebrate shared lineage, and members participate in cultural activities, fostering community connections and strengthening social ties. The Lee family's 2008 national convention in Washington, DC, is one example. The Portland delegation included, from left to right, Thomas Lee, Susan Lee, Kristin Wong, Tim Lee, unidentified, and Louis Lee. (Kristin Wong.)

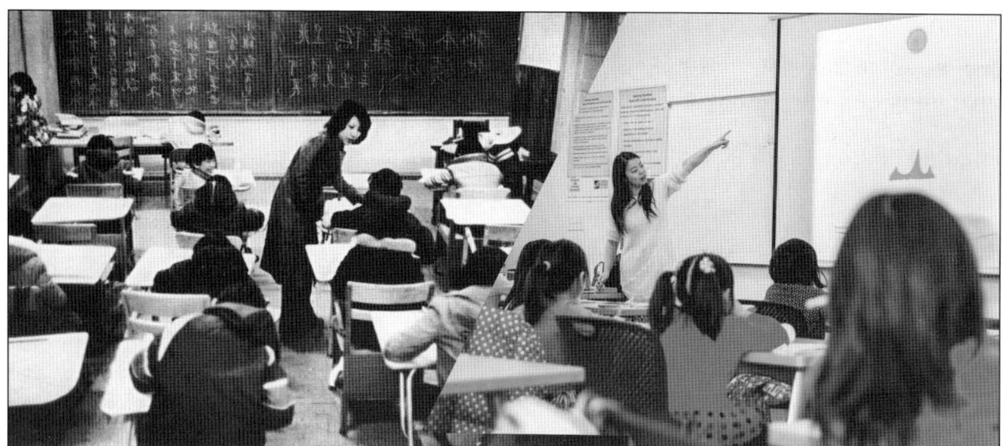

To better serve the growing Chinese community in Southeast Portland, the CCBA Chinese Language School relocated to the Portland Community College campus in the Jade District. Since the early 1900s, the school has educated generations of students and continues to offer Saturday classes for all ages and skill levels. Dedicated instructors teach both written and spoken Cantonese and Mandarin, ensuring a rich and comprehensive language-learning experience. (CCBA.)

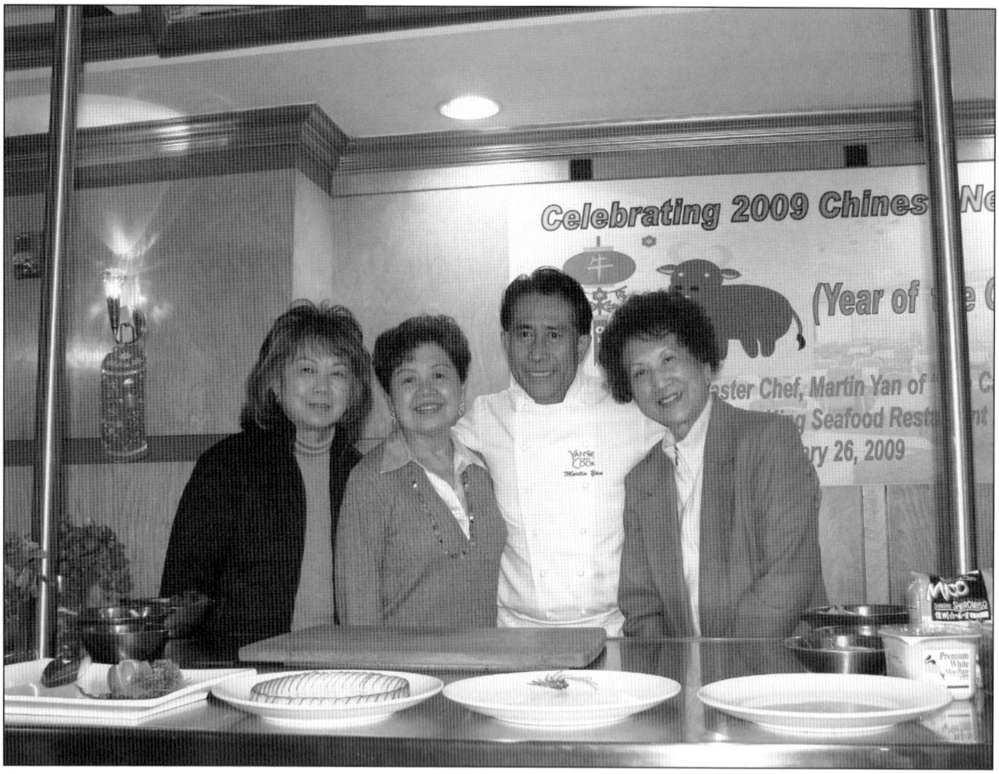

Celebrity chef Martin Yan of *Yan Can Cook* helped bring in the Chinese New Year at Wong's King restaurant in 2009. Through his dynamic personality and engaging cooking demonstration, Chef Yan brought a sense of festivity and culinary excellence to the event, making it a memorable experience. Shown from left to right are Jane S. Wong, Jean Won, Martin Yan, and Mary N. Leong. (Kristin Wong.)

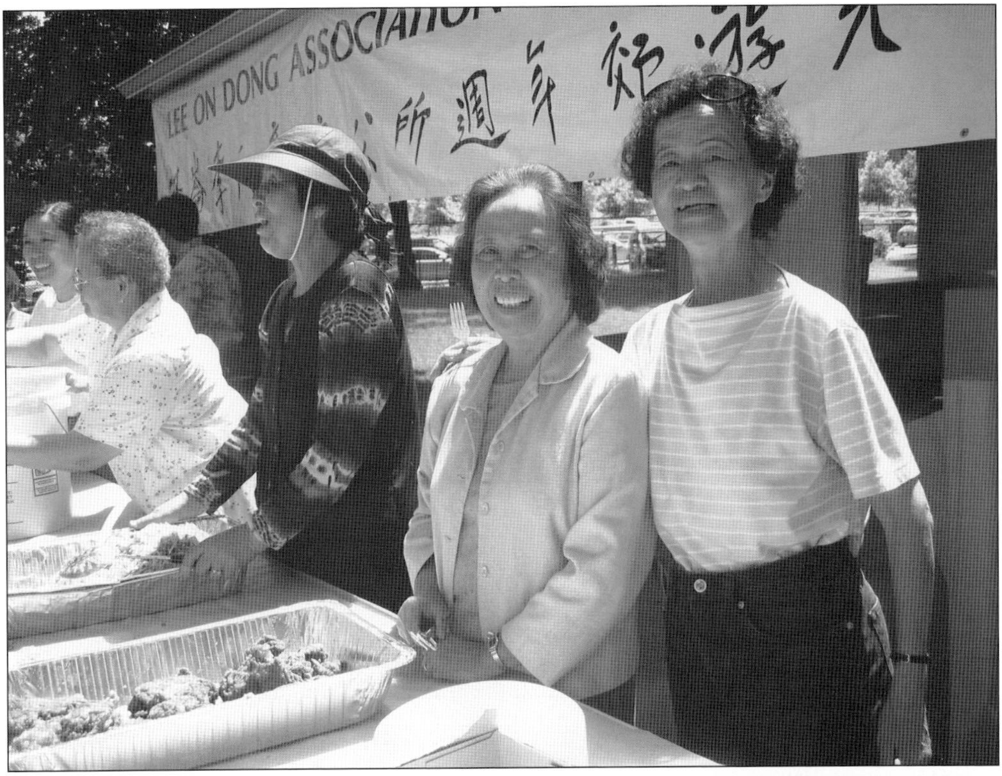

Family associations are dedicated to fostering cultural pride and community involvement among their members, including the younger generations. The associations organize a variety of events throughout the year, such as the Chinese New Year banquet and annual picnic, along with sponsoring youth programs. Shown in the photograph are, from left to right, unidentified, Verna Lee, unidentified, Pui Kwong, and Pearl Lee Wong. (Kristin Wong.)

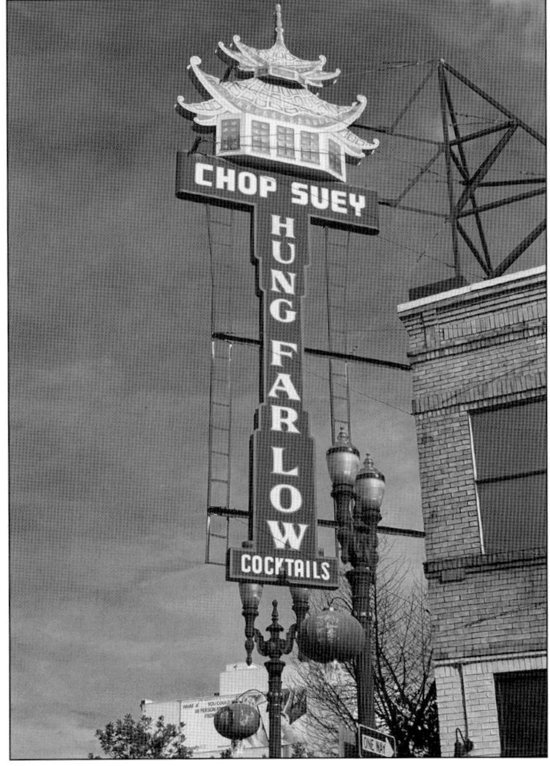

The iconic two-story Hung Far Low sign (Toishan for "almond blossom fragrance") at Northwest Fourth Avenue and Couch Street has been a beloved landmark since the restaurant opened in 1927. In 2010, the community and city came together to restore this historic sign, preserving a cherished piece of Portland's Chinatown heritage. The restoration effort highlighted the community's dedication to maintaining its cultural legacy and supporting significant local landmarks. (Kristin Wong.)

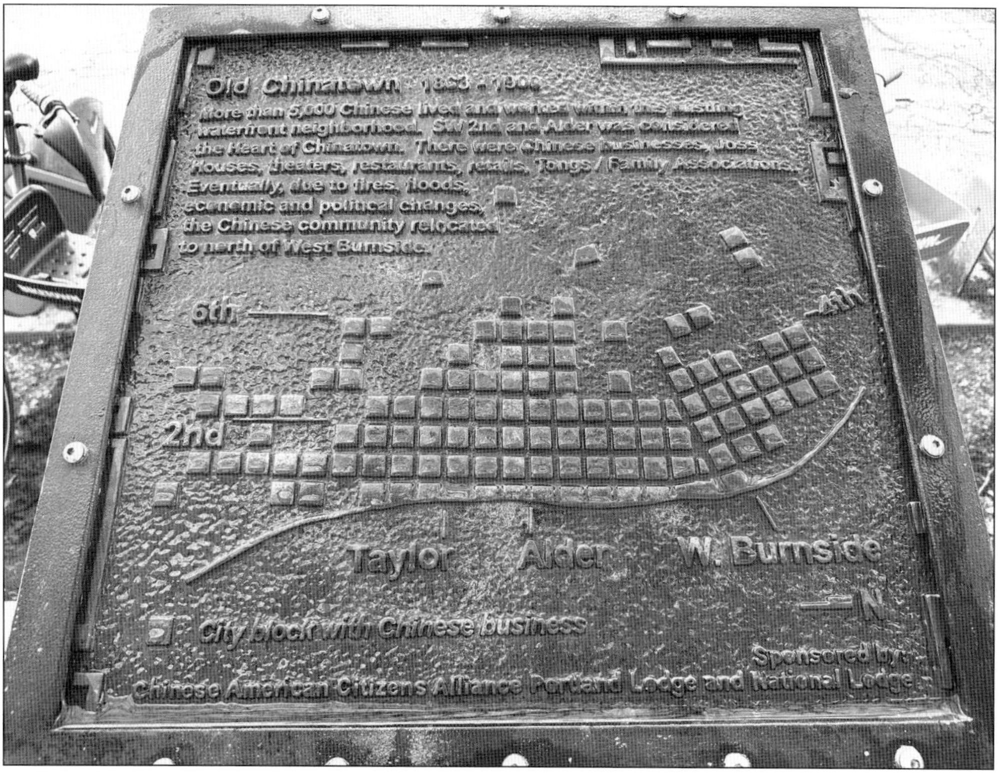

In 2017, a bronze plaque at Second Avenue and Pine Street was designed by Suenn Ho to commemorate Portland's first Chinatown. This project was led by Betty Jean Lee and commissioned by the Chinese American Citizens Alliance. It was dedicated by commissioner Dan Saltzman and transportation director Leah Treat. They also championed SB 280, ensuring Oregon students learn about the history and contributions of Chinese Americans and other minorities. (Kristin Wong.)

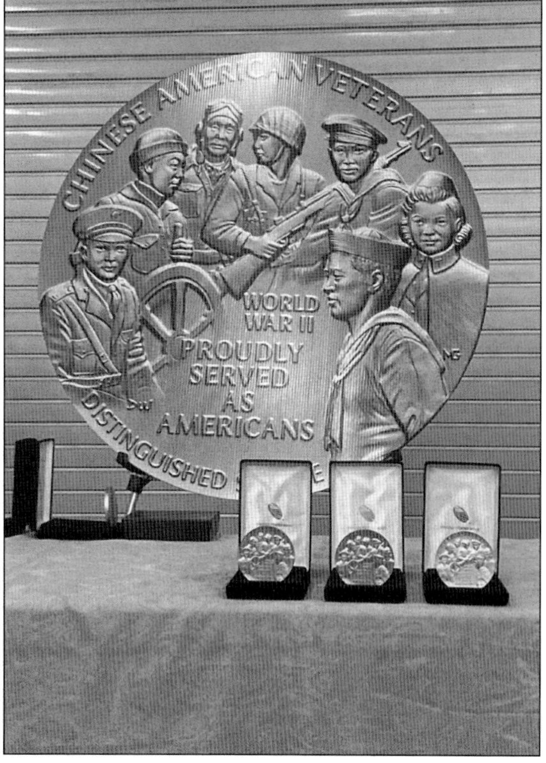

During World War II, 20,000 Chinese Americans served in every theater and branch of the US military, often without citizenship due to the Chinese Exclusion Act. In 2018, the Chinese American World War II Veteran Congressional Gold Medal Act was signed, recognizing their service and sacrifices. Yin K. Leong, who served in the Army, received his Congressional Gold Medal at Camp Withycombe in 2021. (Wing K. Leong family.)

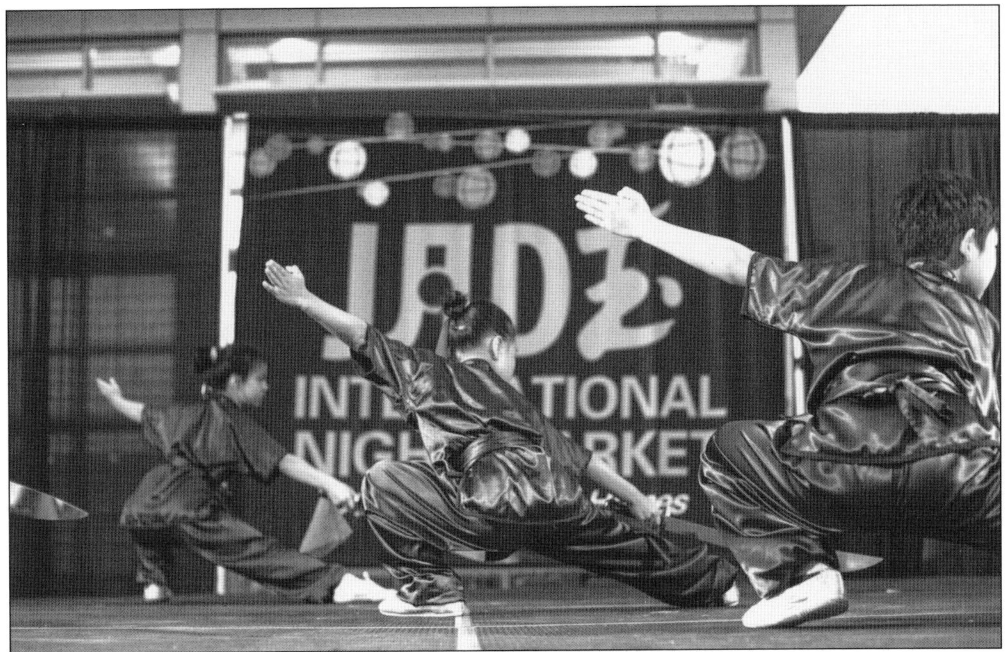

The Jade District, centered at Southeast Eighty-Second Avenue and Division Street, is a vibrant, culturally rich neighborhood known for its Asian-owned restaurants and shops. APANO fosters leadership and promotes equity through advocacy and community development, uniting Asians in collective action. The organization also supports events like the annual Jade International Night Market, which celebrates the community's cultural diversity and heritage. (Photograph by Trey Slyapich, courtesy of APANO.)

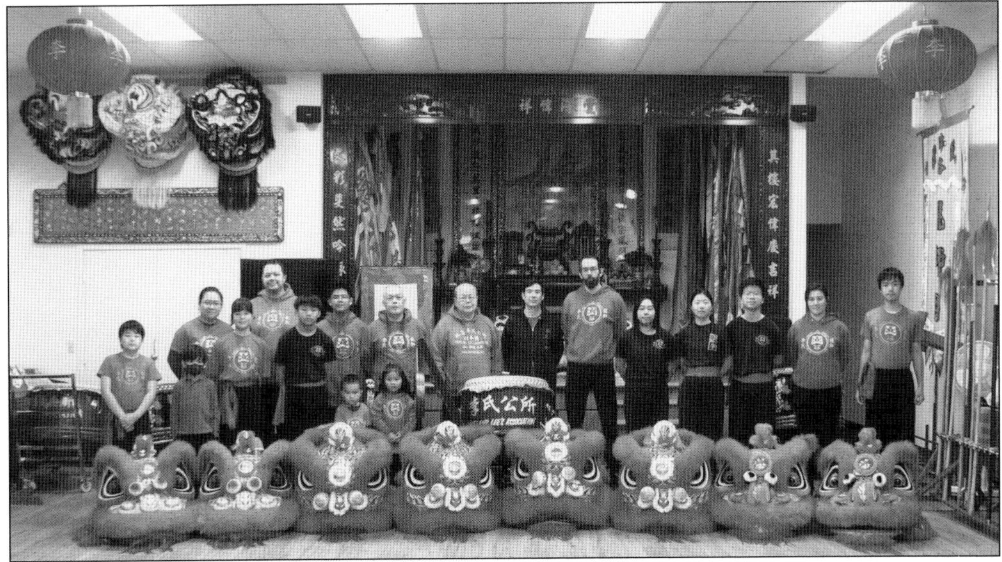

The Lee Association Dragon and Lion Dance Team has been preserving and teaching martial arts along with dragon and lion dance since 2004. From left to right are Alvin Zhang, Rory Hon, Josephine Chen, Azrael Hanson, coach Eric Lee, Jett Chen, Ethan Pham, Justin Lee, Jenny Lee, Phil Lee, coach Terry Lee, coach Nick Lee, Walter Fonseca, Trinity Diec, Kelly Li, Aiden Li, Jamie Millon, and Hanwei Zhang. (Lee Family Association.)

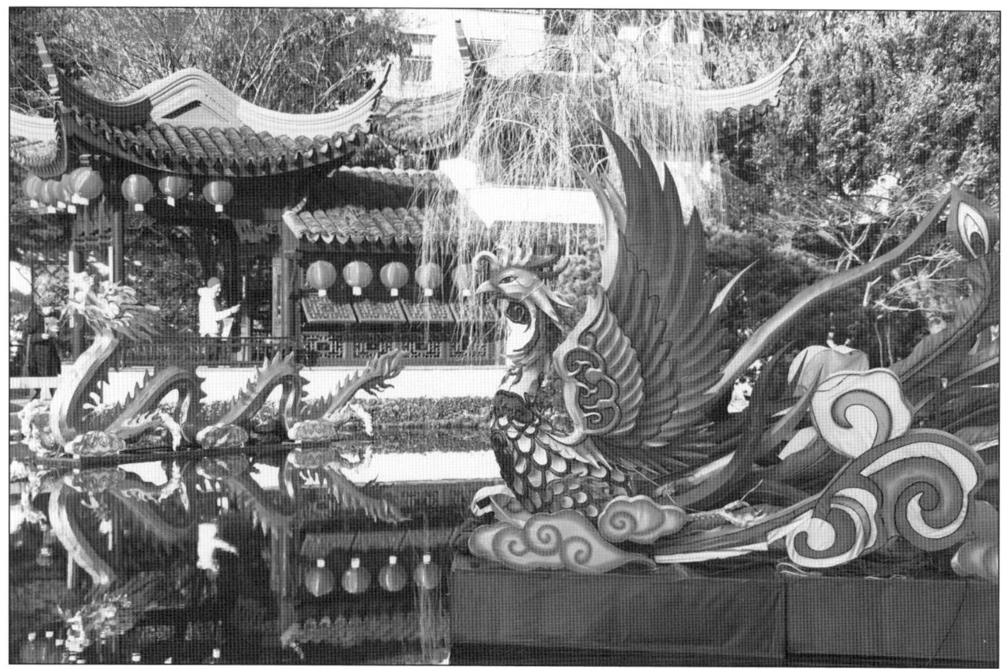

In 2000, the Lan Su Chinese Garden opened at 239 Northwest Everett Street. The garden was a collaboration between Portland and its sister city, Suzhou, China, which is renowned for its tranquil Ming Dynasty scholars' gardens. The garden, the largest in the United States, continues to host educational and cultural events for the community. This photograph shows the Chinese New Year celebration in 2024. (Lan Su Chinese Garden.)

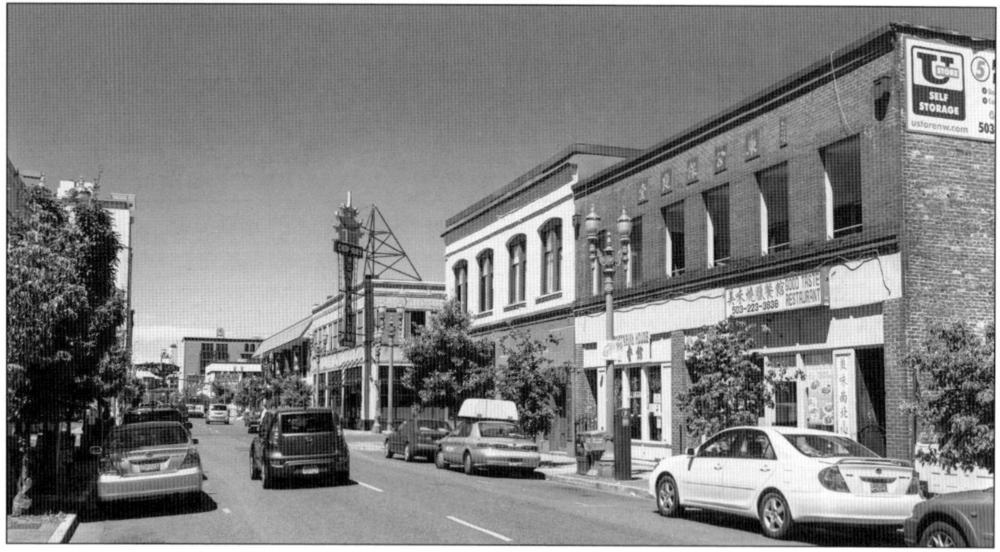

In 1915, Bing Kung Tong, in the building on the far right, merged with Bow Leong Tong, becoming a key fraternal organization in Portland's second Chinatown. Over the years, it has remained influential, fostering community support, preserving cultural heritage, and strengthening business networks. Today, it continues to engage in community activities and to advocate for Chinese American interests, maintaining its long-standing role in Chinatown's civic and economic landscape. (Eric James/Alamy Stock Photo.)

Built in 1881 and located at 203 Northwest Third Avenue, the Mariners' Building initially welcomed sailors. Eventually, it housed various hotels and businesses, including Kung Wo and Company (1920–1924) and Hun Yick and Company (1924–1927), a Japanese laundry, bathhouse, and barbershop, and Jewish businesses. After an extensive renovation, the Society Hotel opened in 2015, restoring this historic Chinatown/Japantown building. (Photograph by Alex Hoxie, courtesy of the Society Hotel.)

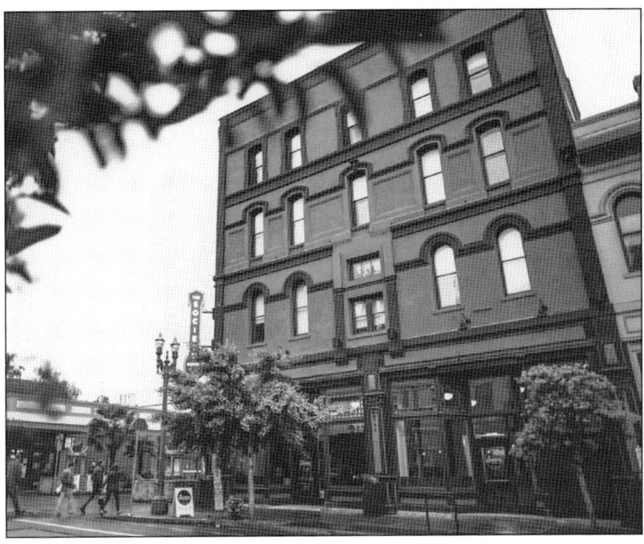

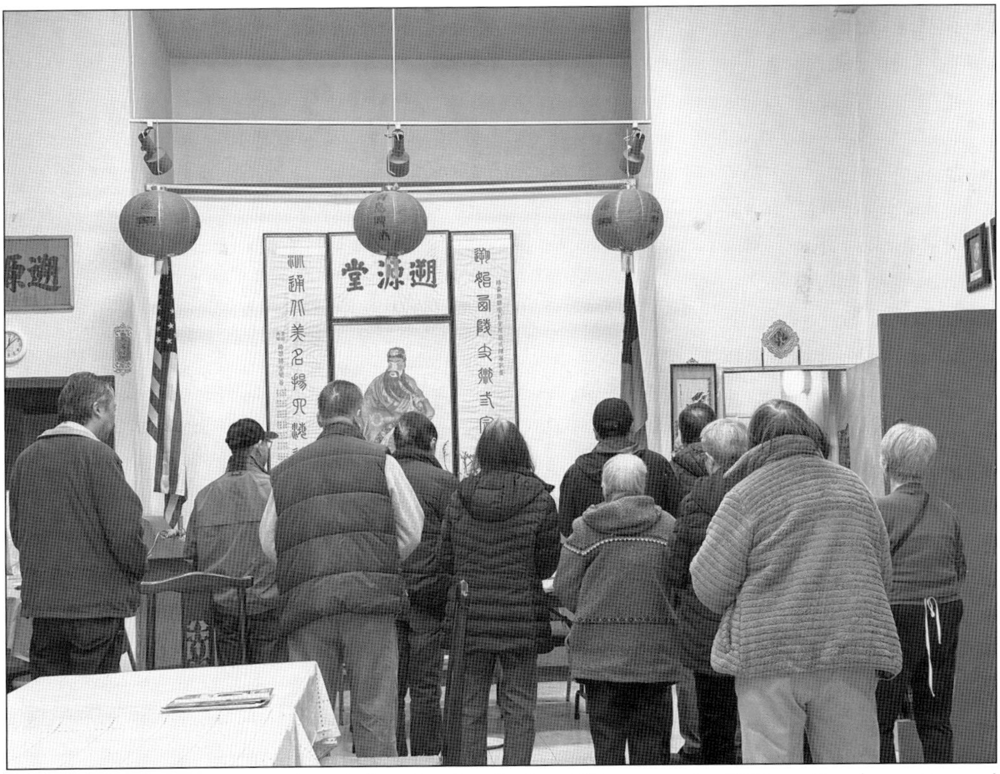

The Soo Yuen Association, founded in Portland's first Chinatown in 1922 on Southwest Second Street, relocated to the New Chinatown in 1981. It continues to preserve Chinese heritage and strengthen the unity of families with the surnames Louie, Fong, and Kwong. This image, taken during the Winter Solstice, shows an offering to Father Louie (Ah Gung), along with honoring ancestral traditions and celebrating with *tangyuan* (glutinous rice balls). (Kristin Wong.)

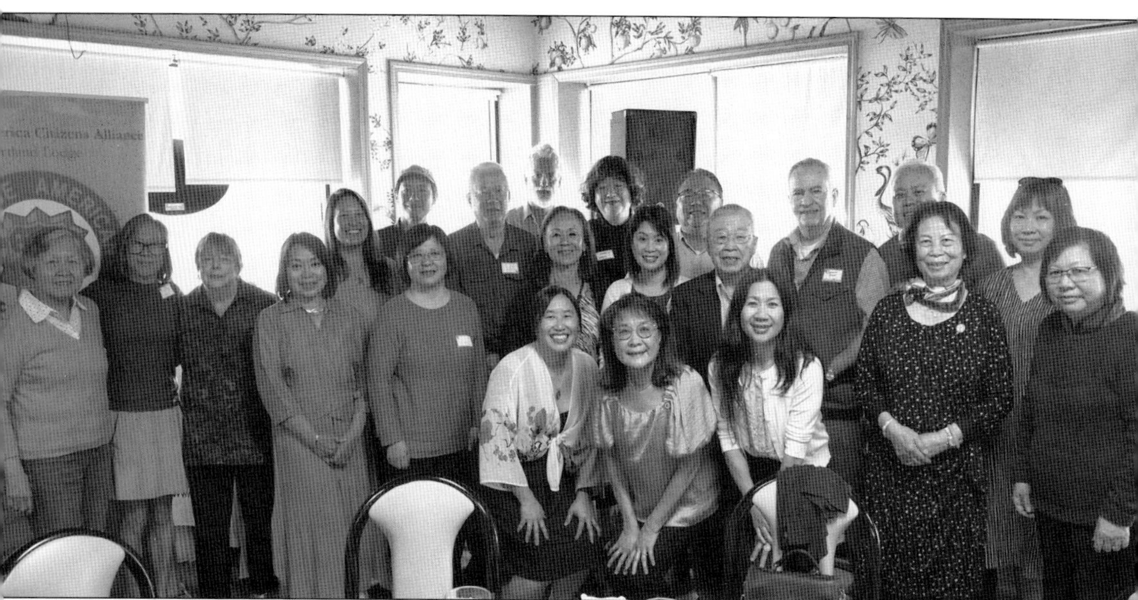

The Portland lodge of the Chinese American Citizens Alliance remains steadfast in its mission to "develop leadership, serve the community, and promote civil rights." Dedicated to combating discrimination, fostering cultural awareness, and advocating for equitable immigration and economic policies, the CACA continues to safeguard the rights and well-being of Chinese Americans. To nurture youth leadership within the Chinese community, the CACA organizes the Asian American Youth Leadership Conference (AAYLC) and offers a national essay contest and local scholarships. There are 20 lodges across the nation. Portland members at the 2024 AAYLC include, from left to right, (first row) Sharry Quan, Suenn Ho, Joan Harvey, Amy Lee, Winnie Ng, Kittie Kong, Helen Ying, Wisdom Ming, Fenge Tam, and Cathy Chinn; (second row) Ocean Yap-Powell, Bing Wong, G.G. Rowe, Dr. Lori Tam, Franklin Quan, Bennett Rowe, Robin Chongkit, and Dorothy Chongkit; (third row) Michael Yun, Michael Mellick, Mary Li, and Stephen Ying. (CACA.)

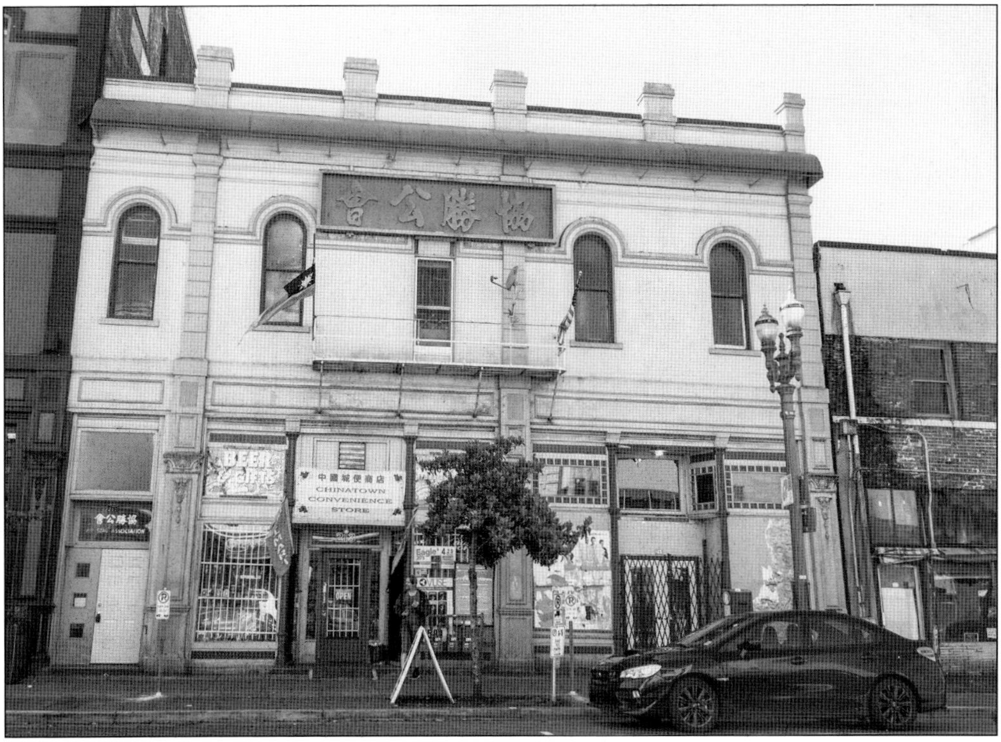

The Hip Sing Association building, at 211–215 Northwest Third Avenue, was constructed in 1889 as an addition to the Mariners' Building. Early tenants included the Japanese-owned Nichibei Company (1910–1940) and K. Mori's shoe repair shop (1930–1933). The Columbia Rooms, managed by Mike Meras, occupied the upper floor from 1930 to the 1940s. Since acquiring the property in 1947, the association has continued to rent its storefronts to businesses in Chinatown. (Erik Lattwein/Alamy Stock Photo.)

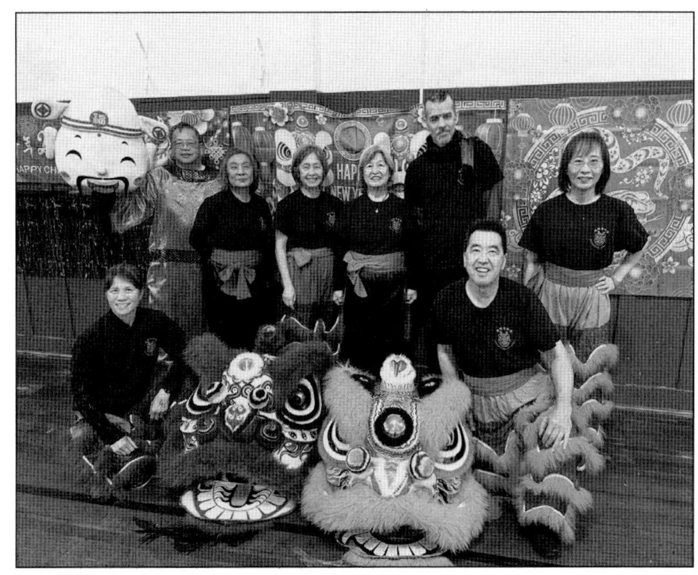

The International Lion Dance team was formed in 2010 and plays a vital role in preserving this tradition by performing at events throughout the year for the Chinese New Year, grand openings, weddings, and other celebrations. Members include, from left to right, (first row) assistant coach Tina Johnson and coach Michael Choi; (second row) Myron Lew, Margie Woo, Sun Noble, May Knotts, Jacob Bleedlove, and assistant coach Miranda Ho. (International Lion Dance.)

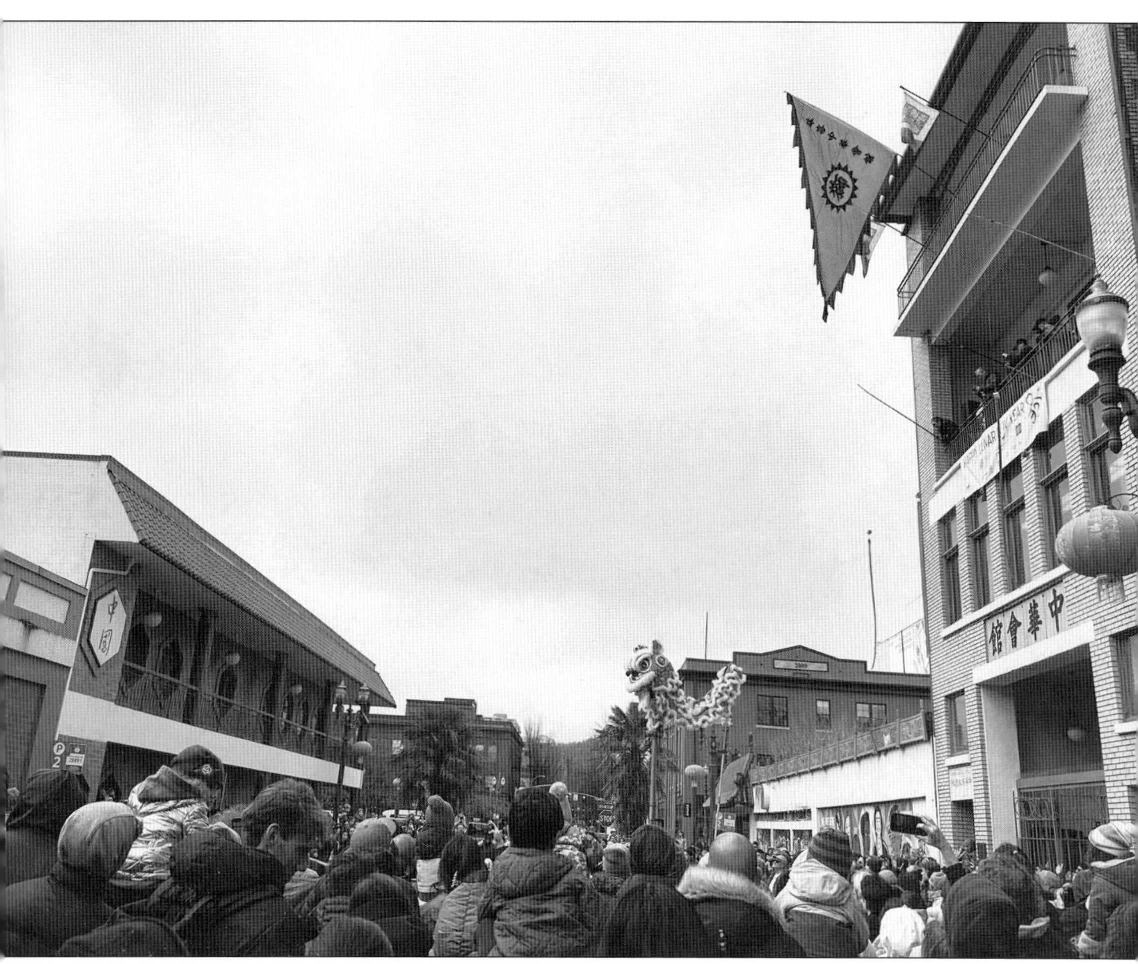

Oregon's Chinese Consolidated Benevolent Association is headquartered in Portland at 315 Northwest Davis Street. It was founded in the late 19th century to assist early Chinese immigrants with essential services like housing, employment assistance, funeral assistance, legal aid, and immigration, helping to ease their transition in a new country. The CCBA continues to embrace all individuals of Chinese heritage, regardless of their origins within the diaspora. The organization promotes civic engagement, advocates for social justice, and preserves Chinese culture in the New Chinatown/Japantown historic area and through events in Portland. The organization works closely with community and city leaders toward the common goal of improving the society we share and preserving the rich cultural history of the area. The CCBA building, shown on the far right in the photograph, serves as a social gathering place, houses its Chinese history museum, and has a rentable auditorium. The Chinese language school has relocated to Portland Community College in the Jade District in Southeast Portland. This image is from the 2025 Lunar New Year parade. (Kristin Wong.)

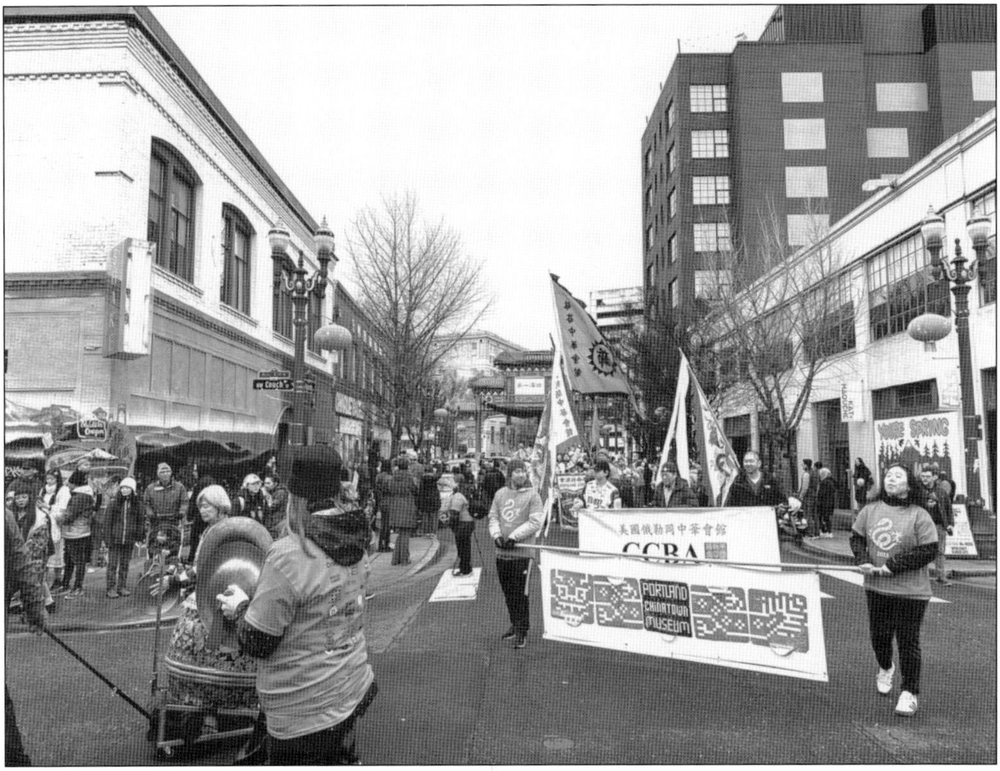

The Portland Chinatown Museum, in partnership with the Oregon Historical Society (OHS), hosts the annual Lunar New Year parade, which begins at the Chinese Consolidated Benevolent Association in Chinatown and concludes at the OHS's Park Plaza. A highlight of the celebration is PoChiMu, the Portland Chinatown History Foundation's 150-foot dragon, mesmerizing spectators with its intricate design and vivid colors. The parade, featuring traditional lion and dragon dance performances, honors a legacy dating back over 175 years to the arrival of Portland's first Chinese pioneers. This cherished event fosters community unity and cultural pride, bringing together the community in celebration. These images capture moments from the 2025 parade. (Both, Kristin Wong.)

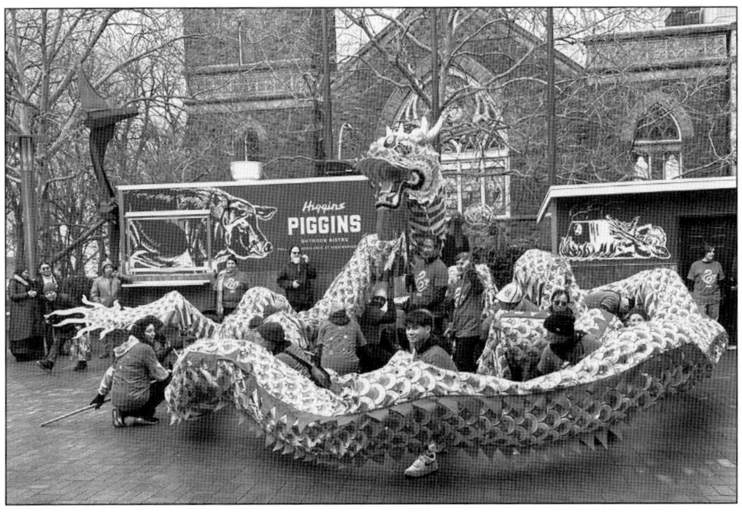

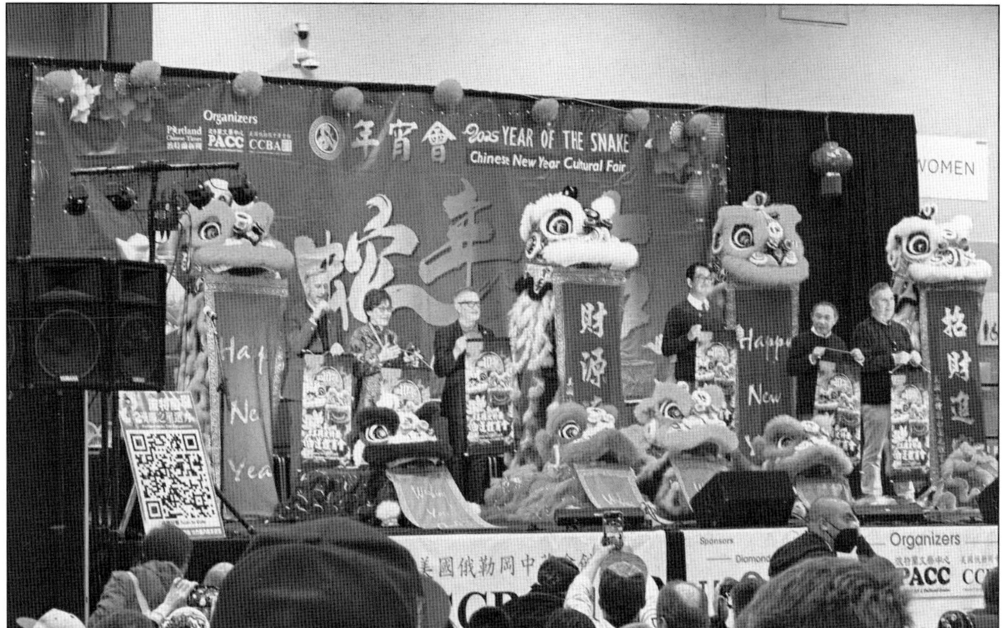

The Chinese New Year Cultural Fair at the Oregon Convention Center features lion dances, martial arts, folk performances, children's activities, music, and vendors. A cherished Portland tradition, it welcomes the entire community to celebrate the New Year. Organized by the CCBA, *Portland Chinese Times*, and Portland Art and Cultural Center, it blends heritage with modern festivities, making it one of the city's most beloved annual events. (Kristin Wong.)

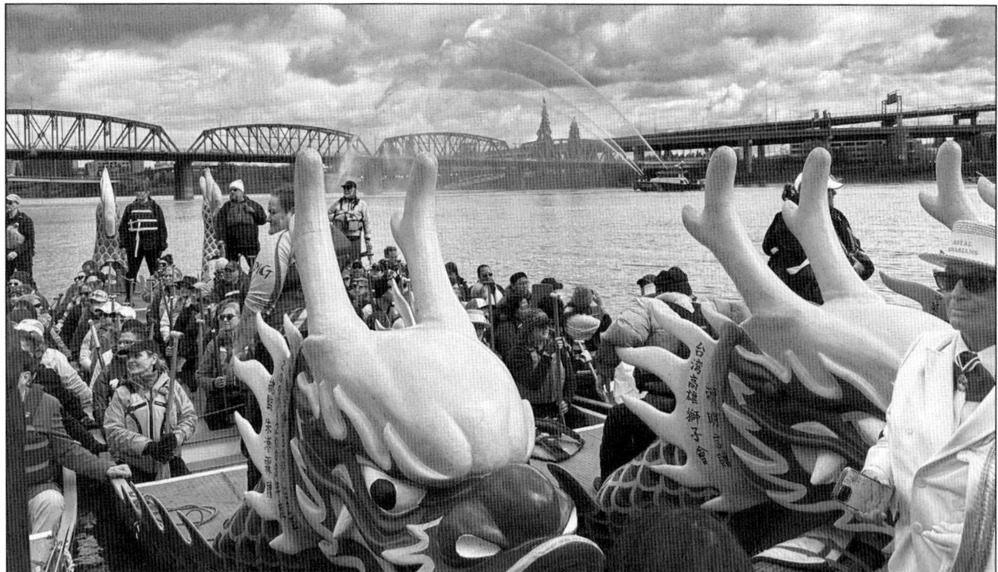

The Portland-Kaohsiung Sister City Association (PKSCA) fosters cultural and educational exchanges between Portland and its Taiwanese sister city, Kaohsiung. Established in 1987, PKSCA continues to organize the annual Portland Rose Festival Dragon Boat Race, participate in the Grand Floral Parade, and also organize goodwill delegation exchanges between the two cities. These initiatives celebrate and promote mutual understanding, enriching both communities. This photograph is from the eye-dotting ceremony in 2025. (Kristin Wong.)

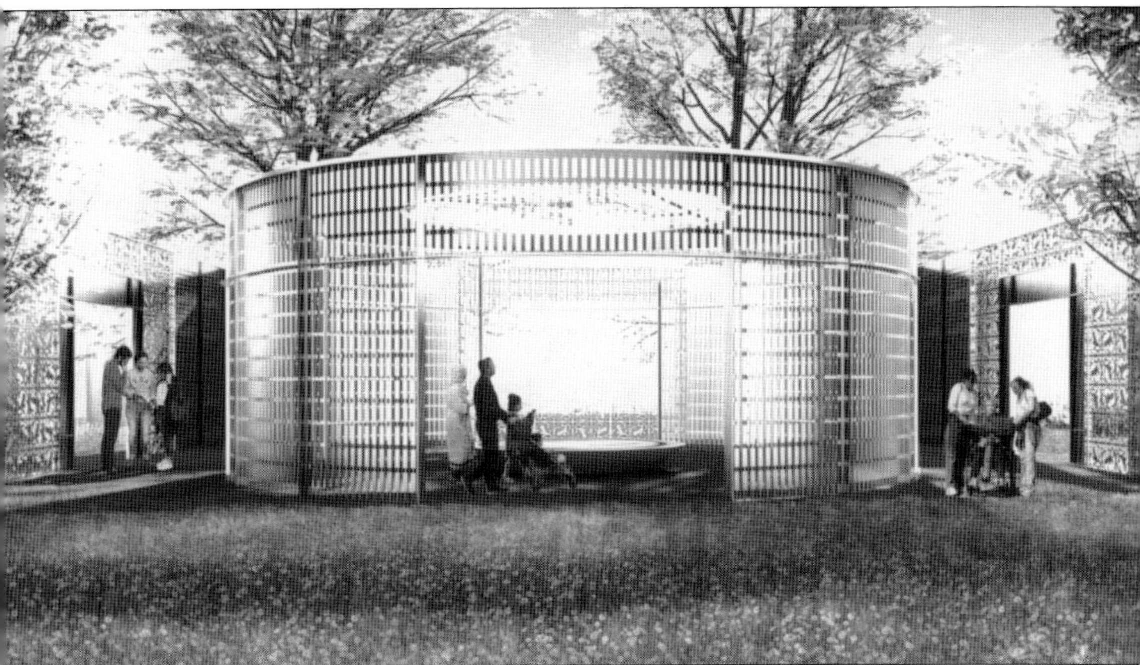

The Chinese section of Lone Fir Cemetery, Block 14, began burials in the 1860s, interring at least 2,892. If there were no local relatives, remains were repatriated to China. In 1928, Multnomah County bought the property, halted Chinese burials, and forced the exhumation of hundreds. A bulldozer was used in 1948 to remove an additional 265 remains, which was culturally insensitive and offensive. Headstones were repurposed, and poor documentation led to uncertainty for these individuals and 13 unaccounted children. In the 1950s, the county extended the Morrison Building over Block 14. After it closed in 2005, the county proposed selling the property for an apartment building. However, in 2004, records were discovered in the CCBA basement, and a subsequent archaeological investigation found more remains. Multnomah County's actions highlight the profound effects of structural and systemic racism, resulting in the erasure of those buried there and a disregard for the dignity of the deceased. A formal apology is in development, and a Chinese Memorial Park at Block 14 will honor the Chinese buried there. (Image by Knot Studio/Allied Works, courtesy of Metro.)

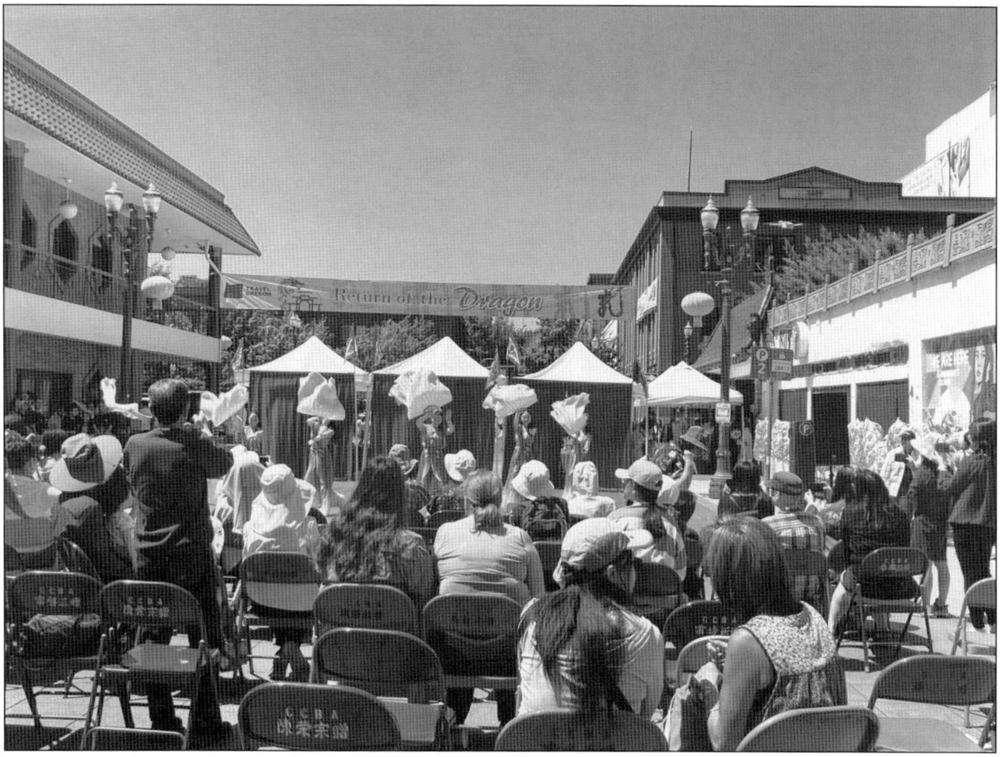

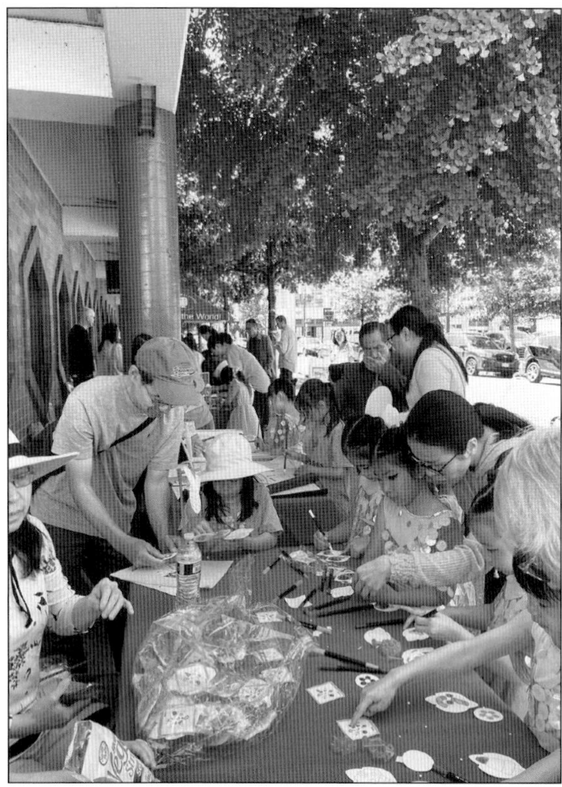

For Asian American and Pacific Islander Heritage Month in May 2025, the Oregon Chinese Coalition, CCBA, Old Town Community Association (OTCA), and cultural heritage allies organized "Return of the Dragon: Revitalizing Portland's Old Town Heritage," sponsored by the OTCA and Travel Oregon. The event featured lion dances, cultural performances, a Chinatown bronze plaque walking tour, food vendors, traditional crafts, tong and association open houses, and special access to the museums (Portland Chinatown Museum, CCBA Museum, Japanese American Museum, and Oregon Jewish Museum) and the Chinese Garden. The OTCA hosts year-round celebrations, including Chinese New Year, Juneteenth, and Nuestro Camino, with festivals, exhibitions, vendors, and street parties. These events highlight the diverse cultural contributions of the area, fostering unity and appreciation for Old Town's vibrant and inclusive heritage. (Both, Lisa Woo.)

Tommy Ly opened Stumptown Otaku, an anime gift shop, in Portland's first Chinatown on Southwest Second Street. Ly partnered with At Nguyen to open GeekEasy Café, Portland's first anime café, next door to the Portland Chinatown Museum. The café offers a selection of specialty drinks, food, and snacks. Their entrepreneurial spirit is part of a broader trend of young innovators revitalizing and continuing the evolution of the historic district. (Kristin Wong.)

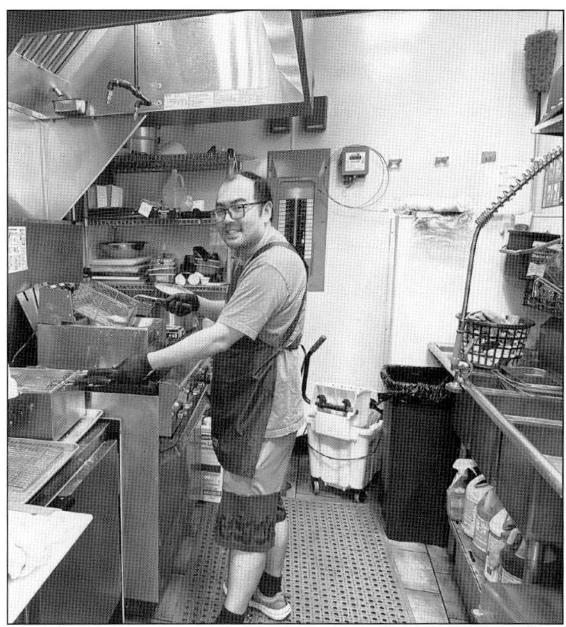

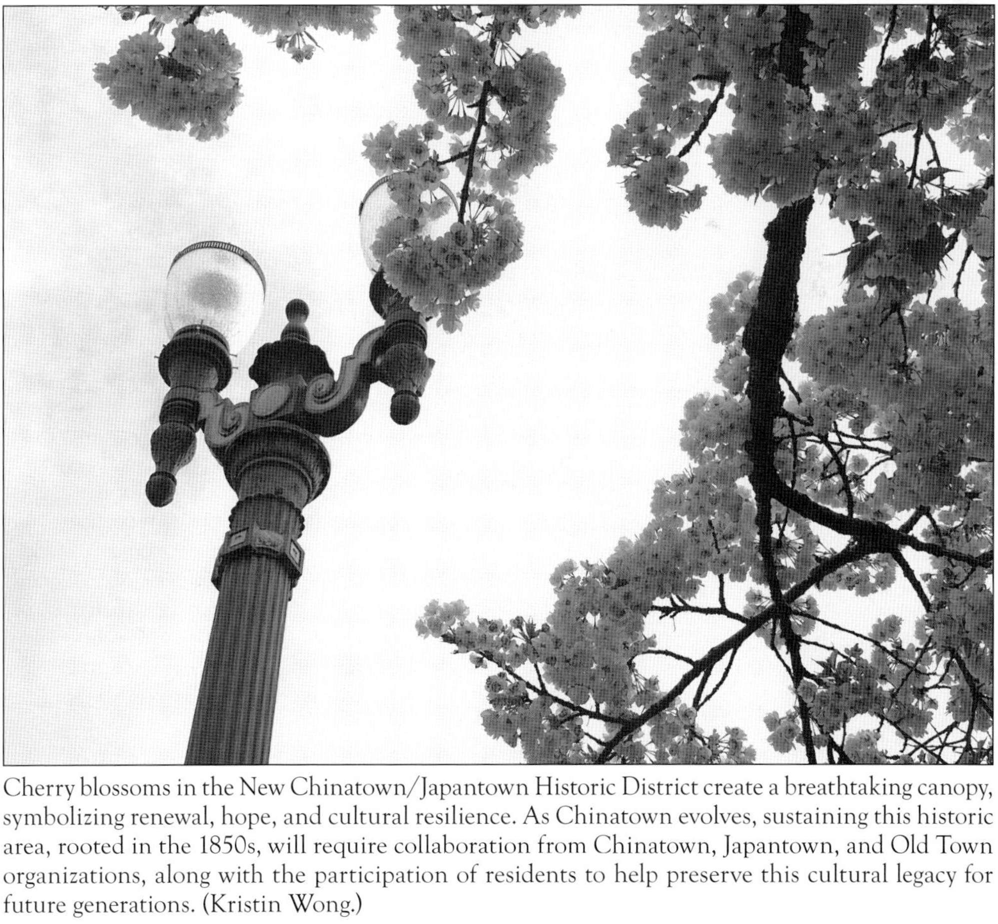

Cherry blossoms in the New Chinatown/Japantown Historic District create a breathtaking canopy, symbolizing renewal, hope, and cultural resilience. As Chinatown evolves, sustaining this historic area, rooted in the 1850s, will require collaboration from Chinatown, Japantown, and Old Town organizations, along with the participation of residents to help preserve this cultural legacy for future generations. (Kristin Wong.)

Consistent with our mission to preserve history on a local level, this book was printed in South Carolina on American-made paper and manufactured entirely in the United States. Products carrying the accredited Forest Stewardship Council (FSC) label are printed on 100 percent FSC-certified paper.

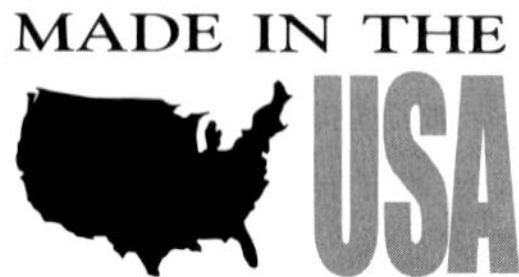